The Linguistics
of Stephen King

D1559612

The Linguistics of Stephen King

Layered Language and Meaning in the Fiction

JAMES ARTHUR ANDERSON

McFarland & Company, Inc., Publishers
Jefferson, North Carolina

LIBRARY OF CONGRESS CATALOGUING-IN-PUBLICATION DATA

Names: Anderson, James Arthur, 1955– author.
Title: The linguistics of Stephen King : layered language and meaning
    in the fiction / James Arthur Anderson.
Description: Jefferson, North Carolina : McFarland & Company, Inc.,
    Publishers, 2017. | Includes bibliographical references and index.
Identifiers: LCCN 2017021219 | ISBN 9781476668345 (softcover : acid
    free paper) ∞
Subjects: LCSH: King, Stephen, 1947– —Language. | King, Stephen,
    1947– —Criticism and interpretation.
Classification: LCC PS3561.I483 Z516 2017 | DDC 813/.54—dc23
LC record available at https://lccn.loc.gov/2017021219

BRITISH LIBRARY CATALOGUING DATA ARE AVAILABLE

ISBN (print) 978-1-4766-6834-5
ISBN (ebook) 978-1-4766-2952-0

Front cover image by Anat Sukeewong (iStock)

Printed in the United States of America

*McFarland & Company, Inc., Publishers
    Box 611, Jefferson, North Carolina 28640
    www.mcfarlandpub.com*

To Lynn Llorye

Acknowledgments

When I first began this project, I had no idea of the enormity of the task ahead of me. First, I would like to thank my wife Lynn Llorye Anderson for her patience and understanding, while I hunched over the computer on so many long nights, and for her willingness to read the manuscript and make helpful suggestions.

I'd also like to thank David Biderman, one of my Stephen King fan friends, for reading my early draft and sharing his insights with me.

Thanks to the Horror Writers Association for awarding me a Rocky Wood Memorial Scholarship for Nonfiction grant that helped me obtain some of the resources that I needed and to my colleagues at Johnson & Wales University, North Miami Campus, who have given me the encouragement that I've needed, not to mention access to databases and resources that were so important in compiling my research.

I would also extend a sincere thanks to Stephen King for writing fiction that is interesting and complex enough to withstand this kind of an analysis (I know you're not a fan of scholars, but I hope you read this book and find some value in it).

I also thank those who have come before me in Stephen King criticism, particularly Michael Collings and Anthony Magistrale, who have paved the way. I am also indebted to my peer reviewers, who provided valuable feedback.

Table of Contents

Preface

When I first discovered Stephen King's fiction, I was working in a factory on an assembly line in Providence, Rhode Island. Armed with my brand new bachelor's degree from Rhode Island College (and unable find work as an English major), I had reached overload with the classics and was now reading whatever junk and genre fiction I could lay my hands on and trying to perfect the craft of writing short stories so I could escape from my job in what I un-fondly called "the hellhole." So at the time, I was particularly attracted to reading genre short stories, so I could figure out how it was done, so to speak. That's when I ran into "The Mangler," a particularly nasty short story collected in King's *Night Shift* anthology.

For those of you who may not remember this early story as vividly as I do, "The Mangler" is about a vindictive machine that comes to life in an industrial laundry, mangling and shredding anyone it can get its gears into. While noted horror fiction critic S.T. Joshi has said of the machine "if one can imagine it" (64), my suspicion is that, with all due respect, Joshi has never had the misfortune to work in an environment with machinery that could maim and kill. I did; this was my kind of story. It spoke to me, since, at the time, I was working for an unscrupulous factory that would remove any of the OSHA mandated safety guards to speed up production whenever it thought it could get away with doing so. These machines, quite frankly, frightened me more than any ghost, goblin, or Lovecraft creation ever had. Sure, I admired Lovecraft's elaborate prose (I went on to write my Ph.D. dissertation on him—and Joshi, whom I do admire, was gracious enough to write a very flattering foreword for it when it was eventually published in book form). I admired Harlan Ellison's way of brilliantly turning a phrase and I just couldn't get enough of Bradbury, whose work I would write my M.A. thesis about ten years later. But this story, "The Mangler," as flawed and unbelievable as it might be—well, it described me and my world, and it fictionalized the real nightmares that I had almost every night.

Now, mind you, never in a million years did I ever think I'd be writing a critical study on Stephen King decades later, let alone have it see publication, and use words and theories that were well beyond the limits of an undergraduate degree in English. I hoped, at best, I would be able to publish some short stories and maybe a novel or two (a goal that I did ultimately reach, but I still am not about to give up the day job, where I am fortunate enough to teach what I love at a respected university and get paid rather well for it). I didn't expect to ever go to graduate school and learn about things like "hermeneutic code" and "metafiction," and I surely never expected that *anyone* would be writing critical studies of Stephen King, least of all me.

But here I am, armed with all of the critical theory I could find from nearly ten years of graduate school, not to mention decades of continuing education, including self-taught courses in linguistics—in order to keep my job, get promoted to a professorship, and be able to write this study.

So why did I write this book? I now hold the rank of full professor and could sit on my laurels, so to speak, until I retire in five to seven years. And this book was difficult to write, a three-year adventure requiring lots more reading and research than my master's thesis and Ph.D. dissertation put together. I wrote this because most of the fan writing, while good, doesn't have the backing of the academy. Although it is changing quickly, most of the early King critics lacked the academic credentials and expertise in literary theory that is required to write studies that would help one be granted tenure. There are, of course, notable exceptions (Magistrale and Collings come immediately to mind), and scholars are now publishing dissertations and scholarly articles and presenting papers at academic conferences. I've enjoyed all of Stephen King's books—even the bad ones, like *The Tommyknockers*—but I always wondered how his fiction would hold up under the magnifying glass (probably more like the microscope) of critical theory. Rather than use subjective criticism of what is "good" or "bad," I wanted to just take the fiction and run it through a more scientific process and see what came of it. And that's how this book was born. I've used a number of different critical approaches in my attempt to pull meaning out of King's books. I began with a linguistic study, since so many of King's stories are about authors and writing, but as I went along I found myself using other theories as well: structuralism, deconstructionism, Marxism, and whatever I could pull from my tool box that seemed appropriate to the particular work under analysis.

Obviously, I could not write an analysis of every story or novel that Stephen King wrote—he writes books faster that I can write the criticism of them. Such an attempt would be too long for any publisher to print. So, for the most part, I chose stories from the canon that best illustrated the writing and language theme in his works. Although the Gunslinger series is intensely metafictional, and, according to King himself, is heavily concerned with writing and the creative arts, I decided not to include it as an extensive study, because it would have turned into a complete book of its own. Finally, I must admit, I chose some stories just because they were my favorites.

Introduction

Since the publication of *Carrie* in 1974, horror has become a genre of its own, and Stephen King, acknowledged as the "king of horror," has indeed become "indisputably a brand name" (Stroby 75) that made the genre popular and inspired new generations of horror practitioners. Before Stephen King, horror was not considered a separate genre and was lumped in with fantasy and science fiction on the bookstore shelves. It is estimated that King has sold more than 350 million copies of his books, most of which have been produced as films. While his popularity cannot be over-rated, King has been the object of very little critical study. Analysis of his work was begun mostly by his peers and fans (Underwood and Miller, Winter) and by a few scholars, most notably Collings and Magistrale. Even today, Stephen King criticism appears mostly in journals and conferences that are devoted to horror fiction and cultural studies (International Society for the Fantastic in the Arts, the Popular Culture Association) rather than in mainstream university presses and conferences. However, when we examine Stephen King's work in light of critical theory, particularly theory that is derived from linguistic studies, his fiction takes on new meaning and generates new critical insights. Indeed, the study of horror and speculative fiction in general have yielded interesting results when subjected to linguistic-based criticism as evidenced by studies by Todorov, Scholes, Barthes, and others.

I would like to begin this study by examining some pure linguistic theory to see how it might apply to the horror and fantasy genre and to the works of Stephen King. J.L Austin, a leading twentieth-century philosopher who sought meaning through linguistics, explained the importance of language in creating reality. Austin identified "performatives" as sentences that indicate "that the issuing of the utterance is the performing of an action" (6) and, thus, bring about a new reality once they are said. In linguistic terms, these performatives are represented by words and contexts, such as uttering "I do" at a wedding, or a jury pronouncing a verdict of "guilty" (5). Thus, we use language to "do things," not to just describe or assert what already exists.

Fiction in general, and horror fiction in particular, can be seen as a metalinguistic "performative" in that it brings an impossible state of affairs into being by its "utterance." The word "vampire," for example, has created an entire genre of vampire stories, from *Dracula* to the *Twilight* series. Without saying so directly, the writer of horror fiction is, in fact, "doing something with words" by creating a world that does not exist and cannot exist under natural laws as we know them. The genre itself, then, serves as a "performative" in that the writer promises a reader that he will enter a new, imaginative world. Writers like Stephen King deliver on that promise.

The philosopher Heidegger, who studied the nature of "being," also asserts the power of language to do more than simply describe what already exists; it can be used to create what exists only in the imagination: "Human expression is always a presentation and representation of the real and the unreal" (1123). According to Heidegger, language not only describes what already exists, but is able to create that which does not, through poetry ("Language" 1125). "Man speaks. We speak when we are awake and we speak in our dreams … only speech allows man to be the being he is as man" (1121). Wittgenstein takes this one step further by saying, "What is thinkable is also possible" (*Tractatus* 35) and "Everything that can be thought at all can be thought clearly. Everything that can be said can be said clearly" (52–53). Searle agrees, saying, "I take it as an analytic thought about language that whatever can be meant can be said" (17), which he terms "the principle of expressibility" (19). Thus, thought and speech can create anything, even a new reality using words.

This speech, expressed as fiction, can and does express both our dreams and our nightmares in the form of fantasy and horror. Horror fiction in particular conjures unreal worlds of darkness and fear and makes them come alive, become real and a part of our culture. As Douglas Winter has observed, "Despite its intrinsic unreality, the horror story remains credible—or at least sufficiently credible to exert an influence that may last long beyond the act of reading" (3). In the hands of a master storyteller, we willingly suspend our disbelief and accept the impossible as the ordinary.

Structuralist critics such as Tzvetan Todorov have posited that metalinguistics—when writing speaks about writing—is the basis of all storytelling and that all stories have the theme of narration embedded within them.

> In a series of striking articles [*Grammaire du Decameron*] Todorov shows that the very subject of such short story-collections as the *Thousand and One Nights* must be seen as the act of storytelling itself, that the only constant of the psychology of the characters ... lies in the obsession with telling and listening to stories [Jameson 199].

"Narration equals life: the absence of narration, death," says Todorov (qtd. in Jameson 199). While this idea might be obvious in a book of stories where the protagonist tells stories, Roland Barthes has analyzed this textual (or metalinguistic) code present in short stories ("Textual") and claims that "discourse must be studied from the basis of linguistics" (*Image* 83). Todorov has shown that a textual code exists in novels:

> *C'est l'historie dans le roman, lintrigue, qui se trouve integree a l'historie de sa creation, historie qui, dans cette perspective, prend la premiere place.... Des oeuvres comme celle de Lacos ou de Proust ne font que render explicite une verite sous-jacente a toute creation litteraire* [In the story of the novel, in its own plot, will be found the story of its own creation, and its own history.... Works such as those of Lacos or Proust explicitly render this truth that underlies all literary creation] [*Litterature et Signification* 49].

This subtext of writing, artistic creation, and imagination underlies all of Stephen King's work and is, in fact, an important part of understanding the deeper layers of his fiction.

In this analysis, I will examine the fiction of Stephen King using critical theory developed from linguistic studies and focus on the textual code, or metalanguage, that forms an important part of Stephen King's fiction, and I will employ other postmodern theories in my analysis, including Marxist, feminist and psychoanalytical criticism when it would be useful to do so. Indeed, most modern criticism has developed from the philosophic and linguistic theories of Ludwig Wittgenstein, Ferdinand de Saussure, J.L. Austin, and John Searle into its various forms of structuralism, semiotics, deconstructionism, and post-structuralism. These theories have been used to both elucidate and deny meaning and will provide a close reading of how King layers language upon language to create both reality and meaning. I will include various theories and critics in places where I feel they will be the most useful, including the theories of Jean Baudrillard, Jacques Derrida, Jean-François Lyotard, Tzvatan Todorov, and others. Of particular interest is the semiotic theory of Roland Barthes (*S/Z*) where he posits that all writing relies on a series of codes in order to create meaning. One of these codes, in particular, comes into play when language calls attention to itself, or when writing speaks about writing. This textual, or metalinguistic, code occurs whenever "language is ... doubled into layers of which the first in some ways cap the second" ("Valdemar" 139). This code will highlight themes dealing with speaking, writing, communication, and what Searle calls the "speech act" (16). Since a great many of King's protagonists are writers or English teachers, the themes of writing and communication have special importance in his work, and foregrounding these themes provides insight and understanding into his fictional universe. And although King has been criticized for his use of "popular" language, slang, and brand names, Wittgenstein's ideas of "language games" (*Philosophical* 10) and "ordinary language," where meaning is based upon a word's use in the language (18) rather than an arbitrary meaning assigned by scholars, clearly show that "the language of every day" is an effective and practical means to say what we have to say (42).

While I will refer to the life of Stephen King, when appropriate, the bulk of this work will involve a close textual-linguistic study of the works themselves. This study will not only provide new insights into the work, but will assist in understanding the mechanics and structure of language, since "literature turns out to be not only the first field whose study takes language as its point of departure, but also to first field of which a knowledge can shed new light on the properties of language itself" (Todorov, *Poetics* 20).

It is my hope that my application of these theories will not only help in an understanding of Stephen King's fiction, but will also expose the complexity of his texts and show that he is more than just a horror writer, more than just a creator of "popular fiction." His fiction is fertile ground for scholarly study, and applying proven literary theory to his work will yield interesting and unexpected results, reveal multiple subtexts and demonstrate the complexity of his fiction. This will, hopefully, inspire further critical study using additional literary theories and will demonstrate that Stephen King does deserve his place in the canon of modern literature.

Chapter 1

Carrie: The Truth Within the Lie

Carrie was Stephen King's first published novel, earning him a $2,500 advance from Doubleday in 1973 and launching his career (he had already written *The Long Walk*, *The Running Man*, and *Rage*, all later published under the Richard Bachman penname). The book's lead character, Carrie White, was a personification of two girls that King remembered from his own high school experience, "the two loneliest, most reviled girls in my class" (*On Writing* 78). Magistrale has written of the book's theme of "unresolved tensions that accompany the transition from adolescence to adulthood" and blood symbolism (*Moral Voyages* 41), territory that I won't revisit here. Instead I would like to examine the book's "dual narrative structure" (Collings, *Many Facets* 42) as a form of meta-language or textual code that weaves its way throughout the novel.

The novel consists of two distinct parts, the fictional narrative as told by the omniscient narrator, interlaced between excerpts from "bogus items of documentation" (Winter 28) that authenticate the incident using several different points of view. These texts range from graffiti scratched on classroom desks—"Carrie White eats shit" (4)—to an academic study published by Tulane University Press. The novel begins with a newspaper story about a "rain of stones" that occurred in 1966 and ends with an excerpt from a letter dated 1988 and foreshadowing another child with telekinetic powers like Carrie (181). The novel also contains excerpts from an autobiography of Susan Snell, one of the survivors of the "Black Prom," and testimony from legal proceedings ("The White Commission Report").

9

From a linguistic point of view, Stephen King is using what Halliday termed "registers," which distinguishes the various forms of use of a language. "The category of 'register' is needed when we want to account for what people do with their language" (*Linguistic Sciences* 87). While this might be considered genre studies in traditional literary analysis, a register accounts for a much broader use of language as it is actually used by the people who write and speak it. "There is no need to labor the point that a sports commentary, a church service and a school lesson are linguistically quite distinct" (87). Halliday is making the practical point, of course, that different registers must be taken into account when teaching language to a non-native speaker, but the point is that different registers are clearly used for distinct purposes and are easily recognized by native speakers of the language.

Stephen King masterfully uses a number of different registers to tell the story of Carrie White and is well aware of the nature and functions of these registers so that he can use them to tell the story from multiple points of view. There is no doubt that he employs the journalism register where describing the rain of stones that fell on the White home, complete with its newspaper "lead" and the follow-up "who, what, when, and where" required of a newspaper story. The graffiti register follows next and an excerpt from the register of an academic article comes next. All of these fictional excerpts utilize the conventions of their respective registers. The fact that they are labeled by King as being a newspaper article, graffiti, and an academic paper is almost linguistically redundant and merely fixes the excerpts in time and place for the reader, who immediately recognizes the linguistic conventions of King's invented excerpts.

A linguistic study of the registers using readability test tools scientifically proves the reader's instinctual recognition of the register. In the first excerpt from *"The Shadow Exploded..."* (*Three Novels* 5), an academic paper that cites Tulane University Press as its source, the readability index rates the piece as an overall grade level of 18. There are an average of 40.33 words per sentence and 16.53 percent of the words are complex. The Flesch Kincaid Grade Level is 19.4 and the Flesch Kincaid Reading Ease index is 27.5, based on a scale from 0 to 100, where a high score means the text is easier to read and a low score indicated more complexity. Interestingly enough, a sample page from Jenifer Michelle D'Elia's Ph.D. dissertation about Stephen King's works registers a very similar score on the readability index: an average grade level of about 16, with 31.67 words per sentence, 16.84 percent complex words, a Flesch Kincaid Grade Level of 16.5 and a Flesch Kincaid Reading Ease index of 33.1. If anything, the software shows that the dissertation is a little less complex than King's make-believe academic study. Contrast this with the readability test results of King's bogus newspaper account "A Rain of Stones" (3), which registers at an 8th grade reading level, with 10.71 words per sentence and 13.33 percent of them complex. The Flesch Kincaid Reading Level is 6.1 and the Flesch Kincaid Reading Ease index is 70.8. This compares closely with a sample internet news story from MSNBC, which had a 7th grade reading level, with 6.51 words per sentence (16.01 percent complex), a Flesch Kincaid Grade Level of 5.7, and a reading ease score of 66. Although this is, admittedly, a short, random sample, these scores show that King's made-up academic papers and news stories accurately reflect the corpus linguistics (the body of work) of their respective registers. Finally, a random sample of King's fictional voice in *Carrie* (*Three Novels* 62, par. 2) shows an average 8th grade reading level, an average of 17.20 words per sentence, 6.98 percent of them complex, a Flesch Kincaid Grade Level of 6.8, and a Reading Ease of 77.2 (easier to read than either the make-believe or the real news story sampled). This easy to read style may, indeed, be one reason that Stephen King's works are so popular (yet the fabricated academic article shows that his prose can be very complicated when such a style serves his purpose).

In using the various registers, ranging from the base letters scribbled on a bathroom wall to the inflated prose of the academic, King is putting the Carrie White story into a larger context, where it is commented on by every layer of society, from the teenagers to the scholars, and each member of society weighs in on the story in language appropriate to that register, as the language would be used by that speaker. Since these registers are used to create "believability" in the fictional story, it is crucial that they accurately reflect the linguistics of their registers. Collings argues that "the interpolations seem critical to the tome of the novel" and they "subvert the fantastic by shifting to logical, rational ... explanations for phenomena an earlier generation of novelists might have asserted simply as supernatural" (42). There is no doubt that King is using these textual devices to make the supernatural plot believable, and, as Collings has observed, "parallels other recent novels that blend the subjectivity of fantasy and horror with the objectivity of science fiction by providing scientific (or pseudoscientific) explanations for monsters, creatures, or other paraphernalia of horror" (41). Various newspaper articles and the New England A.P. Ticker give an unbiased, journalistic account of the events that occurred in Chamberlain, Maine, and serve as a historical record, of sorts, to "prove" that the disaster actually occurred. Additional texts published after the tragedy attempt to analyze what occurred and reach a conclusion about its cause. Some of the pieces, such as the various excerpts from the "White Commission Report," assure the public that the Carrie White phenomenon was a one-time event and is not likely to reoccur. Other documentary pieces, however, like the academic study "The Shadow Exploded: Documented Facts and Specific Conclusions Derived from the Case of Carietta White," conclude that a reoccurrence is both scientifically possible and would be impossible to stop or control. The TK phenomenon is explained as a genetic mutation in this study: "The telekinetic, or TK gene, produces female Typhoid Marys capable of destroying almost at will" (*Carrie* 75). This conclusion, coupled with the letter that ends the novel, is what really turns the novel from a science fiction story into a horror story, however, because it postulates a future where a teenager could develop a terrifying power, as in Jerome Bixby's short story "It's a Good Life" but on a much larger scale.

As Collings correctly points out, "The joke, of course, is that all of King's excerpts are as fictional as the narratives interwoven with them" (*Many Facets* 43); "however, they create the illusion of reality" (44). Thus, King validates his story by using the registers of journalism, magazine articles, scientific studies, letters, autobiographies, and legal proceedings. These invented texts, meta-texts, tell us something about writing and the credibility and authority that we give it. The Associated Press wires and the newspaper articles are unbiased and to be believed, even if they are made up. The same holds true for the scientific and university studies, which refer to other studies that were not directly quoted as text. And the texts also allow us to hear the voices of some of the survivors, in their own documented words, both in their individual written pieces (Susan Snell and Norma Watson) and in their testimony before the White Commission.

While the nonfiction excerpts attempt to validate the Carrie White case and make it real and believable, it is the fictional "reading between the lines" that really brings the story to life, however. "Fiction is the truth inside the lie," King said in *Danse Macabre* (375), his nonfiction study of horror, and *Carrie* serves as a perfect example of this idea in action. The lies, of course, are the texts that King has invented to make the occult believable. And the truth is the fictional story that King has written, for this story tells the truth about people and about life. Carrie becomes a real person in the reader's mind because of the fictional portrayal of her as we enter her mind, observe life through her eyes, and experience her thoughts and actions first-hand.

The nonfictional texts only tell a small part of the story. They speculate on what occurred: "How apparent was Carrie's 'wild talent' and what did Margaret White, with her extreme Christian ethic, think of it? We shall probably never know. But one is tempted to believe that Mrs. White's reaction must have been extreme" (*Carrie* 68). The fictional sections that follow fill in the details and bring the scene to life.

The meta-text admits that the objective news accounts and studies cannot capture the full picture. As the Susan Snell "documentary" says about Carrie White: "They've forgotten her, you know. They've made her into a symbol and forgotten that she was a human being, as real as you reading this…. Nothing can change her back now from something made out of newsprint into a person" (*Carrie* 98). The fictional elements of the novel use several points of view of their own. First, there is the omniscient narrator, who opens the narrative on the first page, right after the news story about the rain of stones:

> Nobody was really surprised when it happened, not really, not at the subconscious level where savage things grow. On the surface, all the girls in the shower room were shocked, thrilled, ashamed, or simply glad that the White bitch had taken it in the mouth again…. What none of them knew, of course, was that Carrie White was telekinetic [4].

The omniscient voice, unlike the metalinguistic texts, has tone of authority that claims the truth, even about things that could not possibly be known for sure. As Dymond has correctly pointed out, the omniscient narrator does appear to be male, as he "frequently employs overtly masculine images in reference to his female subjects" (95), including images of gunslingers, sports, and billiard halls. Yet the narrator does attempt to explore the minds of all of the characters and often translates their thoughts into language that King's readers, who were predominantly male, can understand (it must be remembered that King's earliest published stories appeared in men's magazines). It delves into the collective minds of the high school girls who think of Carrie as "the White bitch" even as it gives background information about Carrie's past with the girls: "Carrie had been going to school with some of them since first grade." This short section sets the time and place, introduces the characters, and illustrates the tension that had been "building slowly and immutably in accordance with all the laws that govern human nature" (4).

This omniscient narrator is interrupted by the grammar school graffiti meta-text and then picks up in the locker room in "Period One" (a raunchy foreshadowing of what happens next). The narrator here, though, is no longer omniscient, but adopts the third person objective point of view. This point of view shows just the facts of what occurred, but it does so with intricate detail, describing the scene in microcosm. Here we see Carrie for the first time through the eyes of this objective narrator: "She was a chunky girl with pimples on her neck and back and buttocks, her wet hair completely without color" (4). She is introduced as a "frog among swans," the "sacrificial goat." The narrator describes the shower room itself, the dialogue of the girls, the gym teacher, and finally the laughter as Carrie emerges from the shower with blood running down her leg. This narrative section is completely objective, even if seen through a male voyeuristic lens, except for the tiny intrusion into Carrie's thoughts as "she wished forlornly and constantly" that the high school had private showers. This section is cinematic in form, as if the narrator is a camera recording the action as it occurs, almost as if the scene were something from an "R" rated film. Here King essentially reads between the lines of the accounts that surround it, the graffiti at one end and the excerpt from *The Shadow Exploded* on the other end. The fictional narrator sees the events occurring in real time and conveys a sense of truth and accuracy. Meanwhile, the *Shadow Exploded* study is based on guesswork and speculation: "We have only skimpy hearsay evidence upon which to lay our foundation for this case" (5).

In the next section, the narrator ventures into the mind of Sue Snell, who "felt an odd, vexing mixture of hate, revulsion, exasperation, and pity." Carrie is shown from the point of view of one of the popular girls, who, disgusted, joins in the hazing, throwing tampons at Carrie along with the other girls: "*There's no harm in it*" (7). For a moment, King brings us into the mob mentality and we, the reader, experience the "bully" point of view as all the jokes against Carrie are recounted (7–8). Only at the end of the section does Sue Snell begin to realize what is happening, and we sense her pity for Carrie emerging.

In the following sections, the narrative voice enters the mind of Rita Desjardin, the gym teacher, then Mr. Morton, the assistant principal, before we finally are allowed access to Carrie White's thoughts. Carrie is seen through the eyes of these authority figures, who offer objective viewpoints of their own as Desjardin glimpses Carrie's power as a light bulb burns out and Morton doesn't even remember Carrie's name. The omniscient point of view shows the truth about Carrie as she is seen by the world at large: disgusting, unattractive, and forgettable. And if, as Dymond suggests, the omniscient narrator has a distinct male persona, that persona is, indeed, indicative of a world where females are judged more by their looks than by what their minds can accomplish, which is why Carrie White, the unattractive girl, is so disliked in the first place.

The reader is really not allowed into Carrie's mind until page 16, when she is walking home after the shower room incident. After setting the scene, the narrator slowly works in Carrie's thoughts, sometimes in stream of consciousness (16–17) as she curses her tormenters, remembers her mother's admonishments, and recalls incidents from the past where she was laughed at. "Stream of consciousness writing differs from omniscient narration in its representation of subjectivity" (Lee 10), which leads to the unedited, raw emotions of Carrie White. These thoughts and descriptions can only be told in fiction, of course, since recoding the thoughts and feelings of a dead character is impossible in any other form, and, thus, the fiction fills in the gaps between the meta-texts. Carrie comes to life through the omniscient narrator, who shares her thoughts with the reader, making her a real person to us. Entering her thoughts allows us to empathize, to feel her pain, so to speak:

> She had tried to fit. She had defied Momma in a hundred little ways, had tried to erase the red-plague circle that had been drawn around her from the first day she had left the controlled environment of the small house on Carlin Street and had walked her way up to the Barker Street Grammar School with her Bible under her arm. She could still remember that day, the stares, and the sudden, awful silence when she had gotten down on her knees before lunch in the school cafeteria—the laughter had begun on that day and had echoed up through the years [17].

Later, when Carrie destroys the town, her actions are understandable. In fact, in some way, the reader is with her, rooting for her as she destroys her tormentors. As King himself says, "I never liked Carrie ... but I came at last to understand her a little. I pitied her and I pitied her classmates as well because I had been one of them once upon a time" (*On Writing* 82).

Ironically enough, Sue Snell refers to a movie that was made about Carrie and the incident (a perfect example of reality imitating fiction, since *Carrie* was brought to the screen in 1976, and the remake released in 2013). Even as King says that "fiction is the truth inside the lie," Sue Snell refers to films, fictional products, as places where we forget: "They finally even made a movie about it.... Whenever anything important happens in America they love to gold plate it, like baby shoes. That way you can forget it" (72). In other words, we fictionalize things to make them go away, yet, according to King, it is the fiction that tells the truth. And, in Carrie, the fiction truly does tell what happened and how, and even why, while the so-called "real" texts can only speculate and propose theories that can merely approach the truth, but never really understand it. As we have seen with recent historical films such as 2013 Oscar nominees *Lincoln* and *Argon*, the film versions of history are what we remember, even if they are fictionalized and contain inaccuracies, or, as Baudrillard claims, "only the medium can make an event" (*Simulacra* 82). And, ironically, mentioning "Carrie" to the average person results in a recalling of the Brian De Palma film, not the novel.

Metalanguage, language that talks about itself, plays an important role in Stephen King's first published novel by creating two intertwining narratives, the fictional "story" of Carrie White and the fictional texts that attempt to make the fiction appear realistic. The two narratives complement one another, one working to give the story logic and verisimilitude, and the other, the fictional story, creating detail and characters that bring the story to life in a more visceral way.

Stephen King also has some fun with the metalinguistic and inserts himself directly into one of the documentary sources: "Carrie White passed in the following short verse as a poetry assignment in seventh grade. Mr. Edwin King, who had Carrie for grade seven English, says: 'I don't know why I saved it'" (52). King was to use this in-joke again, when he made cameo appearances in film adaptations of his work, beginning in 1982 when he played the part of Jordy Verrill in *Creepshow* (and where his son Joe played the role of Billy, a boy who gets in trouble for reading comic books). King has also inserted himself into his novels by using writers as characters, and thus writing about writing that creates a "textual or metalinguistic code" where writers write about writers and writing—King even inserts himself as a major character (writer/creator) in the Gunslinger epic. This phenomenon will be discussed in later chapters of this work.

Finally, from a structuralist point of view *Carrie* can be viewed as a retelling of what Joseph Campbell calls an archetype, "elementary ideas, what would be called 'ground' ideas" (*Power* 61) that are common to all of humankind and form the basis for myths, legends, and stories. While structuralism is no longer the popular critical theory that it once was, it does lend itself to a linguistic study since it claims to be the grammar of narrative rather than the grammar of sentences. Furthermore, stories that do fit into the structuralist archetypes of Campbell and Propp still demonstrate how even contemporary writers are, in effect, writing about writing when they use an archetype story as an objective correlative. In the case of *Carrie*, King has used both the menstruation motif and the Cinderella tale to build his novel.

According to Campbell, "in primary cultures today the girl becomes a woman with her first menstruation" (104). Based upon this cultural norm, *Carrie* can be thought of as the female version of the coming of age story. King, like most writers, is really writing about writing when he retells one of these archetype stories and resets it in the modern world for entertainment, as in the folk tale, or spiritual instruction in the myth (71). Campbell says that while males in the ancient world were systematically taught to turn from boys into men by the use of clearly-defined rituals, girls became women as a result of nature: "her first menstruation happens to her. Nature does it to her. And so she has undergone the transformation, and what is her initiation? Typically it is to sit in a little hut for a certain number of days and realize what she is" (104). According to Campbell, many of the problems of modern society are the result of us not having clearly defined rituals or myths to guide us in our transformation into adulthood. This is clearly a problem for Carrie, since she is not allowed to "realize what she is" in a normal way, but must suffer the unnatural attacks of both her mother and the girls in her high school.

Yarbro, Strengell, and other critics have also pointed out the obvious connection between *Carrie* and the Cinderella story, another female coming of age story, if you will. The Cinderella tale is "the best known folktale in the world ... found nearly everywhere from Alaska to South Africa, from Europe to Indonesia and South America; more than 500 versions of the tale are known in Europe alone" (Leach 233). *Carrie*, however, is Cinderella gone horribly wrong. As Yarbro says, "King knows how to evoke those special images that hook into all the archetypal forms of horror that we have thrived on since early youth" (46). He puts Cinderella into the modern and frightening world of high school, where everything can and will go wrong. The girl does not get to try on the glass slipper, does not get to marry the prince, and, while she has just the briefest moment of redemption and liberation, it all goes up in flames, literally. In our modern world of reality, we all know that fairy tales seldom end happily ever after and that princesses only exist in Disney's Magic Kingdom. This novel is a reminder that women must harness their own power and not rely on others, who will let them down when they are needed most. Unfortunately for Carrie, this was a lesson never learned and she is, therefore, destined for destruction.

In summary, *Carrie* was Stephen King's early attempt to effectively portray a female character (Magistrale, *Decade* 5), one who is plain, unattractive, and disliked by everyone, but who has incredible powers of the mind, a metaphor that is not lost on his readers. As a male who wrote for men's magazines, it is difficult for him to escape from his masculine persona, which does anchor his omniscient narrator, so he employs the use of a number of linguistic registers to verify and codify the story of Carrie White, which might not otherwise be believed. His use of journalistic and academic registers is of particular importance, since these mediums are considered unbiased and trustworthy. Yet the real truth of the narrative lies in the fictional telling of the story, where he employs an omniscient narrator to dig beneath the headlines, so to speak, and explore the mind of Carrie White. While his narrator may be masculine, as Dymond suggests, many of King's readers are also male (Mckay), and his narrator is often able to translate the complexities of Carrie's mind to his male readers, though, perhaps, at the cost of alienating his female readers in the process. And, of course, since Carrie is unfairly judged by a world based upon male ideas of womanhood, it is not altogether unrealistic that the narrator's images be masculine.

Ultimately, though, King is, I think, exploring a different human condition than gender alone, though he is certainly writing a story that reminds women not to put their faith in the Fairy Tales of the past. Carrie is the story of an outcast, an outsider, someone who is judged by physical appearance rather than intelligence or strength of character, and in a world that favors looks and popularity, she falls short. And when she is transformed for the prom, she still won't win her Prince Charming. *Carrie* is the story of a teenager being bullied, a theme King returns to often in his fiction—"The Body" is one notable example. Telekinesis becomes a metaphor for Carrie White's mental powers, which have been completely buried by her physical appearance and which must be "validated" by reputable sources. Horror and the supernatural are King's chosen vehicle for exploring this truth and, in fact, exaggerating it to the point that it cannot be ignored. As Perry has said, "If an author's truth can best be expressed through the supernatural ... then such narratives can still represent an 'honest' narrative, even when it diverges from common perceptions of reality" (31). In *Carrie*, as in most of King's work, fictional horror and the supernatural are indeed the lies that tell the truth.

CHAPTER 2

'Salem's Lot: The Word Gives Being

'Salem's Lot, originally titled "The Second Coming" in manuscript form, was Stephen King's second published novel and appeared in 1975. The paperback edition reached number one on the *New York Times* best-seller list and was adapted into a television miniseries in 1979. The novel, one of Stephen King's favorites (Winter 36), successfully transported the vampire legends of Europe into a small American town.

King, of course, is cashing in on the overwhelming popularity of vampires as one of the favorite "monsters" in the horror genre. According to Fishoff's study in 2005, vampires were ranked number one in popularity of all "movie monsters" by both males and females (16); "vampires engage viewers most because of their intelligence and because they never die of old age" (24) and have "supernatural powers that may be appealing to those who feel powerless" (27). Another positive feature cited in movie vampires is their sexual appeal (24).

The premise of *'Salem's Lot* is brilliantly simple—what if vampires moved into a small, isolated New England town? Reference to the town is mentioned in a short story "Jerusalem's Lot," a sort of Lovecraftian prequel that King wrote in college and was later published in *Nightshift* in 1978. Winter has noted, however, the book is not about vampires, as such, but is about their "victim," the mythical town that lies somewhere in Maine between Falmouth and Cumberland. The protagonist, Ben Mears, is a "mildly successful novelist" (*Three Novels* 191) who returns to his hometown after leaving it in his childhood.

Much like *Carrie*, the beginning of the novel uses newspaper articles to bring authenticity to the story. Mears (who is not named in the prologue) has fled with "the boy" to Mexico and makes a weekly 40-mile trip to get the Portland *Press-Herald* for news of Jerusalem's Lot (193). On page 194, an entire bogus newspaper story (the journalism register) is reproduced—"Ghost Town in Maine?"—and documents that something strange has happened in this tiny Maine village. As in *Carrie*, however, the newspaper can't uncover the truth since the former inhabitants of the town won't speak with the reporter (195), and so there are "unanswered questions" (196). Nonfiction and journalism again fall short, and the truth will emerge in the extended flashback that becomes the novel itself.

It is, in fact, the telling that makes it so, or, as Heidegger said, "the word alone gives being to the thing" (*On the Way* 62). This is demonstrated clearly when the boy enters the church and tells the story: "He made his first confession—and confessed everything" (196). At first the priest does not believe—"I have never heard a stranger confession in all my days of the priesthood"—but Mears assures him that the confession is the truth. This use of metalanguage in the genre of "confession" adds more evidence to the "fact" that an "awful thing, a dark thing" (198) has happened to the boy and is "eating him up." It would be unthinkable to lie about such a thing to a priest during confession, and so the reader is assured that whatever happened, it must have been true.

According to Heidegger, and modern linguistic theory, language not only describes what already exists, but can be used to create new realities (1125). In this novel Stephen King uses language to create a town that doesn't exist and he makes it real. It is important that the town be created first, that it is real and totally believable and with intricate detail. As King has said, "I thought it would make a good [novel], if I could create a fictional town with enough prosaic reality about it to offset the comic-book menace of a bunch of vampires" ("On Becoming" 44). Once we enter the first chapter, driving into town with Ben Mears, the world is described in painstaking detail. A cast of characters is vividly introduced, everyone from Susan, who will become Ben's lover, right down to minor characters like Charlie the school bus driver (242) and Richie Boddin, "the school bully and proud of it" (247). The omniscient narrator slides into each of the character's minds, one by one, and brings them almost magically to life. As Ringel has noted, "The tale owes its power not to ancient European vampire myths, but to the verisimilitude of the down–Maine setting" (207).

According to Thury, vampire stories have become part of modern mythology and have "mythological status" (773). They are classified as "urban fantasy" (772) and "are typically set in a mundane world that is more or less 'normal' except for the presence of vampires" (777). King goes to great lengths to create this "mundane world" before inhabiting it with supernatural creatures. And he chooses a nondescript, out of the way rural town, which, according to Magistrale embodies "the pastoral myth ... [that] represents the last bastion of American values and patriotism" (*Hollywood* 176). Magistrale rightly observes that this town will serve as a "prototype" that King will return to again and again in his fiction, where horror infects rural America. The message, of course, is that if vampires and horror can exist in such a small, insignificant place like 'Salem's Lot (or Derry, Castle Rock, Little Tall Island), then it can exist anywhere and must, by extrapolation, be even more powerful in cities like Los Angeles, Las Vegas, and San Francisco (home to the first Satanic Church) that seem to embrace less traditional values.

The town itself is described in minute detail, beginning, of course, with the Marsten House:

> It was huge and rambling and sagging, its windows haphazardly boarded shut, giving it that sinister look of all old houses that have been empty for a long time. The paint had been weathered away, giving the house a uniform gray look. Windstorms had ripped many of the shingles off, and a heavy snowfall had punched in the west corner of the main roof, giving it a slumped, hunched look. A tattered no-trespassing sign was nailed to the right-hand newel post [206].

Interestingly enough, after seeing the house again, and its no-trespassing sign, Mears feels a "strong urge to walk up that overgrown path" and enter the house, if it were unlocked. This, of course, foreshadows events that will occur later in the narrative.

Obviously the Marsten House, the centerpiece of the horror that would infect the town, would be fully described, as in the tradition of Shirley Jackson's Hill House, or Faulkner's description of Emily's house in "A Rose for Emily." But King goes beyond just creating the haunted house, or the evil place. Virtually every corner of Jerusalem's Lot is painted in realistic detail. The town is given a history (217) and the reader is then provided a guided tour:

> The main street, known originally as the Portland Post Road, had been named after Elias Jointner in 1896. Jointner, a member of the House of Representatives for six years (up until his death, which was caused by syphilis at the age of fifty-eight), was the closest thing to a personage that the Lot could boast—with the exception of Jerusalem the pig and Pearl Ann Butts, who ran off to New York City in 1907 to become a Ziegfeld girl [217–18].

The history is told by an insider, a native, with all of the scandal and trivia as we are shown the intersection with Brock Street, the northeast quadrant, the southeast, southwest, and even the telephone lines. We learn that the town council has biannual public meetings and that there are three selectmen (219). The purpose of this trivia is to figuratively set the cornerstones of the town, anchor it in time and place, and cement it on a solid foundation of belief. The town, of course, is not real—"'Geographically speaking,' King admits, 'Jerusalem's Lot would be about ten feet underwater. Because the geography in the book suggests that, to get there, you would have to drive off where the existing coast ends'" (Winter 197). Yet, it is easy for the reader to suspend disbelief when presented with such descriptive realism. It is important, even necessary, for the reader to believe in the town, to accept it as real, to believe that "nothing too nasty could happen in such a nice little town. Not there" (*Three Novels* 220). Stephen King gives us the insider's tour of his town. As Collings has observed, "King works ... at disallowing any particular sense of horror or dread" early in the novel (*Facets* 72). And then, after over 150 pages of living in Jerusalem's Lot, the vampire appears. By then we have become so immersed in the details of the town and its inhabitants that we believe in the supernatural horror and accept it as well.

If the town is, indeed, the "victim" of the vampire outbreak, it appears to be a willing victim, however, one that is already "infected" with dark secrets. "King's third person narrative is a scathing portrait of small town middle America," according to Magistrale (*Hollywood* 178). As we will see again in *Needful Things*, the town is already suffering from moral decay and the vampire invasion merely makes the secret corruption come to life. As Eads points out, the township has a history of kidnapping and pedophiles (84) and the gossip overheard in the store is about perverts and sexual predators (87). In fact, once the townspeople learn that Ben Mears is a writer, they begin to speculate about his sanity and his writing, which Mabel says is "a sexbook, pure and simple" (*Three Novels* 224). Of course, one must wonder how she knew it was a "sexbook" unless she had actually read it. As Eads also points out, homosexuality is also considered deviant behavior by the residents of 'Salem's Lot, which is no surprise considering that the novel was originally published in 1975, a much less progressive era than the present, and that it depicts the attitudes of a small, conservative town where calling a male "queer" was the ultimate insult. Yet the town does have its resident homosexual in the person of George Middler, who is mocked behind his back and yet accepted as a necessary evil by the townsfolk. As the owner of the town's store, he is not only the object of gossip, but the purveyor of it as well; since the store is the "hub" of the town, so to speak, it is the place where secrets are shared and gossip is passed on.

Although the town is clearly saturated with "secrets," even the most intimate secrets become known through the voice of the omniscient narrator who effectively tells all. In the first section of Chapter Ten, the town itself becomes one with the omniscient narrator. "The town knew about darkness" (412) and in this section, it shares its secrets with the narrator and with the reader, "some that will later be known and some that will never be known" (416). Yet, in the reality of the novel, they are all known, they all become part of the story. And while the town keeps its secrets with a "poker face" (416), it is important that the reader knows them all because this town is not the idyllic, pastoral paradise that is depicted in the small town stereotype. 'Salem's Lot is a place where the great fire of 1951 was an act of arson, where the Reverend dreams of preaching naked to his female congregation, where Hal Griffen keeps pornography hidden in his closet for his masturbation fantasies, and where George Middler likes to dress up in women's lingerie. It is a town full of hypocrites, whose public and private lives do not match. As the omniscient narrator says, "when evil falls on the town, its coming seems almost preordained" (*Three Novels* 414). The town is its own worst enemy, and with its hypocrisy and secrecy, it makes the perfect breeding place for evil. As Magistrale has said, the townsfolk "appear ready to accept and to welcome the evil darkness of the vampire as a vehicle for escaping the financial, marital, and communal misery that typifies everyday life in this American town" (*Hollywood* 178).

In Bram Stoker's *Dracula*, vampirism was a thinly veiled metaphor for sexuality in a Victorian time when sex was not openly discussed and could not be written about. The vampire, in fact, becomes a hero, of sorts. Yet in *'Salem's Lot*, the vampires are more zombie-like, more like an infection or an infestation. According to Auerbach, "King's vampires are so horrible that they look retrograde" (155). They do not have the charm of a Dracula, but are more like mindless zombies. "These floundering, directionless killers pay occasional lip service to Dracula, but they have no access to his individuality, his efficiency, even his tyranny.... They are cousins of the utterly American vampires ... in *Night of the Living Dead*" (161). This concept is developed further when these vampires reappear in the Gunslinger epic.

In the 1970's, when *'Salem's Lot* was written, it was not necessary to disguise sexuality as metaphor: the censors had already effectively been silenced, as Stephen King, who had published his fiction in the "men's magazines," well knew. His vampires are not sexy or seductive in the traditional sense. They were not "selected," as they are in traditional vampire novels; anyone can become infected until the whole town is composed of vampires. Men, women, old people and children, heterosexuals and homosexuals—they all become victims of the disease. Though homosexuality was still not fully accepted by mainstream America when King wrote the novel, his depiction of it is not, I believe, a metaphor of sex or sexuality, but is one of power and corruption, as Eads has pointed out. Sex itself is not the evil, but when it is used as a tool of power it becomes corrupt: "there is neither a potentially monstrous homosexuality or heterosexuality specifically, only a potentially monstrous sexuality in general" (83). The town's secret history of pedophiles and kidnappings point to sins of power rather than sexuality, and these sins are what make the town susceptible to vampirism, which is the ultimate symbol of power and control. "King is primarily interested in using vampirism ... to show how any human desire carries a vampiric potentiality" and that "Barlow only brings out the township's 'inner vampire'" (Eads 82). It is relatively easy for the vampire plague to invade and infest the corrupt inhabitants of the town, who are so busy keeping their own secrets that they don't recognize what is happening right under their eyes. Because of this, the infection is democratic and "open to all," as Auerbach has said, an "epidemic as indiscriminate as fire" (156).

Yet if the vampire exhibits power and control, it can also be the victim of power in the form of language and knowledge. Much of the novel's symbolic code is based upon the binary oppositions of secrecy and knowledge, both of which represent power. Holding and retaining secrets, of course, grants power to the secret holder. The vampires, in fact, gain the power from the fact that their power is secret; the townsfolk do not realize that they are vampires, and since such knowledge is not scientific but is founded in myth and legend, the secret is easy to keep. Even in a small, rural town, twentieth-century Americans are not willing to accept the premise of vampirism, and that is Barlow's trump card, so to speak. However, once the secret is revealed, the balance of power shifts: "once they have been named and referenced, they will be destroyed" (Sanders 153).

The horror novel typically has a three-part structure, which is apparent in 'Salem's Lot. The first part is the set-up of time and place and the gradual understanding of the reader and protagonist that something is not quite right with the world. The second is discovering the exact nature of the wrongness, of the "otherness" and pinning it down. Once that revelation is made, the evil can be destroyed. If it is a werewolf, the silver bullets are created; zombies are beheaded and vampires succumb to the stake through the heart. This concept is the basis for fantastic fiction and, as Austin has said, allows us to create things with words. But just as language can create, so, too, it can destroy. "If we can think the name 'vampire,' if we can allow that such a thing might exist, then we may ... describe it, teach it, settle it, and rule over it.... The vampire's greatest fear, after being made visible, is that of being named" (Sanders 151).

Ben Mears, of course, is a writer whose living depends upon words, who, in fact, does things with words. It is only natural that he is the one who "names" the vampires and ultimately destroys them. But first, it is important that Mears himself be established as an author so that he may play this pivotal role in the story. His character introduces the textual code of writing and authorship into the novel.

King is perhaps having some fun at his own expense as his Mears is "mildly successful" (191) and disliked by the critics—as Ann Norton tells her daughter, "I read a review of this in the Portland paper. It wasn't very good" (222). At the time of its publication, King himself had not yet become a bestselling author.

King also plays with the metalanguage of fiction and nonfiction:

"You think he's a real writer, Park?"
"Sure he is. He's got three books right in this library."
"True or made up?"
"Made up."

Ironically enough, it is the "made up" portions of writing, fiction, that seem to get at real truth and understanding, while, as we have seen in the novel's prologue and in *Carrie*, the metalanguage of truth as indicated in newspaper articles and documents, leaves "unanswered questions." Ben Mears, the author of *Conway's Daughter* and *Air Dance*, seems remarkably like the later Richard Bachman that Stephen King fans would grow to know and love. These books, about a minister's daughter who runs away and joins the counterculture, and about an escaped con who is recaptured, sound mundane and based more in realism than horror or fantasy, and Mears himself wonders "how it ever got published" (209).

King examines the stereotypes of writers through the eyes of the rural inhabitants. "'A man would have to be nuttier than a squirrel to tap-tap-tap away like that, day in and day out,' Weasel Craig, one of the locals, thinks" (244). "And he had heard most of those writers drink like fish" (246).

Aside from the insights and in-jokes about writing, however, the fact that Mears is a writer is thematically significant. First of all, in a metalinguistic layering of language, Mears tells Susan about the book he is writing, which is the theme of *'Salem's Lot* itself: "You asked me what my book is about. Essentially, it's about the recurrent power of evil" (315), "a fiction-

alized sort of thing" (359). At the end of *'Salem's Lot*, when Mears returns
to destroy the vampires in Eva's boarding house, where he lived, he also
symbolically destroys the draft of his book.

> He took the manuscript, threw it in, and made a paper spill of the title page. He lit it
> with his Cricket, and when it flared up he tossed it in on top of the drift of typewritten
> pages. The flame tasted them, found them good, and began to crawl eagerly over the
> paper. Corners charred, turned upward, blackened. Whitish smoke began to billow
> out of the wastebasket, and without thinking about it, he leaned over his desk and
> opened the window [627].

Burning the manuscript not only foreshadows his return to set the entire
town to flames, but also purges evil thematically. Torching the fictional
evil in the draft of his book makes the destruction real. His description
of the burning manuscript is rendered in the same intricate detail as the
description of the town and its characters. And, in Stephen King stories,
"fire, the cleansing agent of evil, gets the upper hand in the end" (Anderson, "Morality" 32). It is the only way to completely destroy the book and
all traces of its evil.

Another important theme of *'Salem's Lot* is confrontation of evil.
"Vampires are the perfect vehicle for demonstrating concerns that we live
in a harsh, dark world and have to contend with diminished expectations
as a result of natural limitations and human greed," according to Thury
(771), which is one of the reasons these stories have become part of modern mythology. The town has been unable to come to terms with the things
that have occurred in the Marsten House, which remains as an eyesore to
remind them of their corrupt past. Even Mabel Werts, "a repository of
town history and town gossip [whose] memory stretched back over five
decades of necrology, adultery, thievery, and insanity" (274), refused to
share gossip about Hubert Marsten's alleged devil worship. "The secrecy
concerning that aspect of Hubie and his wife is almost tribal," according
to Matt (405). These secrets were not spoken of and definitely not shared
with strangers or outsiders.

Writers, however, are seekers of truth. And while journalists might
seek truth in their own ways, fiction writers seek a deeper truth, the truth
inside the human heart. So if "fiction is the truth inside the lie" (*Danse
Macabre* 375), then it only makes sense that the protagonist, a novelist,
would seek the truth about his adolescent experience by returning to
'Salem's Lot and writing about the Marsten House. Ben Mears is the only
one who can pull aside the curtain and discover the truth. "Ben Mears'
role as a writer forces him to confront the secret of the town by acknowledging its essential corruption" (Magistrale, *Moral* 112).

The protagonist takes it further, though, by confronting fears within himself. He is forced "to face (by writing about them) the fears that have troubled him since adolescence. By confronting these fears on paper, Mears learns how to confront and conquer others that await him in real life; his writing is nothing less than an act of self-empowerment" (113). He does this by writing a fictional piece about evil, which turns out to illuminate the truth: "that the Marsten House may have become a kind of evil dry-cell; a malign storage battery" (*Three Novels* 405). Mears' fictional search proves mirror to the actual events that occur. He describes the plot to Matt: "There are a series of sex murders and mutilation. I'm going to open with one of them and describe it in progress, from start to finish, in minute detail.... I was outlining that part when Ralphie Glick disappeared" (360).

In contrast, Father Callahan is a "wannabe" author who wants to write history. "He had been working on the Notes for seven years, supposedly for a book on the Catholic Church in New England, but he suspected now that the book would never be written" (352). As a historian and a resident of the Lot, Callahan should be the one to see the truth first, and as religious leader, he should have been the one to confront the truth and destroy it. Yet, interestingly enough, he is unable to stand up to Barlow. His crucifix is destroyed, Barlow overpowers him and completely destroys his faith, and Callahan flees 'Salem's Lot forever. Mears, the outsider and the fiction writer, faces the truth and stands up to it. His makeshift crucifix, made from two tongue depressors taped together, drives Barlow back. And, of course, Mears is the one who destroys the vampires, and, later in the epilogue, returns with the boy to incinerate the place once and for all, burning it down just as he burned the draft of his fiction based upon the town.

In conclusion, *'Salem's Lot* might be considered just another vampire story, yet it is different from the Bram Stoker model in that it takes the vampire out of the castle and puts him in a small, mundane American town. If the vampire can live in small-town America, then he can exist anywhere and be amongst us (as, he is again, when vampires turn up in New York City in the Gunslinger books). The vampire is, in fact, welcomed by the inhabitants of the town, each of whom is harboring their own dark secrets. Many vampire novels, from *Dracula* to the *Twilight* series make the vampire a heroic figure. King's vampires are not heroic, however. They embody the worst traits in each of us. They are predators, and the humans they turn into vampires don't become heroic or even sympathetic. Whatever flaws they had as humans are magnified in them as they enter the world of the undead.

King's vampires are not about seduction, or repressed sexuality. They are about power and control. They are the pedophiles, the rapists, the bullies and abusers transformed into the supernatural. They are the metaphorical secrets that humans keep, they things we chose not to think about. As King says, "Only *through* fiction can we think about the unthinkable, and perhaps obtain some sort of closure" (*Bazaar* 268). And, in *'Salem's Lot* this closure—the destruction of the vampires in the rural town—is brought about not by the police, the military, or a superhero, but by Ben Mears, a fiction writer. Only Mears can "think about the unthinkable" and thereby destroy it.

CHAPTER 3

"The Word Processor of the Gods": The Writer Creates the World

"The Word Processor of the Gods" was originally published in *Playboy* in 1983 and was adapted into a television episode of *Tales from the Darkside*, which aired in November 1984. The story and was reprinted in *Skeleton Crew* in 1985. While the technological references are quite outdated by today's standards—"at first glance it looked like a Wang word processor" and had an "IBM cathode Tube" (*Skeleton* Crew 307), and a word processor has a cost of $5,000 to $18,000—the concept is still interesting, and as technology closes the gap towards creating artificial intelligence, its theme is more relevant than ever. This story, along with, perhaps, "Ur," exposes its metalinguistic code most clearly and uses writing directly as a symbol for the creation of the world. In this story, writing is seen as the tool of God, or the gods, as it can create physical objects just by writing them down. The plot itself is right out of Austin, "the issuing of the utterance is the performing of an action" (6), and Heidegger, "the word gives being to the thing" (*On the Way* 62). As the first verse of the Gospel of John states: "In the beginning was the Word, and the Word was with God, and the Word was God."

The story opens when the protagonist, Richard Hagstrom, receives a word processor built by his nephew Jon, who was killed in an accident when his drunken father drove the family van over a cliff. The boy, a child genius, has built the machine out of spare parts and assorted salvage.

Richard, a teacher and part-time writer who is trying to earn a living at his craft, isn't taken seriously by his wife or son, and only his nephew and sister-in-law understand him. He lives an unhappy life where he feels like he has been treated unfairly:

> And Richard thought how strange it was—his brother, who had been an utter shit since the age of six, had gotten a fine woman and a bright son. He, himself, who had always tried to be gentle and good ... had married Lina, who had developed into a silent, piggy woman, and had gotten Seth by her [311].

Yet "he had never quite let go of his dream" (309) and relates more to his nephew than his own son, who plays loud "sour bar chords" on his guitar and does "marginal work in the same school where Richard taught" (308). On the other hand, Jon is "just like you, Richard," according to his wife. "Head always in the clouds" (322). Once Richard turns on the word processor he learns that it not only works, but has the power to create, delete, and change the world, not only figuratively with language, but in reality.

From a linguistic point of view, this story is a perfect illustration of the use and power of words. As de Saussure has said, "In language one can neither isolate sound from thought nor thought from sound" (157). Words describe the known world and they name things, concepts and ideas: "MY SON IS SETH ROBERT HAGSTROM" (319). The machine also has the power to create new worlds, however. Once Richard hits the "delete" key and deletes this sentence, then his son Seth ceases to exist, and, in fact, has never existed. This is illustrated most clearly when Richard examines the bannister where his son had carved his initials as a child, had used writing to mark his own existence. After Seth is deleted, "all trace of the initials is gone" (320).

This story harkens in some ways to "The Nine Billion Names of God" by Arthur C. Clarke, a story where monks use a computer to "print" all of the possible names of God, who is supposedly unnamable. Once the feat is accomplished and the correct name listed, God reasserts his power and the world is destroyed. The word processor, like the monk's computer, is God-like. When Richard first brings it in, in pieces, his wife exclaims, "What in the name of *God* is that?" (307). But the machine isn't a god by itself—it needs man to "speak" in order for it to do god-like things like create and destroy. "Wired up like the bride of Frankenstein" (312) the technology brings Jon and his mother back to life, but it needs the words of a man to do so: "I AM A MAN WHO LIVES ALONE EXCEPT FOR MY WIFE, BELINDA, AND MY SON JONATHAN" (324).

As the Gospel of John states, the word was with God and was God. Indeed, every society has articulated its creation stories in words, has written them down, and, for that society, the words have become real. As Heidegger states, "something *is* only where the appropriate and therefore competent word names a thing as being, and so establishes the given being as being.... Therefore ... Language is the House of Being" (*On the Way* 63).

The machine is personified as being alive as it speaks. "Eerily, like a voice from the grave, these words came up, green ghosts from the darkness: HAPPY BIRTHDAY UNCLE RICHARD! JON" (311). The CPU "was humming ... almost roaring" (313); "it began to make an uneven, howling noise" (323) and is "screaming" (324) before it finally dies. Even Jon refers to it as human as he plans to "cannibalize anything worth cannibalizing out of that thing" (325).

The word processor is a high tech version of the "magic eight ball" that Richard had as a child and which also spoke. "Its phony, yet somehow mysterious responses," words also created by men, "included IT IS ALMOST CERTAIN, I WOULD NOT PLAN ON IT, and ASK AGAIN LATER" (314). Yet the machine, even when spitting nonsense, is considered magical. Modern computers, with their ability to compete with chess grandmasters and solve complicated problems, are, indeed not understandable to the average person who uses them. As Joseph Campbell said, the inside of a computer is "a whole hierarchy of angels—all on slats, and those little tubes—those are miracles" (*Power* 24).

Creation stories from many cultures begin with a plea or prayer to God or the gods to supply the words in order to create the story of creation. Hesiod says that the daughters of Zeus "breathed into me wondrous voice, so that I could celebrate things of the future and things that were aforetime. And they told me to sing of the family of blessed ones who are for ever, and first and last to sing of themselves" (4). Ovid asks the Roman gods to "breathe your breath into my book of changes: may the song I sing be seamless as its way weaves from the world's beginnings to our day" (qtd. in Thury 50). The author of the Mesopotamian *Enuma Elish* creation story begins with a time "when heaven above was not yet named/Nor earth below pronounced by name." Then the gods "Lahmu and Lahamu emerged, their names pronounced" (qtd. in Thury 68). According to the creation story of the West African Bambara tribe, the sound "yo" brings the universe into existence (Bailey). These stories all share the theme of the importance of language, both to humans and to the gods; until something was named and could be "sung about," it did not exist.

"The Word Processor of the Gods" can be thought of as a foreshadowing to King's longer work "Ur," which is also about technology creating the world, and which will be discussed at length in a later chapter, and the artist in the Gunslinger series is capable of creating and destruction using pencil drawings. The word processor was built by 15-year-old boy and has bugs and flaws, partly because of Jon's inexperience in building such a machine and partly because he didn't live long enough to perfect it. If we extrapolate a little, though, we can easily understand how a perfected model of this machine could exist and, in fact, in Stephen King's multi-verse, *does* exist. As Richard reshapes his own world by creating and destroying, he is, in effect, creating a parallel universe and putting himself in it. "The Word Processor of the Gods" was written early in King's career, but this multiverse concept becomes a major theme in his fiction, weaving itself through the Gunslinger novels, reappearing in *11/22/63*, *IT*, and "Ur," to name just a few. It is interesting to note that in "Ur" the machine, a pink kindle, is the reading device that opens up each of the multiverses to Wesley Smith, the story's protagonist. With this device he is able to read novels by Hemingway that the author did not write in this universe, but did write in other universes. One might speculate that if a Kindle reader can be used to observe these alternate universes, then might not they have been written on the perfected version of the word processor in this story? Might not all of the worlds in all of the universes have been created on a computer that "writes" them and by an author-god that creates them?

Campbell suggests that the robot or machine has become a modern worldwide mythology, appearing in *Faust* and *Star Wars* in the persona of Darth Vader. "The machine man can provide us with all the means and is thus likely to determine the aims of life itself" (*Power* 24). In "Word Processor of the Gods" the machine creates a better life for Richard. In other King stories (such as *Cell*, for example), the machine is a destructive force that can bring about the apocalypse.

In this story, both the eight ball and the word processor require a writer, however, someone to write the script. In Stephen King's world, the writer is the god and the machines, no matter how clever, are his tools. God, then, was the world and created everything through the word. It is no coincidence that the creator of this word processor was named "Jon," based upon the name of John in the New Testament book that says that the Word came first and the Word was God. Jon, the "God" of this multi-verse, created the machine and no doubt would have perfected it and used it to reshape his own world, had he lived long enough. Instead, Richard wound up with the device, and, as the text shows, Richard is a flawed god.

Not all writers are recognized as "gods" in this world and Richard, who has had limited success, would not be considered for the writer's hall of fame, if there were one. "The one novel he had written had not been lucrative, and the critics had been quick to point out that it wasn't very wonderful, either" (309). His wife, or course, agrees with the critics and she mocks him, even though she seems to enjoy reading "a bodice-ripper paperback" (308). "Why don't you go write a Nobel Prize winning short story or something?" she says (323), displaying her ignorance of writing.

Linguistic theory recognizes that all language is magical, though, and has the power to name, create, and change the world—not just poetic language. And, it is so in this story as well. "I have no son," Richard says, and then thinks, "How many times had he heard that melodramatic phrase in bad novels.... Now it was true" (320). Even the mundane can be changed; when he writes that his wife's picture is on the wall, and then, when he dislikes his words, he deletes them and the picture, too, is gone (315). Rewriting the phrase makes the photo reappear and brings it back to life. Writing, even mediocre writing, creates characters, places, and things. If we believe what King is telling us in this story and in "Ur," writing might, indeed, have created everything.

In this short story, as in a number of King's narratives, the protagonist is a writer, a creator of worlds with language. Magistrale reminds us that in King's fiction, the true writer is a survivor, one who can transcend hardship and emerge stronger. We have seen this in *'Salem's Lot* and the theme will appear again in *Misery*. "If there is strength to be found in staring into the abyss, King hastens to inform us that even greater power is to be had in the act of writing about it" (*Moral Voyages* 120). Richard Hagstrom does more than just survive, though. He goes on to create a new, improved world for himself, one where he is respected and loved. One suspects he is no more successful as a writer in this world than he was in his original one; he seems to be living in the same house, not the mansion of a celebrity, but his quality of life has vastly improved because of Jon's genius and Richard's role as writer and creator. He has, in fact, been a god, at least for a few moments. But it is enough. When Jon suggests not rebuilding the word processor, his new father agrees: "That might be just as well.... Delete it from our lives" (325).

In summary, "The Word Processor of the Gods" is an early Stephen King story. Its technology is now outdated and King himself has perfected his craft, even as "Jon" would have, had he lived longer in the story. I believe this story is an important part of the King canon, however, for several reasons. First, it metaphorically demonstrates the power of words and language, Heidegger's "House of Being," and how language and art creates people, places, things, and ideas basically out of thin air. Language is, indeed, a magical process, one that is only available to human beings in our world. The word processor, named as a tool of the gods in the story's title, represents language, the vehicle with which all creation stories are made. Without language, we could not contemplate even the idea of "being," let alone speculate on where we come from, where we are going, or the meaning of life. Language in general, and literature in particular, allows us to be metaphysical beings. "In 'poetical' discourse, the communication of the existential possibilities of one's state-of-mind can become an aim in itself, and this amounts to a disclosing of existence" (Heidegger, *Being* 205). In other words, we cannot understand the concept of life without language.

Secondly, this story is an important part of the Stephen King canon in that it foreshadows his work to come and his complex weaving of alternate worlds and the existence of a multiverse throughout his fiction. The Gunslinger series forms the hub of this multiverse, which radiates out into much of King's later fiction, including *It, Lisey's Story, 11/22/63, Revival,* and others. We can see how some of this comes together in "Ur," where King creates a machine that allows us to peek into the different universes that are part of the multiverse. This pink Kindle offers a small and secret window into the bigger picture. However, if the pink Kindle is the reading device, could a better developed version of the word processor of the gods be the tool that creates these varied universes? When placed within the larger context of Stephen King's fiction, it seems a plausible hypothesis, even if King didn't realize he was creating the mechanism for his multiverse at the time he was writing the story.

Chapter 4

The Shining:
The Sleep of Reason

The Shining, published in 1977, was King's first hardcover bestseller (Rogak 84), was adapted into film by Stanley Kubrick in 1980, and was remade into a three part ABC miniseries in 1997. The book was banned in school libraries "for portraying a father as being truly evil" (84) and was particularly terrifying because so much of the horror took place in Jack Torrance's mind, causing some interviewers to ask if the book was a ghost story, or just a product of the protagonist's mind. Although he seldom analyzed his own stories, King did make it clear that this was, in fact, a ghost story "because Jack Torrance himself is a haunted house. He's haunted by his father" (*Bare Bones* 104). Although this novel and its derivative film adaptations have had more critical attention devoted to it than any of King's works, I believe a metalinguistic approach can help to sort out the various readings and provide new insights into the work, especially in the context of writers and writing, a theme that King returns to again and again.

The novel begins with an extensive quote from Poe's "The Masque of the Red Death" as King pays homage to the father of the horror story and employs his "spirit of the perverse" as a theme of the novel, a subject that will be examined later.

Following this is a quote by Goya, "The sleep of reason breeds monsters." From a metalinguistic perspective, this quote can be seen as the governing principle of the entire novel—the "sleep of reason" affects Jack Torrance at many levels. His alcoholism, of course, puts his reason to sleep.

But his inability to write, to create, is even more devastating, feeding his alcoholism, his depression, and his madness. His writer's block, a sleep of reason, does, indeed, unleash monsters. Where Richard Hagstrom's writing, though mediocre, kept him going, brought him life and ultimately earned him the greatest gift, the wife and child he dreamed of, Torrance's inability to write allowed the monsters in and destroyed his reason, his sanity, and the beautiful family that he already possessed. Torrance refers to both his wife and son as "extraordinary" on just the second page of the novel (*Three Novels* 650), so it seems that he begins the novel having a perfect family. Very soon, however, we see the cracks in the family, and we quickly learn that Jack himself is the weak link—"daddy ... sometimes he does things he's sorry for later" (660).

In both *'Salem's Lot* and "The Word Processor of the Gods," the writer has been the one in control of his own life. Ben Mears is flung into a horror not of his making and escapes using his wits. And Richard Hagstrom is always the good father, the provider, even if his family is lacking. In *The Shining*, though, Jack is the dysfunctional party and his dysfunction seems to be related to his writing. As his wife Wendy notes: "Her husband was a lush. He had a bad temper, one he could no longer keep wholly under control now that he was drinking so heavily and his writing was going so badly" (697). This is an example of "metafictional determinism," a concept I will explore later in this chapter.

While Magistrale claims that "Jack's dedication to his craft is as strong as any of the other authors found elsewhere in King's fiction" (*Moral Voyages* 107), it seems that Jack really lacks the motivation and work ethic it takes to succeed as a professional writer. He is not very prolific, having written only short stories, and lacking the ambition to write a novel: "he was not ready to stumble into the swamp of another three-year undertaking" (754). Furthermore, he is incapable of holding down a real job while he works at his craft. Once he lands a prestigious teaching job, he turns to drinking and "now thought that part of his drinking problem had stemmed from an unconscious desire to be free of Stovington and the security he felt was stifling whatever creative urge he had" (753). Jack believes that publishing the play may get him reinstated in his teaching position, but if the teaching job stifled his creativity, then it is a no-win situation. Furthermore, Jack relates to George Hatfield, a "lackadaisical, amused sort of student in the classroom" who was "content with C's and the occasional B" and "was familiar with the type from his own days as a high school and college student" (758).

Stephen King himself had toiled in a number of menial jobs while pursuing his writing career, including Worumbo Mills & Weaving, the New Franklin Laundry (*On Writing* 67) and teaching high school English. As King himself admit, "the writing was *hard*" (70). He confesses that "teaching school is like having jumper cables hooked to your ears, draining all the juice out of you. You come home, you have papers to correct, and you don't feel like writing" (qtd. in Rogak 62). With the help of his wife, who made a "critical difference during those two years ... spent teaching" (*On Writing* 73), Stephen King struggled on, completing *Carrie* and working on the novel that would become *'Salem's Lot*. His determination paid off: "if you don't want to work your ass off, you have no business trying to write well" (144), he advises. "If you want to be a writer, you must do two things, above all others: read a lot and write a lot" (145).

Jack Torrance is not willing to put in the work, and, instead, spends his weekends drinking, and even when he gives up alcohol he gets road blocked "in that interesting intellectual Gobi known as writer's block" (753). He thinks that spending a winter in seclusion at the Overlook Hotel will rekindle the muse and he does make some progress. By October he has "rewritten most of the second act" and was making progress on the third, at least mentally. Yet even when he is his most prolific, his writing is uneven at best. "Wendy could hear the typewriter Jack had carried up from downstairs burst into life for thirty seconds, fall silent for a minute or two, and then rattle briefly again.... Jack had not been writing so steadily since the second year of their marriage" (*Three Novels* 768). So even when he is writing, his writing is a series of starts and stops, "irregular bursts" (770) with the typewriter silent for at least twice as long as it is actually working, as Jack is "lost in the world he was making, staring at the typewriter" (771).

The Overlook doesn't provide the inspiration Jack needs, however. Instead, it offers a distraction in the form of records of its sordid history, and Jack has a track record of being easily distracted. Instead of finishing his play, which seems to be nearly half complete, he allows himself to be sidetracked by the prospect of writing a book about the hotel. "It could be a work of fiction, or history, or both—a long book exploding out of this central place in a hundred directions" (802). Once he finds the scrapbook, his play is forgotten and his writing is replaced with a new mission, learning everything he can about the hotel and taking care of it: "He had promised himself he would take care of the place, very good care. It seemed that before today he had never really understood the breadth of his responsibility to the Overlook. It was almost like having a responsibility to history" (807). Jack tells himself he is still working on his writing, working on the book about the hotel. But this is the book he had "semijokingly promised himself" (802) and immediately after finding the scrapbook this book becomes an "if" and not a when. "This would be a part of the book, if he actually wrote it" (807). Instead of working on his play, he goes into town to research the history of the hotel and to call Ullman, the hotel manager, in another attempt at self-destruction. He tells Ullman, "I'm thinking of writing a book about the Overlook Hotel" (829), not that he is writing or will write the book.

As Magistrale has noted, "Jack gives up on his writing at the very moment in which he needs it the most" (*Moral Voyages* 107) and this "lets the monsters out" and leads to his destruction. Mustazza has shown the influence of Poe's "Masque of the Red Death" on this novel, and Winter has said the novel's themes "parallel those of America's guiltmaster, Nathaniel Hawthorne" (50); however, Jack more closely resembles an Edgar Allan Poe protagonist with a self-destructive tendency, with a "broken switch somewhere inside" (755). Poe's description of the "spirit of the perverse" certainly describes Jack's actions:

> Perverseness is one of the primitive impulses of the human heart—one of the indivisible primary faculties, or sentiments, which give direction to the character of Man. Who has not, a hundred times, found himself committing a vile or silly action, for no other reason than because he knows he should *not*? ... It was this unfathomable longing of the soul *to vex itself*—to offer violence to its own nature—to do wrong for wrong's sake only [299–300].

Jack recognizes this trait in himself and wonders if it is true. "Once, during the drinking phase, Wendy had accused him of desiring his own destruction but not possessing the necessary moral fiber to support a full-blown deathwish. So he manufactured ways in which other people could do it" (831). The "spirit of the perverse" is often used in fiction in what Bo Pettersson terms "metafictional determinism," which he defines as the way "a course of action is established by an outline early on" (qtd. in Strengell 246). This is, essentially, a specialized prolepsis, which is "any narrative maneuver that consists of narrating or evoking in advance an event that will take place later" (Genette 40). Rather than just a general prolepsis or foreshadowing, metafictional determinism points specifically to the fact that a character's fate is already determined; the author knows something will happen and is alerting the reader to this fact ahead of time. As Strengell has pointed out, this is a common narrative technique in horror fiction (186) and is an important part of *The Shining*. Jack's alcoholism predetermines his destruction, as does his propensity to violence and poor decision making when he is drunk.

Jack's "metafictional determinism," or "spirit of the perverse" comes in several forms. There is, of course, his alcoholism, "the Bad Thing," which he shares with Poe's narrator in "The Black Cat." He loathes himself for his drinking: "the self-loathing would back up in his throat in a bitter wave.... Those were the times that his mind would turn thoughtfully and sanely to the gun or the rope or the razor blade" (684). Poe's narrator in "The Black Cat" also suffers from alcoholism, and like Jack, his drinking causes him to commit violence, first against his pets, and then against his wife, whom he ultimately murders.

Like Poe's narrator, Jack's temper also gets him in trouble. First he breaks his son's arm when the boy spills beer on his manuscript. It returns again when he loses control and hits a student, George Hatfield: "A slow, red cloud of rage had eclipsed Jack's reason" (662). He loses his temper again when a wasp stings him and he vows revenge, destroying the nest not just for the safety of his family, but in a personal vendetta: "He went down the ladder to get the bug bomb. They would pay. They would pay for stinging him" (763). He loses control again, in the phone call to Ullman, where he antagonizes the manager, screams at him, and hangs up the phone. "*(Why are you baiting him? Do you want to get fired?)*," he thinks and then realizes that he has lost his temper again (830), "made that damned senseless call, lost his temper, antagonized Ullman" (832). These two things alone alert the reader that this character is in for trouble in the story.

Jack's greatest mistake, though was his willingness to abandon his writing, to be distracted by something new and allow it to take over his life. His writing initially offers hope that he will be able to overcome his internal flaws by creating a play. As we have seen in "The Word Processor of the Gods," writing can create new and better worlds, and as we will see in *Misery* and other works, writing gives life. Had his writing become his obsession, it might offer hope that Jack would become the true hero of the novel. Yet, as we have seen, Jack lacks the discipline or the motivation to be a successful writer over the long term. This is another example of metafictional determinism: Jack loves the accolades that come with having written, but he lacks the will that it takes to be a writer. Unlike Stephen King, who seems to be addicted to the act of writing, Jack's only reason to write is in order to achieve some measure of success. Instead of his play, the hotel becomes his new addiction. He allows his reason to sleep and "breed monsters." As Winter explains, "Jack has failed in his responsibilities—to his family, to his writing, to himself" (50). And this is what leads to his downfall.

As Collings has pointed out, *The Shining* touches on language itself. "Words are critical in the novel" (*Many Facets* 70). Jack is a writer and uses words in his craft, but Danny, who cannot read, receives coded messages in words. This novel explores the linguistic question of words and meaning, the "sign, signified, and signifier" of de Saussure. De Saussure's theory "assumes that ideas already exist independently of words" (65). Only in Danny's case, the process is working in reverse; he "sees" the linguistic signs for the ideas before he knows what they are. Language tries to bring the ideas into being, but until the boy can read, the "signs" that he sees make no sense to him. "Language is the House of Being" (Heidegger, *On the Way* 63) is shown as precognition in this novel. "The Shine" illustrates de Saussure: Danny "knows" things. But without the proper words, without language, he cannot explain them or act upon those ideas. This is particularly interesting in the word REDRUM, "that indecipherable word he had seen in his spirit's mirror" (681).

His precognition and ability to read other people's thoughts and to communicate using "the shine" allows him to circumvent language as he reads the pictures in other people's thoughts and sees images sent to him by Tony, including those with written signs that he cannot read. In this respect, Danny symbolizes the contradiction in all language, in all philosophy, a contradiction expressed by Jacques Derrida and the Deconstructionists.

Deconstructionism can be defined as "a reading strategy ... whose essential gesture is to demonstrate that every philosophical position, irrespective of how coherent it seems on the surface, contains within it the means of its own self-undermining" (Buchanan 115).

Derrida postulated that every sign achieves its meaning not only from its history, its definition, but also from the related signs that are absent, and that most meaning occurs in binary oppositions (i.e., light/darkness). He calls this difference "*differance*"; it not only highlights the differences but also illustrates how words defer to each other. It is the *differance* that produces meaning. The meaning of a sign, then, always leads to or defers to another sign, and then another; therefore, in order to communicate, we must suppress unwanted meanings and signs and privilege those that fit best with the meaning we wish to convey. Yet it is the "*differance*" that clouds meaning, since despite the writer's best efforts to subdue unwanted meanings, they are still present, embedded in the language itself, and will ultimately deconstruct the text. "*Differance* produces what it forbids, makes possible the very thing that it makes impossible" (143). Writing, according to Derrida, thus cannot be controlled by the author once the text is written and released. "The writer writes *in* a language and *in* a logic whose proper system, laws, and life, his discourse by definition cannot dominate absolutely" (158).

Although signs aren't everything, there is nothing without signs, or as Derrida says, "there is nothing outside the text" (*Grammatology* 158). This means that we cannot rely on outside "truths" to convey meaning, but must rely only on the text itself. And since every text ultimately contradicts itself, or deconstructs itself, each text is, in effect, an untruth which, paradoxically, attempts to reveal truth. Therefore, if the text is unreadable, we cannot acquire meaning or discover truths.

In *The Shining*, Danny has access to unreadable texts in the form of words ("redrum") and has access to "the shine," the ability to magically experience "truth" though other people's thoughts and through visions of the future brought to him by his imaginary friend Tony. However, since he can't "read" the text, he is unable to fully comprehend the cryptic messages of his future self from ten years later. Interestingly enough, "Tony" (Danny's middle name) is forced to use writing to convey complex ideas such as "murder" to his younger self, who is unable to read them. Thus, true to Derrida's theory, only the text is "readable," yet it is also "unreadable" to the five-year-old boy, who cannot comprehend complex ideas without words, yet hasn't mastered the language enough to understand the words either. So if it is true that ideas are first, and language gives them names, Danny contradicts this, deconstructs it, if you will, by receiving words, names, and language that exist before he understands the ideas. So are the words bringing the ideas to life, or are the ideas creating the words? Derrida would say "neither" and "both" since contradiction is imbedded in language in general and highlighted in writing. And Danny, like readers of texts in general, is unable to nail down a specific truth through the imperfect form of language. He will not understand what happens until it happens, and then his future self, at 15, will be unable to warn his younger self because of this fluidity of words and writing.

Ultimately, the worlds of Jack and his son converge as the novel reaches its climax. Jack Torrance, the writer who has a command of words, writing, and language, is destroyed because he really is not in control of his writing at all; he allows it to become kidnapped by the Overlook Hotel, and so in searching for the truth about the hotel, he loses sight of the truth concerning himself and his family. Conversely, his son Danny gradually learns language in an attempt to understand the messages that "the shine" brings to him, and despite his inability to fully understand the complex symbols and ideas, he survives the cataclysm and lives to not only "speak" to his younger self, but to become the protagonist of *Doctor Sleep*, Stephen King's sequel to *The Shining*, published in 2013.

In summary, *The Shining* is a novel that thematizes the deconstruction of writing. Where writing is a constructive, life-giving force in *'Salem's Lot* and other Stephen King stories, the lack of writing and language is a destructive force in this book. Jack Torrance believes that writing will solve all of his problems, but his lack of commitment to his craft actually brings about his downfall. He is unable to muster the energy and enthusiasm to express himself and complete his play, and, therefore, in unable to exorcise his demons. This allows his character flaws, his alcoholism and temper, to take over his character, which leads to destruction rather than creation.

Language is also deconstructed for both Danny and Tony, his future self, because they are unable to communicate effectively until it is too late. The reversed word "REDRUM" has no meaning for him, and the mirror image of the word itself serves as potent symbol of the "slippage" that is an integral part of words and language. Despite Tony's best attempts, his efforts to communicate with his younger self fail. As Jameson has said, "The sign itself is always somehow impure" (175).

Ultimately, it is "the shine," a form of metalanguage that transcends language, that proves to be Danny's savior, even as it is his curse. This "shine" is a pre-linguistic ability that allows him to understand with his intuition and his precognitive senses, which don't rely on the accuracy of words. Although his precognition creates nightmares that Danny doesn't fully understand, this sixth sense works on a primeval level that doesn't require words or language: it is Heidegger's "House of Being."

The Shining, then, tells us that while language and writing can be equated with life, we must not rely only on the logical sense of words. Jack's problem is that he sees writing as a means to an end and does not experience what Barthes calls *jouissance*, the pleasure of the text, "writing is: the science of the various blisses of language" (*Pleasure* 6). In "The Word Processor of the Gods," Richard Hagstrom, a mediocre writer at best, wrote for the joy of writing, not for the money, and he was rewarded emotionally and, ultimately, by recognizing the ability of language to change his life. Other King protagonists (and King himself) write for the joy of the experience and the joy of creation; they are willing to sweat for their creations. Jack is not and therefore cannot use the life-giving power of language to save himself.

Danny, on the other hand, gives up on the logical but turns towards the instinctual as he uses his illogical ability—the shine—to save himself.

In the "sequel" to *The Shining*, King will show how the adult Dan Torrance uses this pre-linguistic talent to comfort those who are dying, bringing, not life, but a pleasant and respectful death to those who are terminally ill and to ultimately reignite his "shine" to do battle with evil paranormal creatures. In becoming "Doctor Sleep," Dan puts reason to sleep and allows his instincts, imagination, and creativity to take over, something his father was unable to do.

CHAPTER 5

Pet Sematary:
The Spoken Secret

Selling 657,000 hardcover copies in its first year of publication, *Pet Sematary* was both a commercial and a critical success, gaining positive reviews from *Publishers Weekly* and others (Beahm, *Stephen King Story* 109–110). Initially King felt that the book was too terrifying to publish when he completed the draft in 1979 and it didn't see print until 1983 when he used it to conclude his contractual obligations to Doubleday (Winter 131–132). The story was originally inspired by the death of his daughter's cat, Smucky, which was hit by a car and subsequently buried in the neighborhood "Pets Sematary" that the local children created; King didn't want to let his daughter know that he'd found the body of the cat, but his wife convinced him that it was time for his daughter to learn about death (Beahm 84). The incident caused King to wonder about what would happen if pets could come back from the dead, which led him to speculate about human reanimation.

The literary inspiration for the story came from several sources, including W.W. Jacob's 1902 story "The Monkey's Paw," where parents wish for the resurrection of their son, only to learn the lesson of "be careful what you wish for" (an excerpt of which is reprinted in *Pet Sematary* on page 378), and Algernon Blackwood's 1910 novella "The Wendigo," where this Native American mythical being first appeared in horror fiction as "a sort of great animal that lives up yonder" and is "quick as lightning in its tracks, an' bigger'n anything else in the Bush" (162). In Blackwood's story, set in Canada, the creature runs so fast that its feet turn to fire. As Winter has correctly pointed out, The Wendigo legend is not part of Maine mythology, but dates back to the Native Americans of the Cree nation, which were translated by Howard Norman in 1982 (a fact that might have contributed to the family's last name, Creed). According to this legend, the Wendigo is described as "a giant spirit, over 15 feet tall … with glowing eyes, long yellowed fangs, and overly long tongues" (Taylor). The being, according to the myth, was created when desperate people resorted to cannibalism, an allusion that King refers to when Jud explains the mysteries of the old Micmac burial ground to Louis Creed (156). The Cree believe that a person can "'go Windigo'; that is, a Windigo spirit … could take over that person's behavior" and this behavior often includes "becoming a cannibal" (Norman 3). The Cree also use Windigo place names to mark places where these creatures have been seen or are likely to be found (Norman 13).

Of course, *Pet Sematary* has obvious associations with Mary Shelley's *Frankenstein* novel. The major difference is that Shelley uses science to bring a human being back to life; King uses the supernatural. The book has also become part of the Zombie genre, only in King's book, the zombies return individually and not as part of a major zombie uprising or apocalypse. According to Redfern and Steiger, King's novel mirrors a real story that occurred in the English city of Exeter in 1996 when the Halden Hills' pet cemetery was "transformed from a place of tranquility to one of outright terror" (236) when an "unholy, zombie-like humanoid" in ragged clothes was said to haunt the place, disturbing the graves, digging them up and devouring them, and finally threatening a young female visitor to the place. The incidents ended in 2004, according to the stories.

Pet Sematary, "the most frightening book Stephen King has ever written," according to *Publishers Weekly*, is primarily a novel about death. Set in a small Maine town somewhere between Bangor and Bucksport, the book begins when Louis Creed, his wife Rachel, daughter Ellie, who is about to enter the first grade, and his son Gage, a feisty toddler, move into a house in the country set on the side of Highway 15. Their back yard blends away into miles of open land that belongs to either the state or the local Indian tribe, depending on the outcome of decades of litigation. Louis, a medical doctor, has taken a job with the University of Maine to be in charge of their on-campus clinic. The family immediately meets Jud, the neighbor from across the road, who, in an obvious case of narrative determinism, warns them about the dangers of trucks speeding down the road and how many neighborhood pets have been killed on the highway (22). From that point on the reader knows that the highway will bring tragedy to this family. And, of course, the prediction is fulfilled as both the family cat, aptly named "Church," and then the two-year-old boy are killed by trucks on the highway.

Jud, who becomes a father figure to Louis, introduces him to the Pet Sematary behind the Creed house, where children bury their dead pets, and, later, to the "real" Pet Sematary, which is much deeper in the woods and has the power to bring the dead back to life.

The "constant reader" who is hoping that the novel will help one understand and cope with death will be disappointed, since the book, really does neither. As Nash has said, "King has transformed the Gothic tale in an exciting and truly horrifying fashion, but, in doing so, he has made something so much more frightening that we forget to confront death" (174). Nash is correct; however, I don't think the book is asking us to deal with the fear of our *own* death. Instead, we are asked to confront our grief and cope with the death of a loved one. "King's novel does not deal with death," Nash says. "It deals with a fear that replaces the fear of death, and that fear is the return of the dead" (175). Although the return of the dead is horrifying in this novel and triggers basic human fears of ghosts and zombies, I think that fear is merely a side-effect and not the main point of the book. The real theme is handling and accepting the death of someone we love, even the death of one's child, and how we recover from this loss. Death is not about the person who has died—it is about those who are left behind to mourn.

Almost everyone has experienced the grief of losing a pet; as children, it is often our first experience with death. King uses Church the cat as a metaphor for this loss and extrapolates it to include the death of any loved one. The Pet Sematary that the children have built shows an acceptable way of dealing with this tragedy. Since ancient times, humans have used ritual as a means of coping with death, and the children instinctively pick up on this idea, creating a graveyard for their pets, with markers and words: "SMUCKY THE CAT ... HE WAS OBEDIENT" (43), reads one marker, memorializing the cat that had belonged to King's daughter Naomi. Ellie's first fear of death comes not with the contemplation of her own mortality, but when she considers that her cat might die and be buried in the Pet Sematary. "I don't want Church to ever be dead! He's my cat! He's not God's cat! Let God have his own cat!" (51). When she says this, Louis realizes that "the horror had been articulated," the horror that she might lose a beloved pet—or perhaps her mother or father.

Rachel is the character most terrified of death and she refuses to face it or talk about it. Yet she doesn't seem to worry about or even contemplate her own death. Her fear stems from the loss of her sister Zelda, who died a long and torturous death from spinal meningitis while she, still a young girl, had to watch. She does not want to talk about death or face its possibility because for her it was embodied in "Oz the Gweat and Tewwible" (207), the demon-like disease that slowly consumed her sister and turned her into a monster. The terrible secret that Rachel cannot face is that she actually wished for her sister's death (203). Although Rachel can't articulate her emotions about this in the beginning of the novel, her real fear is of losing another loved one: "no one is going to *die* around here," she insists (54). For her, death is an outsider, an intruder. "There is nothing natural about death," she says (56), and "no one wants to talk about it or think about it" (60).

As a doctor, Louis has become intimately familiar with death and for him it is "a part of life" (52), something that is very natural and inevitable. "You could go to school for twenty years and you still couldn't do a thing when they brought a guy in who had been rammed into a tree hard enough to open a window in his skull" (85). And although Louis thinks "you learn to accept it, or you end up in a small room writing letters home with Crayolas" (33), it isn't that easy to accept when the dead person is someone you love. So he, too, succumbs to his emotions and, as Heldreth says, he "like Victor Frankenstein, yields to temptation, and brings the dead back to life" (149).

Pet Sematary is a cautionary tale that shows that our fear of death is selfish—we are not weeping for the person who has died, but for ourselves, since we have to continue to live without them. Although death hits Rachel the hardest, it is Louis who is the worst failure since he is unable to be there for his family when they need him the most. As a physician, he has seen the grief of families who have lost loved ones. In fact, he experiences it on his first days at his new job when Victor Pascow is killed and soon afterwards he speaks with the dead student's father. He, of all people, should know that his wife and daughter need his strength and support. When he is with his friends and Rachel at lunch, his wife breaks down and he does nothing. "They were waiting for him to comfort his wife. He couldn't do it. He wanted to do it. He understood it was his responsibility to do it. All the same, he couldn't" (243). Finally, Steve, his co-worker, puts his arm around Rachel. Later, when his daughter needs reassurance, he fails once again. "Louis did not try to comfort her but only brushed her hair back from her forehead" (251).

It is Louis Creed's inability to accept his son's death, his inability to realize that there are things worse than death, and his inability to console his family that bring about the horrors of the last part of the novel. One might argue that once he learns of the reanimation powers of the Pet Sematary, he no longer has a choice, that the power of this place changes him, in effect making him insane, and so he has no control over what happens next. Since the power of the Wendigo and the poisoned burial ground is in control of him, he is not responsible for his actions. If this is so, then the Wendigo has used basic human selfishness to bring about its horrific vision.

When Jud brings Louis to the Pet Sematary, he tells his friend he is doing so as a favor to him, in gratitude for his saving Norma's life. But even at the time Louis thinks that Jud is hiding his true motive. Later, Jud confesses that he is, in fact, sharing the secret because he wants to: "mostly you do it because you want to" (168). Even at the time, Jud realizes he is doing something wrong, but he can't help himself. Secrets need to be told. Jud is telling the secret for his own selfish reasons, not as a public service to Louis or the town.

Bringing Church back to life is also a selfish act, done for the family, not for the cat. Louis brings Church back because he loves his daughter, not because he loves the cat. Pet owners often prolong the life of a pet despite its suffering because they can't bear to let it go. Allowing a human loved one like Zelda to suffer is an equally selfish act. As Jud says, "Kids need to know that sometimes dead is better" (166). Finally, Louis brings Gage back to life out of selfishness. "It is not little Gage who wants to come back; it is his father who will not let him go" (Nash 170). Even Louis knows this. *"Have you ever thought, Louis, that you may not be doing your son any good service? Perhaps he's happy where he is"* (334). But Louis continues and in his fantasy he and his resurrected son are riding in the medical cart at Disney World, waiting for an opportunity to save lives in the happiest place on earth. It doesn't matter that his son might return to life deformed or unable to think or take care of himself. Just like it didn't matter to Bill Baterman that his son Timmy was more of a zombie than a human: "They had no right to take my boy" (270), he says, and, selfishly, he brings back his son—"God never helped me. I helped myself."

Winter has suggested that Louis suffers from the flaw of rationality: "he has apparently acquired the ability to return the dead to life—and he cannot help but use it" (134). Yet Louis only seems rational when it suits his purpose. Yes, he does rationally plan his method, how he will convince his family to leave town, exhume the body, bring his son back to life, and even kill him again with a syringe if things don't work out the way he wants them to. But his rational thinking fails him more often than not, perhaps clouded by the power of the Windigo in the marshes beyond the edge of his back yard. He never develops a real plan to explain the reappearance of his dead son to his family or to the community. His idea of leaving town and going to Disneyworld is a fantasy, at best. He doesn't rationally think about how Church came back "changed," despite being buried almost immediately. Finally, he doesn't even rationally think through the mundane things, such as building a fence between his yard and the highway to prevent such a tragedy from happening in the first place. He succumbs to the power of the supernatural forces in the Pet Sematary, and his rational mind, which knows that "the dead do not return; it is physiologically impossible" (83), takes an extended vacation.

Death is one major theme of the novel, one that King obviously intended. But another theme, that of truth, lies, and secrets, is equally important. As Magistrale correctly pointed out, "*Pet Sematary* is a novel about secrets" (*Landscape* 59). Indeed the binary opposition between truth and lies forms a linguistic symbolic code that runs throughout the novel and ties the work together, exposing the theme of kept secrets.

While at first glance, the residents of this small town seem to be wholesome and well-adjusted, unlike those of 'Salem's Lot, a look beneath the surface shows that truth is a rare commodity in this place. The only people capable of telling the whole truth, it seems, are children and the Windigo when it appears in the persona of Timmy, the first resurrected boy, and then later in the form of Gage. As Norma herself says, "only children tell the whole truth" (105). Timmy is also more than happy to announce all of the town's secrets, and we find that even Jud, a respected senior citizen and likable man, a father figure to Louis, even he has had a history of visiting prostitutes to do things he wouldn't ask his wife to do. Ironically, Gage, having returned from the dead, voices the truth that Norma was also having affairs with a number of men, apparently doing those things that Jud wouldn't ask his wife to do with him. Since Gage represents the voice of the Windigo, which, according to Jud, told the truth, even if the only truth it told was "only the bad" (273), we must believe the accusations about Norma.

But the private secrets of the townspeople are only the tip of the iceberg. Each of the characters also keeps much deeper, darker secrets. Jud and the town keep the secret of the polluted burial ground and only share it in order to keep it alive, for if the secret is totally forgotten, the evil place will no longer have any power. It exists because it is known, but only to a few who feel the compulsion to share its secret in order to feed its power. Jud is very quick to introduce the Creed family to the harmless Pet

Sematary of the children, which immediately causes grief to Ellie and Rachel. It is inevitable that he will share the secret of the darker place, thus giving it the possibility to manipulate Louis and perhaps even Gage.

Once Louis learns the secret, he, too, keeps it. Rather than telling his wife or daughter what really happened, he engages in a systematic set of lies in order to conceal the truth and keep this secret. While he claims to be a bad liar, he is actually quite an accomplished one; although everyone realizes something is wrong with Church, no one suspects that Louis had anything to do with it. He also lies in order to make his family leave town after Gage's death, deliberately breaks the promise he solemnly swore to Jud just hours before, and lies to his family about his whereabouts and what he is doing while they are away. It is carefully orchestrated, and although they suspect something is wrong, it is only Ellie's version of "the shine" that finally reveals to Rachel that something is terribly wrong and requires action. Louis, in fact, does have a history of lying and keeping secrets even in the novel's backstory. He also visited a prostitute, which Rachel never knew about, and he successfully kept the secret about her father's attempt to pay his way through medical school in exchange for him breaking up with Rachel. Louis even manages to lie to himself on more than one occasion, as he tells himself that Church wasn't really dead when he buried him, and then that Church was really okay (152), and finally that Gage will be just fine when he is brought back to life.

Rachel has kept her own secret for years, the secret that she wished for her sister's death. And her family kept the dying girl a secret from the world, hidden away in the back bedroom, a "dirty secret" (202). As Winter has observed: "Secrets are the dark undercurrent of *Pet Sematary*: not simply the secrets that divide man and woman, husband and wife.... The ultimate secret ... is that of death" (135).

The narrative structure of *Pet Sematary* is different from that of the typical horror novel or film, which is often divided into three parts—realizing something is wrong, discovering what it is, and then defeating it. The reader knows what is wrong very early in the novel and senses what is about to happen. The horror isn't in the mystery so much as in the knowledge of what will happen and the inability of anyone to stop it. In a television interview promoting *End of Watch*, Stephen King retells how Alfred Hitchcock defined the difference between horror and suspense: "Horror is when a bomb goes off. Suspense is when you see a bomb under the table, and the people are having a normal conversation and they don't know it's there, and the time is ticking down" (*CBS This Morning*). Despite its classification as "horror," *Pet Sematary*, by this definition, is really suspense because the reader sees the bomb ticking down from the very beginning and the actual horror, the visceral "explosion," so to speak, only occupies the last 30 pages of the book.

Stephen King makes strong use of narrative prolilepses as metafictional determinism to show the "ticking bomb" under the table. While this technique, signaling to the reader that something very bad is going to happen long before it does, is a staple of horror fiction, King takes it to new levels and never is it more evident than in this novel. As early as page 22 he alerts us to the dangers of the trucks on the highway, signaling that they will play a major role in the story. On page 33, in referring to Ellie's first day of school, he reminds us that "everything that would follow this first day was simply inevitable," a seemingly innocuous statement at the time, but one that, in retrospect, reminds us that the supernatural forces beyond the Creed's back yard, coupled with the character flaws in Louis, make everything that happens in the book look like falling dominos, with one terrible event leading to another, all caused by fate and bad decision-making. On page 70, with the novel's action still on the rise, Louis gives a preview of things to come when he says the "nightmare" really began when he brought the fatally injured student into the infirmary. On page 144 the narrative states that "a great many other inexplicable things happened as that year darkened," pointing ahead to the doom and mystery that would follow. Page 193 tells us that Norma would soon die and page 224 signals that "Gage would be dead in two months."

These prolipses are especially important in this novel in that they not only create suspense, but also show that Louis Creed and his family really had no free will, that the events that were to occur were being orchestrated by the Windigo and could not be changed. Looking back, there were obvious things that Louis could have done to prevent disaster—building a good fence would have been one of them—but one gets the impression that neither that or anything else would have helped. If Gage hadn't been hit by a truck, he would have choked on a marble, or fallen down the stairs. Neutering Church did not prevent the cat from being run over on the highway; in this world where the Wendigo had such a powerful influence, a fence would have been equally ineffective. This is stated directly in the novel itself in a passage of metafiction that explains much of the horror/suspense genre:

> When you're watching a horror movie, everyone in the audience knows that the hero or the heroine is stupid to go up those stairs, but in real life they always do—they smoke, they don't wear seat belts, they move their family beside a busy highway where the big rigs drone back and forth all day and all night [256].

The reader knows that Louis will break his promise and bring his son back to life and the reader also knows that the result will not be pretty. The novel is about the anticipation of this event, however, not about the horror that ultimately results from it.

Another metafictional element can be found in Jud's attempts to explain the horror that occurred when Timmy was brought back to life. Although Jud tells a good story and uses description and detail, he admits that "I can't make it as bad as it was" (271). This, of course, once again points out to the failure of language to really capture meaning. Our words, our stories are merely an attempt to come close to the truth, but as the deconstructionists argue, we ultimately fail. Despite Jud's best attempt, he, too, fails, since he is unable to convince Louis to leave things alone and not try to play god and bring his son back to life.

From a linguistic standpoint, the novel has a number of deliberate misspellings—the misspelling of "Oz the Gweat and Tewwible," the misspellings on the graveyard markers in the Pet Sematary, and the misspelling of the "Sematary" itself all come to mind. On a practical level, these misspellings represent, of course, the attempt of children to recreate and pronounce adult language; at one point it is even remarked that children sound like immigrants when first learning the language—the babbling of infants is capable of reproducing every sound in every language and then they "forget" as they adapt to their native language. But on another level the misspellings, particularly of the Pet Sematary itself, indicate that something is off, that the world isn't quite right. Furthermore, the misspellings seem to be associated with death, both on the grave markers and in reference to Oz as a metaphor for death.

Examined in light of King's later books, such as *Revival*, for example, and set against the backdrop of the Gunslinger series, we might wonder if the poisoned burial site in *Pet Sematary* is not some sort of portal leading to a different section of the multiverse. As we will see in chapter 22, Conrad Morton, an astronomer, is driven mad when he experiences the multiverse—he, in effect, also comes back "different," his mind a vegetable. In *Lisey's Story* King again takes us to an alternate place, only more directly, where Scott buries his dead brother (275) and this place is also inhabited by "bad things" (286). Perhaps, then, the Wendigo might also be living in a place where alternate parts of the universe touch. As in much of his work, Stephen King makes direct references to other places in his universe. He refers to Cujo (28) and mentions Jerusalem's Lot (358). It is interesting to note that he also quotes the line made famous by the Kubrick version of *The Shining*, released in 1980, which King disliked: "All work and no play make Jack a dull boy" (147).

At the time of its publication, *Pet Sematary* was considered to be one of King's best works, not only because of its horrific appeal, but because it dealt with a real life problem that faces everyone—coping with the death of a loved one. Winter says, "As *Pet Sematary* makes clear, the horror story—at the most penetrating, important moments, those of which immaculate clarity of insight which we call art—is not about make-believe at all" (136). While the book does not help the reader understand death or be able to face his own demise, it does teach the lesson that there are things worse than death. It accomplishes this by bringing Church and Gage back from the dead, showing that it is better to be dead than undead. But I think the message is conveyed with even more power in the story of Zelda, who suffered a very real prolonged and painful death from spinal meningitis. While the return of zombies makes for exciting fiction, the average person is much more likely to be confronted with the lingering death of a pet or loved one. If the suffering creature is a pet, a dog or a cat, then a difficult decision needs to be made, and prolonging the suffering of the animal is usually a result of its caretaker's selfishness. No one wants to lose a beloved pet. The humane thing, of course, is to relieve the animal of its suffering.

But what do we do when the dying creature is a human suffering from a terminal illness, or dementia, or brain damage? The decision is not so easy, nor is euthanizing people even legal. This is the true horror of King's story: that Zelda, an innocent child, must suffer until she becomes a monster; even her family fervently wishes for her to die. And yet she lingers, terrifying her younger sister with every moment of her existence and traumatizing her even into adulthood.

Pet Sematary is a novel about death, about secrets, and mostly about the fact that death is somehow a secret, something that, like the sun, we must not look at directly. In the novel, "death was a secret, a terror, and it was to be kept from the children" (193). And this, King says, is true in real life as well as we tell mourning relatives the same things that Louis is told at Gage's funeral, that the person is in a better place, or did not suffer, or is with the angels. *Pet Sematary* suggests that we face death head on, accept it, grieve and move on. As Louis knows in the beginning of the novel, death is a natural thing. Unfortunately for him, he never really does understand the lesson that Jud tries to tell him—"that sometimes dead is better" (166).

CHAPTER 6

Misery: The Death
of the Author

Misery, published in 1987, was originally slated to appear as a Richard Bachman book (Rogak 152); however, the penname was discovered before the book was printed. This novel followed King's detour into fantasy with *Eyes of the Dragon* and his sister-in-law's announcement in *Castle Rock* that he would be retiring from writing (152). According to Beahm, *Misery* was inspired, at least in part, by fan disappointment with *Eyes of the Dragon* and was King's metaphor of being imprisoned by the horror genre. King admits that his constant battle with drugs and alcohol also played a part in the creation of the novel: "I was writing about my alcoholism and didn't have a clue" (qtd. in Rogak 153). While such themes are, no doubt, legitimate, *Misery* lends itself very well to a metalinguistic interpretation, since it (and perhaps *The Dark Half*) is the Stephen King book most concerned with writing and authorship.

In his landmark essay "The Death of the Author," Roland Barthes, in effect, created the "reader response" theory of criticism, which takes control of the text from the author and places it in the mind of the reader. "It is language that speaks, not the author," Barthes says (143). Since each reader brings his or her own history and culture to the text, multiple meanings are not only possible, but inevitable. "A text is made of multiple writings, drawn from many cultures and entering into mutual relations of dialogue, parody, contestation, but there is one place where this multiplicity is focused and that place is the reader, not ... the author" (148).

Authors, of course, find this idea difficult to accept; however, the concept makes sense—if a text were written and no one ever read it, would it have meaning? Barthes says it would not. "The reader is the space on which all the quotations that make up writing are inscribed without any of them being lost; a text's unity lies not in its origin but in its destination" (148). The result is that the author of a work, "a modern figure, a product of our society" (144), produced a text that is, by Austin's definition, a "performative," a linguistic act of creation that takes on a life of its own once it reaches a reader, a "multi-dimensional space in which a variety of writings, none of them original, blend and clash" (146). Barthes goes on to say that "the birth of the reader must be at the cost of the death of the author" (148). According to this viewpoint, *Misery* can be seen as the struggle between the author and the reader, with the author struggling to stay alive and exert power and the reader trying to take control. It is about the conflict between the reader and the author, the "death of the author" versus the hidden presence of the author as a sort of wizard hiding behind the curtain, pulling the strings and pressing the buttons.

As an author, Stephen King understands the skill and craftsmanship it takes to create fiction, and this understanding is very clear in *Misery*, where King reveals some of his secrets, even if his audience (in this case Annie Wilkes) isn't interested in how the mechanisms work. King understands the difference between a good novel and a bad one and through his alter ego, Paul Sheldon, is able to produce both kinds. "He was Paul Sheldon, who wrote novels of two kinds, good ones and best-sellers" (*Misery* 7). The irony, of course, is that his "hack" work is popular, while his good novels aren't.

King is also aware of the fact that the novel is the creation of the author and he justifiably takes pride in this work. "He had spent most of his adult life thinking the word *writer* was the most important definition of himself" (29). Even Annie, the Constant Reader, admits that "a writer is God to the people in a story, he made them up" (36). Authors write for themselves, Sheldon says, and not for anyone else. Even after being forced to write *Misery Returns*, he thinks, "*It was never for you, Annie, or for all the other people out there who sign their letters 'your number-one fan'*" (303).

Michael Foucault observes a "kinship between writing and death" (1623) that also becomes a theme of *Misery* as the author struggles to stay alive, both physically and metaphorically. "Storytellers continued their narratives late into the night to forestall death and delay the inevitable moment when everyone must fall silent" (1623). In writing *Misery's Return*, Sheldon becomes "his own Scheherazade" (*Misery* 244) and must continue writing in order to stay alive: "*and so began the thousand and one nights of Paul Sheldon*" (149).

Sheldon says it is "good to have produced, to have caused something to be" (313), a statement that reflects J.L. Austin's concept of writing as a performative, a linguistic act of creation. Sheldon does feel a sort of post-partum depression once the work is completed. "He felt as he always did when he finished a book—queerly empty, let down, aware that for each little success he had paid a toll of absurdity" (312). It is at this point, of course, that the author must relinquish control, first to editors and publishers and finally to readers and critics.

Sheldon does complete the novel and uses it as an instrument to finally kill Annie and free himself from his prison at the book's conclusion, thus retaining control of his creation, at least as far as Annie is concerned. According to Dowling, her death is "a figurative rape in which he rams his burning manuscript down her throat, screaming 'suck my book,' and delivering the death blow by smashing her skull with his typewriter, the object of his slavery" (12). He, in essence, kills her with his product "ramming her full of what she has been demanding all along" (12). So to Stephen King's character, Paul Sheldon, the author is not dead. But his reader from hell certainly is.

Interestingly enough, Stephen King, the author, intrudes into the novel on page 211 with an offhand mention of the Overlook hotel, a setting from his earlier novel, *The Shining*. This reference to the hotel and the crazy caretaker who burned it down reminds the reader that King is still in control, pulling the strings behind the curtain, that the author behind the author is still alive and well and manipulating the entire show. Writing has its "autoerotic side," Sheldon admits (244), and King shows this side when he makes references to his other works, or when he makes cameo appearances in films adapted from his books, and even as a character in the Gunslinger series.

The reference to writing techniques also reinforces the idea of the author being in control. He calls attention to the *deus ex machine* technique used in Greek drama (108), the concept of subject dictating form (21), and even the business side of writing, down to the detail of what type of paper to write on—"write long-grain mimeo" (74)—to name just a few. Annie, the "Constant Reader," becomes "lost in a specialists' world of which she had not the slightest knowledge" (71).

Yet the author is not in complete control. "Writing unfolds like a game that inevitably moves beyond its own rules and finally leaves them behind," Foucault reminds us (1623). When Annie asks Sheldon how the book will end, he refuses, not only to prolong the story (and his life), but because he can't. He has two possible endings and hasn't exactly figured out which one will occur.

> When I write a book I always *think* I know how things will turn out, but I never actually had one end *exactly* that way.... Writing a book is a little like firing an ICBM ... only it travels over time instead of space. The book-time the characters spend living in the story and the real-time the novelist spends writing it down. Having a novel end exactly the way you thought it would when you started out would be like shooting a Titan missile halfway around the world and having the payload drop through a basketball hoop [279].

When it comes right down to it, both Sheldon the author and Annie the reader are hooked on what King calls "*the power of the gotta*" (249), that cliffhanger technique used in old serials and chapter books, the linguistic technique that Roland Barthes refers to as the "hermeneutic code ... the various ... terms by which an enigma can be distinguished, suggested, formulated, held in suspense, and finally disclosed" (*S/Z* 19). While the author might seem to be in control of the "gotta," Sheldon admits that the story does take on a life of its own. "Misery's death had been something of a surprise to him.... She had died a mostly unexpected death" (*Misery* 35).

For Sheldon, and presumably for King, writing can be an escape into the world of dreams: "there were times when he had gone to the work not just because the work ought to be done, but because it was a way to escape whatever was upsetting him" (170). He can easily lose himself in the work, and the writing keeps him alive emotionally and mentally and gives him the will to continue on. "When it was very good, he could see through the paper" (122). The author feels as if the book is his, "the work, the pride in your work, the worth of the work itself" (29) belongs to the author alone. And though there might be millions of copies of his novels, "there was no copy of Paul Sheldon" (55).

The importance of the act of writing is graphically shown in *Misery* where King doesn't just tell about the writing of *Misery's Return*, but actually writes it, first a very poor draft that "cheats" the reader (101–105) and then a longer, 25-page version that had "heat baking out between the lines" (149). In order to maintain verisimilitude, the typeface is changed to that of an old, manual typewriter and each of the broken "n's" is neatly written in. The signet paperback edition also has an inside facsimile cover of *Misery's Return*, complete with the stereotyped bodice-ripper cover art. As Grace has noted, *Misery* "is most overtly metafictional in its frequent reflections on how Paul's current circumstances are akin to the world of fiction" (64), as, for example when Paul sees himself as a character in a fictional account (*Misery* 11).

Annie, of course, is the personification of the reader. "Annie Wilkes was the perfect audience, a woman who loved stories without having the slightest interest in the mechanics of making them. She was the Victorian archetype, Constant Reader" (63). However, as Sheldon's "number-one fan," Annie (and the audience in general) feels that the author owes her for his success, that she has some control over what he writes, even though "she saw the story's creative course as something outside of her hands" (107). Interestingly enough, just before the release of *Misery* in 1987, it was announced in *Castle Rock* that Stephen King would be retiring from writing (Rogak 152), an announcement that outraged many of his fans and echoed Annie's statement that "she only wished he would write them faster" (*Misery* 9).

According to Barthes, the author loses control of the text once it is read. "As soon as a fact is *narrated* ... this disconnection occurs, the voice loses its origin, the author enters into his own death, writing begins" ("Death of the Author" 142). Even Sheldon realizes he cannot control his texts or his fans once the books are released. "*Turn the pages of the manuscript into paper hats if you want,*" he thinks (20). Once the reader gets the book, it is out of the author's hands. Readers create their own reality, based upon the fiction.

This fact is graphically illustrated in the case of a fan named Mrs. Roman D. Sandpipper III who "had turned an upstairs room into Misery's Parlor" (251) and had sent Sheldon Polaroid photographs of the project.

> It had been like looking at photographs of his own imagination, and he knew that from that moment on, whenever he tried to imagine Misery's little combination parlor and study, ... [the] Polaroids would leap immediately into his mind, obscuring imagination with their cheery but one-dimensional concreteness [251–252].

The conflict between Sheldon's desire to write "serious fiction" and Annie's demand to write more Misery books is the battle between the author and his readers. In interviews after *Misery* was published, King was careful to show his appreciation for his fans, some of whom thought the book showed contempt for them (Rogak 153). In the text, Paul Sheldon does, in fact, show contempt for his readers and doesn't understand why they won't accept his more serious work. "*She doesn't understand the new book because she's too stupid to understand what it's up to,*" he thinks (*Misery* 27).

> Was she so different in her evaluation of his work from the hundreds of thousands of other people across the country—ninety percent of them women—who could barely

wait for each new five-hundred-page episode in the turbulent life of the foundling who had risen to marry a peer of the realm? [27].

When he does write what he considers "good" books, he receives "protesting letters from these women, many of whom signed themselves 'your number-one fan.'"

Annie Wilkes, however, becomes every author's worst nightmare. Not only does she not like his "good" book, *Fast Cars*, but she forces him to destroy the only existing copy of the work, and he must do it of his "own free will" (45). This isn't the first time a Stephen King character has destroyed a book. As we have seen in Chapter 2, Ben Mears burned his book in *'Salem's Lot* in an effort to destroy the evil of the Marsten House and Jack Torrance burned his play (and the entire Overlook Hotel) in a fit of madness in *The Shining*. But this case is different. *Fast Cars* is a novel that Sheldon considers his best, possibly a recipient of the American Book Award (15). The manuscript is "190,000 words and five lives that a well and pain-free Paul Sheldon had cared deeply about" (44) and even Annie acknowledges the magnitude of what she is making him do: "I know this hurts you almost as badly as your legs do" (46). She makes him burn the first page and the last one, and, in the process, the fire goes out; then on the second try, it burns so quickly that Paul is afraid it will set the room on fire. Once the book is destroyed, it is gone, and Sheldon has little hope of recreating it. In this instance the reader, Annie Wilkes, has metaphorically killed the author. "Linguistically, the author is never more than the instance of writing" ("Death of the Author" 145). The burning of *Fast Cars* foreshadows the ending, where Sheldon plans to burn *Misery's Return* as part of his plan to catch Annie off guard, brain her with the typewriter, and escape from the prison, a theme we will return to later.

Unfortunately for Sheldon, his readers aren't looking for deep meaning or truth, or literature. They are seeking what Barthes terms *jouissance*, the ecstatic, almost orgasmic pleasure of the text ("Work to Text" 1470). Annie doesn't care if it's serious work. She just finds pleasure in it in the same way that she enjoyed the chapter-plays at the movies when she was a girl. "Annie spoke of these things with an affection which was bizarre in its unmistakable genuineness" (*Misery* 108). These "cliffhangers" didn't have to be realistic, "as long as they played fair. The people who made the story." Annie, as Constant Reader, is hooked on the "gotta," and after seeing a favorite chapter-play, she would wait all week to see what happened next, spending an incredible amount of time trying to figure out what was going to happen: "I didn't just think about Rocket Man once in awhile that next week; I thought about him *all* the time" (110).

To Annie, the characters in the novel are real, even if they are not Sheldon's idea of "realistic." Sheldon might have created them on paper, but the "Constant Reader" brought them to life. They have brought her the only joy she has known in life, a fact that is illustrated by the photograph of her in jail reading *Misery's Quest* as she waits for the verdict of her murder trial (199). So when Sheldon kills Misery in his latest book, Annie considers it "not playing fair" and she shows her insanity. "*Misery Chastain* CANNOT BE DEAD!" she screams (34).

Annie has metaphorically "killed" the author by making Sheldon burn *Fast Cars*; now she gives birth to the reader by making him bring Misery Chastain back to life in a new text. She tells Sheldon: "I want *her*! You killed her! You *murdered* her!" (34). Of course, Sheldon has no choice but to comply, and he begins: "*If you don't find a way to bring Misery back to life ... she's going to kill you*" (112).

His first stab at a new Misery novel goes badly "because he was cheating and he had known it himself" (114). Annie calls him on it—"The Constant Reader had just become Merciless Editor" (106)—and he begins again, with more seriousness this time. He realizes that he has to please his audience, or his death will be more than just a metaphorical one. "The rules for this part of the game were Annie's exactly. Realism was not necessary; fairness was" (117). The reader is in control of the book at this point. Plot is Sheldon's strong point, though—"*That's how I survive*," he thinks. "*If you want me to take you away, to scare you or involve you or make you cry or make you grin, yeah, I can*" (117–118). Before long, the text becomes his again. As Magistrale has noted, "The typewriter is a power source ... [that] functions as a tool for both his mental and physical recovery" (*Second Decade* 130) as he uses it like an exercise weight to strengthen his muscles. At first he gives his latest draft to Annie as he finishes each day, and she becomes his "coauthor" by filling in the missing "N's." But then he makes her wait, tells her she can't see the finished product until it is completed. This, of course, is part of his plan to save himself, to keep the author alive as long as possible, so to speak. The book that he does not want to write becomes his obsession and takes on a life of its own. It winds up not just keeping him alive, but it gives him the very will to live. He admits to himself that everything he writes, even this book, was done for the love of writing. "He understood—now, finally—that he was a bit of a dullard at doing this trick, but it was the only one he knew, and if he always ended up doing it ineptly, he at least never failed to do it with love" (313).

Sheldon's initial plans are to burn the book, but if he does it will be a suicide, of sorts. This text, like that of *Fast Cars*, will be gone. And though he had no problem killing the character of Misery in *Misery's Child*, "Misery—thank God for large favors—was finally dead" (14), destroying a text is another thing altogether, and he can't bring himself to do it. He hides the manuscript under the bed and burns a title page and old drafts (323). Then, after Annie's death and his escape from her prison, he turns the manuscript over to his agent and publisher, who orders the printing of a million copies that will be reborn in a million readers' minds, a million Constant Readers who would cause the book to "outsell everything in the world" (332). As Barthes said, the birth of the reader comes through the death of the author ("Death" 148).

A final metalinguistic meaning is revealed in *Misery* by the antique typewriter, a heavy, ancient thing with the letter N missing. According to the deconstructionist critics, language is an imperfect tool, the "slippage" that occurs between de Sausurre's sign and signified, between the word and the actual object. This slippage causes "its own self-undermining" (Buchanan 115). Because of this slippage, Paul de Man argues that all language is ambiguous and resists interpretation and that acts of meaning produce temporary, not final meanings. "Two entirely coherent but entirely incompatible readings can be made to hinge on one line, whose grammatical structure is devoid of ambiguity" (12). "Literature ... is condemned ... to be forever the most rigorous and, consequently, the most unreliable language in terms of which man names and transforms himself" (19). Language, then, is a broken tool, which leads to multiple meanings of the text, some which contradict themselves.

The antique Royal typewriter that Annie gives to Sheldon is a perfect metaphor for the inadequacy of language. With its broken "N," it signifies the deficiencies of language. "N" is the sixth most common letter in the English alphabet and the second most common consonant. It also happens to be present in both Sheldon's name and Annie's. So even the best text will be flawed when written on this machine, just as the best literature will still be inadequate at conveying perfect meaning. Perhaps it is merely a coincidence, but in mathematics "N" also is a symbol for a varying quantity, even as language has varying quantities of meaning, depending upon the reader.

The typewriter is heavy, clumsy, and old, "as solid as the woman and also damaged" (60), as is written language itself, and "promising trouble" (59). As any writer who has struggled to find the correct word can testify, language is "trouble" and looking at the writing instrument, be it a computer, a number two pencil, or a broken Royal typewriter, can be "a little like looking at an instrument of torture" (63).

Paul Sheldon considers his new novel, *Fast Cars*, to be a candidate for the National Book Award, while *Misery's Child* is simply genre fiction, simplistic and for the uneducated. There are many different factors that define the complexity of a piece of literature, of course, but a readability study of a sample of the *Misery Returns* novel shows that it is written at a higher grade level than King's own fiction. The results of running a 300-word sample of the first chapter of *Misery's Return* (pages 123–124) shows that it is written at an average grade level of 11, with a Flesch Kincaid Reading Ease of 62.1 out of 100, with 100 being easiest to read. In the random sample, 11.84 percent of the words are complex, the average sentence length is 21.71 words, and there are an average of 1.45 syllables per word. The first 300 words of Stephen King's actual *Misery* novel are written at an 7th grade level, with only 4.85 percent of the words being complex. There is an average of 16.26 words per sentence and there is an average of 1.28 syllables per word. In Paul Sheldon's first draft of *Misery Returns*, (pages 101–102) the one that Annie calls a "cheat," King splits the difference. It is written at a 9th grade level, with a Flesh-Kincaid Reading Ease score of 71.8. This draft contains 7.43 percent complex words, with an average of 19 words per sentence and an average of 1.37 syllables per word. While these are, of course, merely random samples (the first 300 words of each book), the results do show that the mock romance novels, even the one that is a "cheat," are more linguistically complex than King's own work. This might be due to King's attempt to duplicate the purple prose of the romance genre, but it does show that the readers of such novels, at least as King perceives them, must have a relatively high level of reading skill. This, at least from a linguistic point of view, contradicts Paul Sheldon's opinion that his readers aren't very intelligent. Of course we are not given the opportunity to do a readability study of Sheldon's *Fast Cars*, but, from what Annie says of the book and it's inappropriate language, one would imagine that Sheldon's "good" novel is written at a low grade level, at least in linguistic terms.

There is, of course, much more to great literature that readability indices. Hemingway and Faulkner, both Nobel Prize laureates, would score on opposite extremes of such indices. According to Shane Snow, Hemingway scores just above 4th grade, while Stephen King rates just over 6th grade, overall, and Tolstoy is just above 8th grade. The Affordable Care Act, by comparison, is written at a 13th grade level, which means it probably was never intended to be understood. Since 50 percent of all adults, according to Snow, read at below an 8th grade level, readability is in important criteria for a best-selling author.

In writing actual samples of *Misery Returns*, King is deliberately trying to show examples of "bad" writing. One of his criteria, apparently, is its readability—the easier it is to read, the "better" it is. And since even Tolstoy writes at just an 8th grade level, there seems to be some merit in this argument. Paul Sheldon and, hence, his alter-ego Stephen King, have other reasons than just purple prose for considering *Misery's Return* inferior, however. Sheldon tries to tell Annie that a "good" book relies on technique, where "the subject dictates the form" (21). He tries to explain to her that *Fast Cars* jumps back and forth in time because the protagonist's mind is confused; such shifts in time, of course, are a trademark of Faulkner, whose complex plots are like a tangled thread and not a straight line. The Misery books, apparently, are strictly chronological. The sample of *Misery Returns* that appears in the King novel also relies heavily on weak "to be" verbs, passive constructions, and archaic words and forms: "dotage" rather than home and "ye" instead of you, for example. The sentences are slow and plodding: "His name was Colter. He was one of the church sextons. To be brutally frank, the man was a gravedigger" (124). King's writing, on the other hand, is tight, built around action verbs, the active voice, and realistic dialogue. In *On Writing: A Memoir of the Craft*, King advises writers to "omit needless words" and "speed the story" (282). *Misery Returns* not only has needless words, but it tends to tell the reader, not show. In short, the mock romance novel needs some serious editing. And that doesn't even address the issues of stereotypical characters and hackneyed plotting.

Some of King's fans expressed anger when *Misery* was published (Rogak 152), believing the book to be an insult to them. Lant goes so far as to interpret the book as the "rape" of King's "Constant Reader" and sees it as reflecting "more extensive hostilities toward women" (149). I believe this criticism is harsh for several reasons. First, Stephen King is as popular among male readers as he is among females. A 2014 survey by Goodreads showed that readers prefer books written by an author of their own sex (Flood) and King's novel *11/22/63* is part of a Goodreads listing of "books for men." On the other hand, 91 percent of the consumers of romance novels are women (Rodale). The Paul Sheldon's "Misery" series, then, would have a predominantly female audience, while King's audience would include men. Annie, then, is a caricature of the audience that reads these type of "bodice-ripper" books and who expect these novels to be written to an exact formula.

Secondly, Lant claims that King characterizes writing as a masculine activity and equates his manhood with his writing. While this may be true in King's case—he is, after all, a man, and men do tend to identify themselves in terms of their profession—this does not mean that females cannot write, as he well knows since his wife Tabitha is a prolific author. He does portray writing as an active endeavor—and anyone who writes will agree that it is—while reading is passive, as anyone who has ever fallen asleep with a book can attest. Yet, as Roland Barthes has shown, reading is active in a different way, as readers take the story and make it their own, leaving the author's intentions in the background. And if King seduces the reader, causes the reader to have an affair with his novel, then the sexual metaphor is true and appropriate, for what reader (male or female) doesn't just love a good book? Yes, we curl up with it, take it to bed with us, and, in the case of our favorite books, keep it always close to our heart. *Misery* does, in fact, speak to a reader's love affair with a book, only in the case of Annie Wilkes, it isn't a healthy love affair, but an obsession that turns into something truly demented. Stephen King is certainly not saying that all of his fans are like Annie—yet he, like any celebrity who has been plagued by stalkers and unstable fans, worries that some of them might be.

King has suggested that *Misery* may also contain a subtext about addiction and that is probably true. But his major addiction is not to drugs, alcohol, or painkillers, but to writing itself. Even after he promised to "retire," he never did, and he has published more than 50 books as of this writing, with no sign of stopping anytime soon. *Misery* is about the act of writing itself, about the struggle of the author to stay in control, about the constant battle between the author who wants to create good, serious work and the reader who wants to be entertained. The book is about both the misery and the joy of writing and about obsession that writers have with their craft. To Stephen King, and to most writers, writing is really about becoming Scheherazade. It's more than just a job; it's the thing that brings meaning to their life, gives them the will to live and to survive despite the mental and emotional hardships that come with art.

In conclusion, *Misery*, as Lant says, "is probably King's most thorough and complex exploration of the powers of his own mind, of the powers of the artist, of the pressures of the audience, and of the workings of creativity" (145). It does symbolize the struggle between the author, the creator of a literary work, and the reader, who interprets that work and gives it meaning, based in a large part on the reader's own experiences. It also symbolizes the author's loss of control, not only to readers and audience, but to publishers, editors, and marketing demands. And, of course, the book does articulate the price of success and of celebrity status, what Stephen

King sees as the downside of his celebrity status, a theme he will return to in "Secret Window, Secret Garden."

Misery also attempts to graphically show the difference between good and bad writing and makes the case that a good writer can switch gears and write outside of his genre, as King himself has done; despite being typecast as a "horror writer," he has published mysteries (the Bill Hodges Trilogy), fantasy (the Gunslinger series), and mainstream pieces like "The Body" and "Rita Haywood and the Shawshank Redemption." In *Misery*, King asserts his right to write any kind of story that he wants to, and in the decades to follow, he will do just that, publishing more complex books such as *The Green Mile*, *Lisey's Story*, and *11/22/63*. But King's exploration of the psychology of writing would also continue in *The Dark Half*, which we will examine next.

CHAPTER 7

The Dark Half:
The Duplicity of Language

In his best known book, *A Theory of Literary Production*, Pierre Macherey uses the Marxist approach to, in effect, deconstruct the idea of the author and authorship. According to Macherey, the author is a "producer of texts" (41); "his narrative is discovered rather than invented" (48) and we "always find, at the edge of the text, the language of ideology, momentarily hidden, but eloquent by its very absence" (60). This idea of writing as a consumer product that meets the demands of a waiting audience is an interesting one when applied to an author that has been referred to as "Bestsellasaurus Rex" (Beahm 7). In *The Dark Half*, published in 1989, King confronts that idea directly in fiction.

Published five years after the Richard Bachman pen name became public, *The Dark Half* is, to some degree, truth turned into fiction as King explores his own writing and that of his alter-ego, Richard Bachman. With the release of a heavily-promoted *Thinner* in 1984, questions began to arise about the similarities of Bachman and King's writing. In fact, fans accused Bachman of copying King (Rogak 137). The Bachman pseudonym was confirmed by a fan who worked in a Washington, D.C., bookstore, and King officially went public in February 1985, releasing the information to the *Bangor Daily News* (Brown 115).

While truth and fiction obviously deviate (Bachman didn't come back to life and become a serial killer), there are some parallels. Although the Bachman books were similar in style to King's, they were a different genre (thrillers) and they did have a darker tone. And King did admit to being a different character when writing under the penname: "When I write as Richard Bachman, it opens up that part of my mind. It's like a hypnotic suggestion that frees me to be somebody who is a little bit different" (qtd. in Rogak 139). King acknowledges his debt to Bachman in his author's note: "This novel could not have been written without him."

At any rate, King's intention in *The Dark Half* was to once again explore the psychology of the writer. "*Misery* ... tried, at least in part, to illustrate the powerful hold fiction can achieve over the reader," King says. "*The Dark Half* ... tried to explore the converse: the powerful hold fiction can achieve over the writer" (*Four Past Midnight* 250). So, if King survived the attempts of the reader to kill the author in *Misery*, the psyche of the author himself tries to self-destruct in *The Dark Half*.

The plot of the novel is simple. Thad Beaumont is a critically successful novelist and professor whose books aren't very popular. When he finds himself in a writer's block, he begins to write crime novels under the pseudonym of George Stark, who is "not a very nice guy" (18). Beaumont creates an entire personality and biography of Stark (much as King did for Bachman) and Stark becomes a bestselling author. As *The Dark Half* begins, Beaumont has revealed the identity of Stark in a *People* magazine article and has ritualistically "killed" the pseudonym, even going so far as to create a mock gravesite for Stark in the magazine article, complete with photographs. Stark, unfortunately, refuses to stay buried and the "ghost" of the penname comes to life and wants revenge. King attempts to make this plot "scientific" by using the phenomenon of teratomas to explain the source of the horror. Once called dermoid cysts, the teratoma is a form of cancer mostly "due to abnormal differentiation of fetal germ cells that arise from the fetal yolk sac" (Adkins). Although "modern doctors resist dubbing them failed twins or aborted embryos" (Fielder, *Freaks* 225), the evidence is still unclear. In his exploration of twins, conjoined twins, and "one-and-a halfs," Fielder asks the question that is central to *The Dark Half*:

> What troubles me most, I think, is the realization that sometimes the second self so troublingly revealed in the series that runs from unjoined twins to joined one to autoparasite can also be carried on in secret, until like an unsuspected pregnancy or an undiagnosed disease, its presence is betrayed by pain. But where, and when, I am left asking—no longer sure that one body equals one self, and one's self one's own body—does my own "I" begin and end? And how will I ever know till the brother I perhaps carry unseen and unfelt declares himself in malignancy? [225].

This concept of "the self" is, indeed, the backbone of King's novel and is metaphorically flushed out in the persona of the author.

There are a number of metalinguistic codes that run throughout this novel and warrant further examination. The book is, of course, about writers and writing, and the killing of Stark is right out of Barthes' "Death of the Author." The book also deals with the binary poles of "literature" and "popular" fiction. *The Dark Half* is also a model for Macherey's notion of the visible and the invisible, the conscious and the unconscious, which displays itself in the theme of "the evil twin." Finally, the work contrasts Rousseau's emotion of the spoken word with the logic of the written. I will examine each of these themes in more detail though a critical perspective.

First of all, *The Dark Half* speaks of the voice of the author, even as one of the authors (Stark) is killed. While Barthes claims that the text is given voice by the reader, Macherey says that the book is given life by the writer, but it is not the writer and the writer's use of language that gives it life:

> It is characteristic of all language to constitute a special object which has no existence until the moment of utterance: the conformity between discourse and the world of things is always illusionary.... Language speaks of itself, its forms and its objects. The bias of things is the bias of language [59].

The author is not "dead" in this world. He manipulates signs and structures in order to create books that people read. "Readers are made by what makes the book.... We must not replace a mythology of the creator by a mythology of the public" (70). This reflects the idea presented in the African Bambara creation myth that sound created the universe and from it the gods who created everything else. This *ex nihlo* concept that sound and the word came first (as in the Christian gospel of John) makes language itself the creator, not either the author or the reader. The author merely manipulates the words, using them as tools, and the reader then re-manipulates them according to his own background and experiences and reinvents meaning.

The work is not solely the creation of the writer; it is created by its history, society, and the marketplace: "Art is not man's creation, it is a product" (67). This Marxist approach makes literature a commodity, of sorts, and the demand for the product determines, to a large degree, what will be written. It is also this society that decides what defines literature and what is merely writing: "society, which consumes the author, transforms project into vocation, labor into talent, and technique into art; thus is born the myth of fine writing" (Barthes, "Authors" 188). The author creates literature and is an artist, while the writer is a tradesperson who creates merely a product.

In *The Dark Half,* Beaumont's two novels, while praised by the critics, did not meet the demands of the market. His nomination for the National Book Award "swung some heavy weight with literary critics, but the breathless celebrity-watchers of America didn't care a dime about Thad Beaumont" (19). This theme, already explored in *Misery*, makes the claim that just because a book is a best-seller, it doesn't necessarily deserve literary merit. Thad Beaumont, then, is the "artist," the "author," while George Stark is the "writer." However, Beaumont, the artist, has his "dark half," his evil twin, if you will, who is a writer—and a highly successful one at that. The disturbing fact is that both men are one and the same, that Stark's *Machine's Way* comes from the same mind as the two novels written by the award-winning author.

Stephen King suffers from much of the same literary schizophrenia himself. On one hand, King is one of the highest selling authors of all time, so, according to the myth, his work must not be "literature." Yet King's work has been studied and written about, not only by "fans" of the horror genre, but by academics as well. King refers to himself as "the literary equivalent of a Big Mac and a large fries" (*Different Seasons* 506), yet in the same essay makes fun of "important" writers who "only publish a novel every seven years" and "brilliant" writers who "write obscure books for bright academics" (503). He "endorses the idea of the 'sub-text'" in his essays (Herron 133) and often refers to themes and ideas that have inspired his work. He has always had aspirations of more than just financial success: "there are lots of people who will tell you that anyone who writes genre fiction ... is in it for the money and nothing else. It's a lie" ("Acceptance"). Magistrale posits that the Bachman alter ego "permitted King to indulge in his darkest fantasies and speculations" (*Second Decade* 63), which is the same role that Stark played to Beaumont. So the question becomes, is Stephen King Beaumont, or Stark, or neither?

While I am not sure this question can be answered here (it is really the matter of determining whether Stephen King is worthy of inclusion in the literary canon), a look at Macherey's concept of the visible and the invisible might provide some insight into the matter. "The work is revealed to itself and to others on two different levels: it makes visible, and it makes invisible" (88). "We must show a sort of splitting within the work: this division is *its* unconscious, in so far as it possesses one ... this is why it is possible to trace the path which leads from the haunted work to that which haunts it" (94).

In *Misery*, the reader forces the writer to write her novel. But in *The Dark Half*, the work itself takes over, in the form of the margins of the author who produced it. In *Misery* King "blames his popular reader, embodied by Annie, for taking away that sense of craft that transcends genre fiction, but is more angry with himself for allowing her to" (Dowling 9). But in *The Dark Half* Beaumont has no anger at himself about selling out and publishing the popular novels. He creates a pseudonym to do the dirty work for him. Stark serves as that unconscious, that invisible force that drives the author to create the work. And since *The Dark Half* is about the ghost of an author taking over the living writer, trying to kill him, the story exposes both the visible plot of the bestselling horror story and the invisible plot of the "evil twin" that lives in every writer, that creative force that comes to life and takes over once the writing has begun. That "dark half" is really nothing other than those dark demands imposed by society, culture, and the world we live in, demands that may force an author to write the kind of stories that readers demand, rather that stories that he really wishes to write. The conflict within the author comes to life once the pseudonym takes the physical form of George Stark.

As we have seen in *Misery*, King has a love/hate relationship with his "Constant Reader," who demands entertainment rather than truth. As Dowling has said, "King loathes himself for wallowing in the filth of low culture—if he created Annie and Annie likes Liberace and figurines, then he is (at his worst), a producer of kitsch, or so he is confessing" (3). Yet King is attempting to be true to his craft, to seek truth in his fiction, as he says in his National Book Award acceptance speech: "We understand that fiction is a lie to begin with. To ignore the truth inside the lie is to sin against the craft, in general, and one's own voice in particular." King goes on to say, "Horror isn't a hack market now, and never was. The genre is one of the most delicate known to man" (qtd. in Underwood *Bare Bones* 14). He then cites "the greatest authors of all time who have tried their hands at things that go bump in the night, including Shakespeare, Chaucer, Poe, Henry James, William Faulkner" (14). So we have this dichotomy where King wants to please his readers, yet also please himself and the literary establishment. In *The Dark Half*, Beaumont makes the critics happy, but it is Stark who appears to the readers. The conflict between the two fictional writers is the conflict that all writers face. Who is the audience, the critics or the public, and can you please them both? In a time where "most of the world sees writing as a useless occupation" ("Acceptance"), this conflict is a serious one for King, for, as Strengell says, "more was required to satisfy his ambition than the sale of books" (qtd. in Dowling 6).

King writes horror because it is in demand; he has been "type cast" as a horror writer and his readers complain when he drifts off into new areas. But the irony lies in the fact that the horror genre didn't exist as a separate entity until King; he, in effect, created his own monster, just as Beaumont created Stark, and once that creature has been let loose, it is difficult to put it back in the cage. At least at some level, King deliberately chose horror as his genre; early in his career, he could have written anything he liked, but once 'Salem's Lot and *The Shining* were published, the die was cast, and he became "the King of Horror."

To return to Macherey's visible and invisible, it is obvious that the visible or conscious message is that King wants to be considered a literary writer and not just a popular one. His heroic characters, Paul Sheldon and Thad Beaumont, both strive to achieve literary recognition. Sheldon attempts this by killing his popular character, Misery, while Beaumont does the reverse—writes a critically successful book, only to turn to the dark side and write the *Machine's Way* novels. Both show contempt for bestsellers, yet both continue to write them until a turning point happens and they kill their characters off.

Ironically, once the characters are dead, they are forced to bring them back to life, but though they both claim to do it reluctantly, they actually find secret joy in their new creations. As we have seen, Sheldon can't stop writing the new Misery book, and, in fact, saves it from the fires and publishes it. Beaumont, though he claims to want nothing to do with Stark, secretly wants to write another of the *Machine's Way* novels. When the manuscript he and Stark are working on burns up in the flaming house, he reacts with sadness: "Thad Beaumont slowly raised his hands and placed them over his face. He stood there for a long time" (431).

King, also, revels in writing "bad" books, so it seems. He writes entire chapters of the Misery books and *The Dark Half* is peppered with excerpts from the Stark novels. Once Beaumont and Stark collaborate on the new book, actual text is written and placed in the novel. This is the invisible theme, the unconscious part of the writer who becomes someone else when creating new worlds and new characters. This part of the writer is invisible, yet important. "Thinking about writing under a pseudonym was like thinking about being invisible," Beaumont reflects (23). King himself echoes the thought: "Writing, it seems to me, is a secret act—as secret as dreaming" (*Four Past Midnight* 250). Whether or not King is a literary writer, one thing is clear—he does use the trappings and clichés of the genre and builds on them, as Harron has pointed out (138). Beaumont admires Stark, a fact that frightens his wife—"I know how Thad was about him," she says (*Dark Half* 185)—and is reluctant to give him up. In fact, his wife recognizes the love and the bond between them. "He made me more nervous with each of the four books he wrote" (182). He admires Stark and has created many of the characteristics in him that he lacks himself. Stark is strong, confident, and not clumsy, while Beaumont is an academic, suffers from writer's block and self-doubt, and is clumsy.

The writer is, in effect, deconstructed. He wants to be accepted, win critical acclaim and awards, but that dark side just won't let him loose. He craves critical attention and awards, yet feels like he owes his audience "a good ride on the roller coaster" (qtd. in Underwood *Bare Bones* 78). King himself sees the answer in all of this; the pop writers and the academics must come together, instead of being two halves of the same creature. "For far too long the so-called popular writers of this country and the so-called literary writers have stared at each other with animosity and a willful lack of understanding" ("Acceptance").

Applying the theory of deconstructionism to *The Dark Half* leads to some interesting observations. Even before Derrida and de Man, Rousseau recognized that "writing, which would seem to crystalize language, is precisely what alters it" (21). Macherey adds: "What is important in the work is what it does not say" (87). According to this concept, what is left between the lines is the real meaning of the text, because the author cannot possibly capture the entirety of his culture and society in the work. "*The impossibility of the work's filling the ideological frame for which it should have been made.* This is where we can locate the personal intervention of the author in a work of literary production" (198).

So what *isn't* King saying in *The Dark Half*? The novel tells us that the popular fiction of a George Stark that appeals to a mass audience obviously sells more copies than the "literary" fiction of a Thad Beaumont, and it seems that the popular fiction is entertaining and tells a good story. We see what this looks like in both the *Misery* books and the *Machine's Way* series, sections of which are reproduced in the respective novels. So we have Stephen King, the popular writer, purposefully writing "hack" fiction as an example of what is popular but not critically successful. Neither the *Misery* novels nor the George Stark novels were ever nominated for any awards in the Stephen King universe.

Yet the work deconstructs itself when we look at King's own definition of a "good story." As the editor of *The Best American Short Stories* in 2007, King "read hundreds of stories between December ... and January 2007" ("Introduction" xiii) in order to determine which ones should be included as "the best." Of those chosen for the anthology he claims, "There isn't a single one ... that didn't delight me" (xvi). According to his own criteria, a good story, one that should be considered among the best of the year, should be, above all, entertaining:

I want the ancient pleasure that probably goes back to the cave: to be blown clean out of myself for a while, as violently as a fighter pilot who pushed the EJECT button in his F-111. I certainly don't want some fraidy-cat's writing school imitation of Faulkner, or some stream-of-consciousness bullshit about what Bob Dylan once called "the true meaning of a peach" [xvii].

One of Thad's readers, Dodie Eberhart, read one of the Beaumont novels and "thought it an exquisitely stupid book" (68) and "had been about ready to throw the boring piece of shit across the room and forget the whole thing" (69). She was, however, a fan of George Stark's novels, which obviously have more of that "ancient pleasure" that King refers to.

After the critical success of Beaumont's first novel, he suffered from serious writer's block, probably because he was trying to live up to his reputation with a second book. As King says, much literary fiction is "written for editors and teachers rather than for readers" ("Introduction" xvi). The George Stark persona, then, was built from this inability to write a second book—under the pen name Thad could "write any damn thing I please without *The New York Times Book Review* looking over my shoulder the whole time I wrote it" (*Dark Half* 22). As King said, "writers—even those who claim to spurn Shakespeare's bubble reputation—write for whatever audience is left" ("Introduction" xvi).

The Dark Half is a metaphor of deconstructionism, how we say one thing and mean another. Thad, the novel's "hero," writes "literature" that is admired by the critics, even if he isn't popular. Stark, his evil twin, wins no awards or praise from the critics, yet is a best-selling author. The surface narrative of *The Dark Half* blames the unsophisticated audience for not being bright enough to appreciate quality writing when they see it. Yet by King's own definition of how he judges the worth of a story, the Beaumont novels fail. These stories are "show-offy rather than entertaining, self-important rather than interesting, guarded and self-conscious rather than gloriously open, and—worst of all-written for editors and teachers rather than for readers" (xvi). A Thad Beaumont story, then, would probably not be picked by Stephen King for inclusion in a year's best anthology. However, a George Stark story might. One of King's selections, "Where Will You Go When Your Skin Can't Contain You," by William Gay, is edgy by anyone's standards and includes a woman getting her face blown off by a shotgun by her ex-lover, who then shoots himself; the protagonist, an ex-con, steals her corpse from the funeral home. This is a George Stark type of story.

Once Beaumont gives birth to his pseudonym, even Thad himself would really rather write Stark novels, and, in fact, only gives them up when the ruse is exposed. "If I'd kept the secret, the temptation to write another George Stark novel would have been too much for me. I'm as vulnerable to the siren-song of money as anyone else" (*Dark Half* 28). Thad also tells the *People* magazine reporter that "Stark was running out of things to say" but three lines later admits to himself that was "utterly full of shit" (28). When he is finally forced to write the novel, he reminds himself to "*remember what you're doing,*" which is, of course, killing George Stark. "But a part of him—the part that really wanted to write *Steel Machine*—protested" (408).

Macherey says, "The work has *its margins*, an area of incompleteness from which we can observe its birth and its production" (90). In these margins we find a different meaning of the story, a narrative where Stark is, indeed, the hero, in a twisted sort of way.

While George Stark is "not a very nice guy," a gross understatement to be sure, we are attracted to him just the same. He has fans who are upset when he is ritualistically killed (111). His books are emotional and exciting: "*Machine's Way* ... became that year's surprise success, going to number one on the best-seller lists coast to coast. It was also made into a smash-hit movie" (27).

In an attempt to expose the reader to George Stark's world, the novel gradually changes its point of view. We are first let into Stark's world in short excerpts: "Beaumont's [books] were on a higher shelf. That was wrong, but he had to assume this bitch just didn't know any better" (132). By chapter 19, however, Stark has an entire chapter told through his point of view. Here it becomes apparent that he is fighting for his life. In previous King novels, we have seen that writing equals life, and in this chapter Stark is struggling to write. "If he could write *on his own*, all would be well and he wouldn't need the wretched, whining creature up in Maine at all" (260). When he can't write anything but his own name, he experiences fear and panic. Physically, he is "losing cohesion" (266) since in his "*perfectly* nondescript face ... the perfect face, one no one would be able to describe afterwards." His "face," of course, isn't a face at all but a literary creation of Thad. In order for Stark to become whole, to become real, to permanently come to life, he must create his own reality by writing on his own.

Stark is writing out of self-defense. "He had no responsibility to lie down and die without a murmur of protest, as Thad Beaumont seemed to think he should do. He had a responsibility to himself—that was simple survival" (305). If George Stark is "Not a Very Nice Guy," it is through no fault of his own—after all, Beaumont created the alter ego and his personality, and Stark merely inherited it. "He had, after all, built George Stark from the ground up" (143). The reader almost feels sorry for the evil twin as he asks Beth, "What would you do if you were in my position? ... Do you really blame me for wanting something so simple as survival?" (313).

Looking at the writing of George Stark from a linguistic point of view offers some interesting observations. Each major section of *The Dark Half* opens with an excerpt from a George Stark novel. The first except, on page 13, reveals that it is written at an average grade level of 7, with a Flesh Kincaid Reading Ease level of 80 out of 100, making it very easy to read. The Flesh-Kincaid grade level is 5.2, there is an average of 12.33 words per sentence, and there is an average of 1.35 syllables per word. This makes George Stark much easier to read than Paul Sheldon's *Misery* novels, discussed in the last chapter, and brings it in line with King's own writing, which is also written at an average grade level of 7, as we have seen in the previous chapter of this study. Perhaps even more interesting is the fact that the George Stark excerpt does not contain a single form of the verb "to be." Every verb in the excerpt is an action verb, and the writing is tight, with a fast narrative pace and no needless words, a style that King himself recommends in his memoir *On Writing*. Unlike Sheldon's *Misery* novels, the Stark books, then, are not "bad" in stylistic terms and, in fact, mirror King's own writing and the kind of writing he finds effective. This leads one to again believe that George Stark's work (stylistically "stark") would be more likely to make the cut in Stephen King's "Best Stories of the Year" than Thad Beaumont, whose last name mirrors the French *beau mot*, or "beautiful word."

In most of Stephen King's novels, we have seen fiction as the window to truth. Yet, we are also told that fiction is a lie: "a novelist was simply a fellow who got paid to tell lies. The bigger the lies, the better the pay" (*Dark Half* 28). So, as we have seen in previous chapters, it is the lie that tells the truth. This idea is compounded in *The Dark Half* because we have multiple layers of fiction. There is the fiction of Thad Beaumont, of course, the award-winning novelist. And there is the fiction of George Stark, the popular, best-selling novelist. Thad is a fictional character created by Stephen King. And George Stark is a fictional character, "a fiction by a fiction" (112), created by Beaumont, who is created by King. So if fiction is the means to truth, which fiction are we to believe, Beaumont or Stark? The text seems to be saying that Beaumont is the "correct" version, yet Stark wins by popular vote. The interplay of these binary oppositions gives probably the best answer, as we realize that there may be a George Stark living inside each of us. As Thad's wife says, "George was there all along. I'd seen signs of him in some of the unfinished stuff that Thad did from time to time. It was just a case of getting him to come out of the closet" (22). That was when "George Stark woke up and started to talk" (28).

King plays with the fiction versus reality concept throughout the novel. A favorite device is his references to the way fictional stories are written against what happens in the real world. "Small town murders in real life, he had found, rarely bore any likeness to the small town murders in Agatha Christie novels" (49). There is a reference to *Alfred Hitchcock Presents* stories (56) and even to Stephen King's own previous novel, *Cujo* (48). But this fiction versus reality deconstructs itself because Stark's novel is "a fiction by a fiction" and that is doubled in *The Dark Half* itself, which is another fiction. At one point, Thad is speculating on his theory of the pseudonym coming to life. "Suppose for a second ... that it *did* happen the way I suggested.... It would make a hell of a yarn" (97).

In conclusion, ultimately, truth is revealed in the "lie" of fiction, and, sometimes, the bigger the lie, the bigger the truth. The fantastic is the sometimes only device that can successfully tell the truth, since it allows the reader to step back and look at life through a different perspective. In *The Dark Half* we are shown two faces of reality: the brutal realism of Stark, filtered through the prose of Stephen King. Ironically, popular fiction consistently outsells "literary" fiction, a point that King makes in his introduction to "The Year's Best Fiction." So if "truth" is to be shared and disseminated, the vehicle of popular fiction is a more efficient means to do so. Genre fiction and "pulp" fiction enjoy much more commercial success than "literary" fiction, which is hidden away on what King calls "the bottom shelf in the bookstore" ("Introduction" xv). *The Dark Half*, then, illustrates that commercial success and truth are not necessarily mutually independent. George Stark's novels, while graphic and gruesome, do show a version of truth, even if it is not the type of truth that we want to face head-on. And Stephen King, in his novels, does the same, by taking truth, reflecting it through the sideshow mirror of the funhouse fantasy and then reflecting it back to us.

CHAPTER 8

"Secret Window, Secret Garden": The Writer's Secrets

When it was published in 1990, as part of the collection *Four Past Midnight*, Stephen King said in the introduction to "Secret Window, Secret Garden" that "it is, I think, the last story about writers and writing and that strange no man's land which exists between what's real and what's make-believe" (*Four Past Midnight* 250). This story, "an exploration of a writer's worst nightmare" (Beahm 218), explores the idea of authorship and plagiarism. The plot is about a writer named Mort Rainey who is accused of stealing a story from one of his fans, John Shooter, who terrorizes him and demands he show proof that the story is original. The story ends with Rainey learning that Shooter is really the other half of his split personality, a character that he had created that was so vivid that he came to life.

In a form of life imitating art, King was sued by a New Jersey woman who claimed he had broken into her house numerous times and stolen manuscripts from her, including the manuscript for *Misery* (Beahm 160). The lawsuit was dismissed; however, the woman sued King again in 2005, claiming that he stole her identity and used her character for his miniseries *The Journals of Eleanor Druse: The Kingdom Hospital Incident*, which had aired in 2004 (Klein). These and other nuisance lawsuits have been dismissed.

Stephen King himself claims that the novella asks "what happens to a wide-eyed observer when the window between reality and unreality breaks and the glass begins to fly?" (*Four* 251). Since this story is about fantasy and reality, and, in fact, straddles the line between horror and mainstream fiction, an examination of this work using the genre theory of Todorov can prove insightful.

According to Todorov, "the fantastic is that hesitation experienced by a person who knows only the laws of nature, confronting an apparently supernatural event" (25). If the reader decides that the supernatural event can be explained, the story drifts into the subgenre of "the uncanny," and if the supernatural event is accepted as being supernatural, the story enters the genre of "the marvelous" (41).

However, "Secret Window, Secret Garden" begins without a super-natural event as Mort Rainey is confronted by a man who claims that he has stolen his story. Rainey thinks that the man *"doesn't look exactly real. He looks like a character out of a Faulkner novel"* (*Four Past* 254), yet immediately rationalizes the incident: "he was probably dealing with one of the Crazy Folks. It was long overdue, of course; although his last three books had been best-sellers, this was his first visit from one of that fabled tribe" (255).

Since this is a Stephen King novel, and King has been typecast as "America's Literary Boogeyman" by George Beahm and others, it is only natural for readers to be on the lookout for ghosts, vampires, spooks, and just about anything that goes bump in the night. John Shooter seems real enough throughout the novel, though—until the epilogue, the closest King comes to the supernatural is when Rainey is trying to understand what he is: "The word 'phantom' came to mind" (356). Yet, King has gone to great lengths to describe the man in detail:

> The man who had rung Rainey's doorbell ... looked about forty-five. He was very thin. His face was calm, almost serene, but carved with very deep lines. They moved hor-izontally over his high brow in regular waves, cut vertically downward from the ends of his thin lips to his jawline, radiated outward in tiny sprays from the corners of his eyes. The eyes were bright, unfaded blue ... [254].

The irony, of course, is that the character who is not real, at least physically, is described in vivid detail. The other characters in the novel are not. John Kintner is never described physically except in stereotype, "Southern-fried cracker" (368), by his speech, "mumbled and stumbled" (370), and by the fact that he was a better writer than Rainey. His wife Amy is also introduced by her voice, as Rainey speaks to her on the telephone. Some of her more annoying personality traits are shown (270), but her physical description is left to the reader's imagination.

King goes out of his way to create realism in this story in a number of other places, though. For example, when he is using the toilet and the phone rings, he makes a point of not only describing the scene, but telling the reader that it is a realistic situation, not a fictional one. "He had that miserable, embarrassing I-didn't-have-time-to-wipe feeling, and he guessed it happened to everyone, but it suddenly occurred to him he had never read about it in a book—not one single book, ever" (358).

The divorce subplot is also realistic, even though it does involve the contrived device of the cheating wife. "There had been a lot more wrong with their marriage than Amy's real-estate salesman" (272). He cites her annoying way of making him "explain" himself, and Amy tells him "even when you were here, you were gone a lot.... Your work was your lover" (364). King acknowledges that good fiction doesn't exactly replicate real life: "It was too close to real to be good" (259). "In novels, everything has a connection, but my experience has been that in real life, things sometimes just happen," Rainey says (314).

To return to Todorov's definition, "Secret Window, Secret Garden" is an example of the genre of the "uncanny" until the last two pages. The reader begins to suspect that Shooter is a creation of Rainey's mind, a result of another "nervous breakdown," and this idea is fully explained in the epilogue. It is a classic example of a narrator who is suffering from madness, and creates a world of horror because of this madness. But at the very end of the novel, Amy says "I think there was a John Shooter.... I think he was Mort's greatest creation—a character so vivid that he actually *did* become real" (398–99). Then she pulls out the "message from a ghost," which suddenly plunges the story into Todorov's definition of the "marvelous," since the message cannot be explained.

Actually, we have both genres (the uncanny and the marvelous) at play in this story, and the novella resides in both of them at the same time. Rainey's madness does explain everything except the note at the end; he is obviously the person who killed his cat, burned his house, and murdered two of the local residents. Yet Tom Greenleaf, one of the locals who was killed, had claimed "he thought he might have seen a ghost" (397). To complicate matters, though, Todorov says that this imperfect tense (he didn't see a ghost—he thought he might have) introduces ambiguity, "creating further distance between the character and the narrator" (38), an ambiguity that brings us back to the realm of the uncanny.

This discussion of genre underscores King's theme of what is real and what is not—just when the reader believes all the questions have been answered and the story has a logical explanation (Rainey's madness), then a note from Shooter appears with no explanation. The reader must decide whether the supernatural can be explained or not (the genre of the fantastic) and whether the story is "uncanny" or "marvelous." Even the ghost is suspect—is it the ghost of John Shooter or the ghost of an insane Mort Rainey? That question cannot be definitively answered and thus the window between reality and unreality shatters.

One interesting piece of this dilemma rests with the title of the story itself: "Secret Window, Secret Garden." The title used in the novella is the one that Shooter, the deranged Rainey, gave to his work, not the original title of the published story. So in the end it is the madman who takes over—the novella is his story, not Rainey's, which makes it more plausible for his ghost to return at the end of the work and not the ghost of Mort—though, of course, the word "mort" means "death," adding another layer of ambiguity. This may reflect King's own career, as he has vacillated between being a horror writer and a realistic writer. Some of his stories, such as "The Body," for example, are rather mainstream, with no supernatural elements. In *Misery*, *Cujo*, *Gerald's Game*, and others, he has tried to distance himself from horror. *Mr. Mercedes* and *Finders Keepers*, the first two novels of the Hodges trilogy, are straightforward detective novels, but in the last novel, *End of Watch*, the supernatural element appears, as the Mercedes Massacre killer develops the power to kill once again through paranormal powers. The "Dark Half" always returns in King's novels, and in some of his latest books, such as *Doctor Sleep* (the sequel to *The Shining*) and *Revival*, rely on his trademark supernatural stories.

Of course the true horror of "Secret Window, Secret Garden" isn't about the supernatural at all, but involves several important fears, fears that are especially terrifying for writers: the fear of losing one's sanity, the fear of running out of ideas, and the fear of unintentionally plagiarizing someone else's work.

The first fear, losing one's sanity, is paramount in Rainey's unconscious mind, though he has managed to repress it. We do not learn that he has suffered a previous mental breakdown until late in the story, nor do we learn that he has plagiarized a fellow student, gotten away with it, and has been plagued by guilt over the incident. He has managed to forget this incident (which might have contributed to his previous breakdown), but the guilt has secretly plagued him ever since.

Stephen King admits to having had doubts about his own sanity. "One of my biggest fears as I was growing up was that I was going to go insane.... For a long time, I was very much afraid of going nuts" (Underwood-Miller 40). He claims he has since "learned what a tough, resilient organ the human brain is, and how much psychic hammering it can withstand" (40), yet "you have to be a little nuts to be a writer because you have to imagine worlds that aren't there" (qtd. in Rogak 4).

The protagonist also reflects every writer's fear of running out of ideas: "He hadn't written anything worth a damn since he had left Amy. He had sat in front of the word processor every day from nine to eleven, just as he had every day for the last three years" (259). When his agent asks him about how the new book is going, he lies and says it is coming along, even though he has only written a few pages. And when he does write, he erases what he has produced.

This was happening in King's life at this time—he had given up drugs and alcohol and he feared he wouldn't be able to write. "His primal belief was that alcohol made it possible for him to write, and ... without a crutch he was deathly afraid that his writing would shrivel up and blow away" (Rogak 158), and "when he's not writing, his brain and body go into withdrawal" (241). "All those addictive substances are part of the bad side of what we do," King says. "I think it's part of that obsessive deal that makes you a writer in the first place.... Writing is an addiction for me" (qtd. in Rogak 2).

As mentioned earlier, King has been the subject of a number of nuisance lawsuits by people claiming he has stolen their ideas or stories, and this theme about writing is most obvious in "Secret Window, Secret Garden." This probably reflects King's secret fears about where his story ideas come from, and if, perhaps, some have been unconsciously taken from others. According to Rogak, this may have happened to him when he wrote "The Body," which was later made into the film *Stand by Me* (119–120). According to his college roommate, George MacLeod, King had asked him what he was working on, and he told him the story about some kids finding a body on the railroad tracks. "He stole it from me," MacLeod says (qtd. in Rogak 120). Then he goes on to admit that "Steve has always had an ear tuned for a good story, whether it comes from a book, a movie, or a friend's story." When MacLeod later wanted credit in the film version and King refused, the friendship ended.

Rainey, like most writers, takes such accusations seriously. "You come out of nowhere and make just about the most serious accusation a man can make against a writer" (*Four Past* 285), he says to John Shooter. He feels guilty even though he knows he has not plagiarized "Secret Window, Secret Garden" (265): "It was the generalized guilt he guessed all writers of fiction felt from time to time" (275). Then he begins to reflect upon where ideas come from. "The idea was often the result of seeing or sensing some odd connection between objects or events or people which had never seemed to have the slightest Connection before" (267). King himself uses the analogy of "unearthing stories that already exist" (Rogak 180) when describing his writing. Rainey says, "when you got a story idea, no one gave you a bill of sale.... Nobody gave you a bill of sale when you got something for free.... The item came to you free, clear, and unencumbered" (267).

Writers, of course, know that there are no new ideas: "Mort himself believed there were at least six stories: success; failure; love and loss; revenge; mistaken identity; the search for a higher power, be it God or the devil" (335). In speaking about "The Body," King defends his work: "A lot of 'The Body' is true but most of it is lies.... As a writer, you tell things the way they should have turned out, not the way they did" (qtd. in Rogak, 120). While writers may take stories from wherever they find them, it is the way of the telling that makes them original, that transform an idea into a piece of fiction. Copyright laws only protect the creative expression in regards to the use of words and creation of characters or fictional place; an author can't copyright a general idea.

However, since John Shooter shows all of the signs of being a writer, Rainey is worried about "Sowing Season" and "Secret Window, Secret Garden" being nearly identical. "*He* TALKS *like a storyteller*, Mort thought" (280). "Maybe Shooter *was* a writer. He fulfilled both of the main requirements: he told a tale you wanted to hear to the end, even if you had a pretty good idea what the end was going to be, and he was so full of shit he squeaked" (281).

At first Rainey tries to come up with a logical explanation and thinks that perhaps Shooter unintentionally plagiarized him. "He *had* come around to the idea that Shooter might have no conscious memory of committing the plagiarism" (285). Then he begins to wonder if he had ever stolen a story (335). His friends wonder if he didn't just "dream him up" (337) and he himself wonders, "*Had* he hallucinated Shooter?" (338).

Finally, when he recalls his college years, Rainey remembers John Kutner and the story he had stolen from him, "Crowfoot Mile," and "what he had done with 'Crowfoot Mile' had been one of the most shameful events of his own life" (371). Plagiarism is the worst career crime an author can commit, and though Rainey "had *known* the possible consequences" (372), he takes the easy way out in order to place a story with the fictional *Aspen Quarterly*.

Since stealing someone else's work is considered a heinous crime in the literary world, Stephen King must make this horror real—Shooter cannot turn out to be a ghost or one of the "Crazy Folks" that plague writers and file frivolous lawsuits. In order for this horror to be real, Rainey must, in fact, be guilty of the crime. His own guilt brings that "dark half" of his mind to life. Unlike in *The Dark Half*, however, this evil twin is not seeking survival or to take over Rainey's writing. He is seeking a form of justice where Rainey writes a story for him, essentially returning "The Crowfoot Mile" to its rightful owner.

Interestingly enough, Shooter wears a Quaker hat; when Rainey wears the hat, he becomes his "evil twin." According to Jones, the original Quaker hat and costume was a "protest against the extravagance of the age of Elizabeth." While the common custom was for a man to remove his hat out of respect, Quakers did not remove their hat, or tip it, even during a church sermon:

> With his firm belief in the absolute equality of man, the Quaker continued to wear his hat, seeing no reason why he should remove it even during a sermon, for such came from the lips of a man; but when he addressed God in prayer, then all arose, removed their hats and stood uncovered before one supreme being [Jones].

Although Shooter is portrayed as a caricature from a Faulkner novel, he is as "good" as Rainey, and in his simple way accuses Rainey of arrogance: "I suppose that kind of man just assumes that everyone in America, if not everyone in every country where his books are published, reads what he has written" (278).

Shooter also writes his manuscript on a beat-up old typewriter, similar to the one Stephen King himself used as a child, a "secondhand Underwood" with the letter "M" broken off (Rogak 23). John Shooter's "manuscript had been typed on good bond paper, but the machine must have been a sad case—an old office model, from the look, and not very well maintained" (261). The broken typewriter, as we have seen in *Misery*, can be regarded as a metalinguistic symbol for language as an imperfect tool, yet in this case, Rainey's version of the story, "Sowing Season," is perfectly typeset and printed in book form. In either case, writing is never perfect: although it was "no 'Tell-Tale Heart' ... he had done a fair job of painting Tom Havelock's homicidal breakdown" (264). In both cases, the tool wasn't the typewriter or the pencil, but the language itself, which, even when it is good, always falls short.

The plot of "Sowing Season" brings up another interesting point. The story is about a man who goes insane, kills his wife and plants her in the garden. The plot of King's "Secret Window, Secret Garden" mirrors this idea, as Rainey goes insane, adopts the persona of John Shooter, and commits murder. He buries the dead cat in the garden and seems to have the same plans for Amy, his wife. The story, then, is plotted like a set of nesting dolls, with the larger story carrying Rainey and Shooter's stories inside it. Rainey had never written another story like it, and Shooter says "it's not like any of the others. Not one bit" (281).

While it is not the last word King writes about writing, "Secret Window, Secret Garden" does fully explore the theme of plagiarism and examines how writers must maintain a balance between reality and make-believe. This novella straddles the line of the fantastic. Just as Rainey and the reader see that "all the pieces of the puzzle were there, and when he saw the old Royal typewriter, they began to fly together" (380), and we are shown the logical explanation for the entire, unbelievable story, King pulls the rug out from under us in the last two pages of the story and pulls us back into the realm of the supernatural once again, causing us to question what is real and what is not.

In summary, this novella forms the third part of what almost may be considered a trilogy about writing, completing the cycle that was started with *Misery* and continued in *The Dark Half*. In *Misery* King confronts his audience and its demand to be entertained, and in *The Dark Half* he confronts his "evil twin" Richard Bachman and the conflict the writer faces between being "literary" and selling books. In "Secret Window, Secret Garden," King examines the legal problems of being a writer, as well as the practical problems of coming up with new and different stories to tell. In doing so, he walks a tightrope between the genres of mainstream literature and horror, playing the roles of both George Stark and Thad Beaumont at the same time. King knows that creative minds do walk a fine line between creativity and madness, between sobriety and addiction, and between success and failure. He understands that the creative well could metaphorically run dry at any time, and he worries that his imagination, like that of many writers and artists, is, perhaps, enhanced by drugs and alcohol; without this crutch he may, indeed, run out of ideas.

Fortunately for King and his readers, his getting sober did not have a negative impact on his writing, and he has gone on to write some of his most insightful work since the publication of "Secret Garden." He does return to the theme of an extended writer's block again in *Bag of Bones*, when one of his fictional characters is unable to write. But for King, writing is his real addiction and must be fed. Thus, he continues to be prolific and successful.

CHAPTER 9

"The Body": Portrait
of the Artist

"The Body" was published in 1981 as part of *Different Seasons*, a collection of four novellas with hardcover sales of 140,000 in the first year (Beahm 100). Written just after he had completed the first draft of *'Salem's Lot* (Winter qtd. in Beaham 100), this story was the first, and one of the best, examples of King's non-horror fiction, and it is considered to be one of his best pieces of work. It was made into the highly successful film *Stand by Me* in 1986, with King's involvement downplayed in the credits. In fact, many people who think of King as a pulp writer are surprised to learn that he authored this story (Beahm, *A to Z* 23).

"The Body" is a coming of age story and, in many ways, quite autobiographical. It could, I believe, be thought of as King's version of *A Portrait of the Artist as a Young Man* since it is about an event that helped to shape the life of a writer when he was just 12 years old. The plot is simple, but effective: a group of boys set out on a journey to find the body of Ray Brower, a boy who was reported missing, and whose body was found by some older boys beside the railroad tracks in rural Maine, but have kept it a secret. The protagonist, Gordon Lachance, tells the story in a first person point of view as an adult looking back on the incident. Gordie goes on to become a successful writer whose books sell and are made into "smash hit" movies, much to his surprise (*Different* 435), and now looks back upon the incident of finding the body as a pivotal moment in his life as he relates the tale.

The novella fits into the formula of Campbell's mythic hero story, as outlined in *The Hero with a Thousand Faces*, a book that King says he "was particularly taken by ... [and] definitely had an effect on me" (qtd. in Magistrale, *Second Decade* 3). "The Body" begins with the "call to adventure," when Gordie and his friends are asked if they want to see a dead body (299), and there is a refusal of the call when a couple of the boys make up excuses why they shouldn't go on the hike (305). Gordie and his friends receive "supernatural aid" when Chris takes his father's pistol; Gordie accidentally fires it, shooting a hole in a trash can, and says that "it was the work of an evil conjurer" (329). Later in the story, of course, the gun makes a reappearance when Chris uses it to drive away his brother and the older boys who threaten him and his friends. Gordie undergoes a refusal of the call when he considers going back home after the incident in the junkyard when he is chased by "Chopper" (352), but he continues, crossing the first threshold as they make their way across the railroad trestle, where he enters what Campbell calls "the belly of the whale" where he is "swallowed into the unknown, and would appear to have died" (*Hero* 74) as the train goes past, nearly killing him and his friends. He emerges alive and meets with the goddess when he sees the doe (*Different* 393); this vision of the deer is described almost as a religious experience by Gordie, who is unable to even put it into words at the time it happened. Gordie and his friends go through the mandatory road of trials, symbolized by the train tracks. "The rite of passage is a magic corridor ... our corridor was those train tracks" (402), Gordie says. The apotheosis, the point where the hero receives enlightenment, occurs when they find the body of the dead boy and Gordie, for the first time, understands death. Although he couldn't really comprehend or process the death of his own brother, this act of seeing it in person, so to speak, brings about the climax of his journey. The result is that he makes a stand with Chris when the older boys arrive on the scene and the older boys are forced to leave. Their "magic flight" home is their walking all night without incident, where they re-cross the threshold. Gordie becomes the "master of two worlds" (Campbell, *Hero* 196) when he can look back on the adventure, write about it, and see it from the perspective of both an adult and a child. Because he was able to complete his journey, Gordie is allowed Campbell's "freedom to live" (205) and goes on to become a successful writer and have a wife and a family. The story reflects the hero's journey, only in the case of this story, it reflects the writer's journey as well.

From the very opening line, in a sort of miniature prologue, this story deals with language and writing, and, like the deconstructionists, King laments the paucity of language to tell a story: *"The most important things are the hardest things to say. They are the things you get ashamed of, because words diminish them—words shrink things that seemed limitless when they were in your head to no more than living size when they're brought out"* (*Different* 293). Even simple words are subject to different meanings depending upon the audience. "So if I say *summer* to you, you get one set of private personal images that are all way different from mine" (341), King says. This doesn't concern him, or the narrator of "The Body" when he is just trying to entertain, as in the "Le Dio" stories that Gordie "made up on the spot" and were "not very good" (387). But the dilemma occurs when he tries to capture real truth. For example, when he sees a deer in the forest, Gordie doesn't tell the story because he's afraid the words would spoil it:

> It was on the tip of my tongue to tell them about the deer, but I ended up not doing it. That was one thing I kept to myself. I've never spoken about it or written of it until just now, just today. And I have to tell you that it seems a lesser thing written down, damn near inconsequential. But for me it was the best part of the trip, the cleanest part, and it was a moment I found myself returning to, almost helplessly, when there was trouble in my life [393–94].

This idea becomes a refrain, "the most important things are the hardest to say" (394, 399), he repeats. *"And you may make revelations that cost you dearly only to have people look at you in a funny way, not understanding you at all"* (293). However, both Gordie the narrative writer and Stephen King himself tell the story eventually in the text of "The Body," even if the truth is diminished. Gordie tells the story of the deer and King tells the story of his growth as a writer, and neither of them expects to be understood. But it doesn't matter. It is a story that they *have* to tell.

When it comes to love, friendship, and relationships, words also are difficult to come by. After they return home from their adventure, Gordie is unable to tell his friend what he's thinking and how this event has changed their lives and cemented their friendship. "I wanted to say something more to Chris and didn't know how to" (425), he says, and "even if I'd known the right thing to say, I probably couldn't have said it. Speech destroys the functions of love, I think—that's a hell of a thing for a writer to say, I guess, but I believe it to be true" (426).

Ernest Hemingway said in *A Moveable Feast*, "all you have to do is write one true sentence. Write the truest sentence that you know" (22). "The Body" is about the author's attempt to do just that, to discover the truth and then write about it. Throughout the novella, Stephen King uses the voice of his first-person narrator to show that writing, indeed, has to be true in order to be believable. "In my stories, there were always rounds.

Never bullets" (364), Gordie says. As if to prove the point, the text reprints two stories that Gordie told during the boys' adventure to find the body, which he later wrote and published. The first story, "a fiction within a fiction," is titled "Stud City" and was originally published by King in *Ubris* in 1969 before being revised and included in "The Body" (Beahm, *A to Z* 221). "Stud City" is about the kid, like Ace Merrill, who could not escape his dead-end life, the kind of kid that Gordie himself might have become if he hadn't succeeded as a writer. "It was the first story I ever wrote that felt like *my* story—the first one that really felt *whole* after five years of trying" (326), Gordie says. "It was the first time I had ever really used the place I knew and the things I felt in a piece of fiction" (327).

This was a lesson that King himself had learned as he used people and places that he knew to create "true" writing in novels like *Carrie*, *'Salem's Lot*, and, of course, "The Body." His fictional version of Maine, much like Faulkner's Yoknapatawpha County, has appeared in many of his books; events from one story are often referred to as being true in another (he mentions *It* on page 312 of "The Body" and *Cujo* on page 336).

The second story within the novella is titled "The Revenge of the Lard Ass Hogan," which King originally published in *The Maine Review* in 1975 (Beahm, *A to Z* 176). Gordie's friends enjoy this gross-out story about a kid who gets revenge at a pie-eating contest but they want to know more and ask "then what happened?" (*Different Seasons* 377). When Gordie tries to tell them that it's the end of the story and he doesn't know what happens next, Vern and Teddy, the least intelligent of the boys, become annoyed. When Chris tells them they are supposed to "use your imagination" Vern replies: "No I ain't!... *He's* supposed to use *his* imagination! He made up the fucking story!" (378). Gordie makes up an ending to try to satisfy them and Teddy lets him know "that ending sucks." Gordie knows it and responds, "That's why I didn't want to tell it" (378); his ending appeals to a more sophisticated audience than Vern and Teddy.

King's narrator is very careful to tell the reader that this story is a true one, a real one, and not just another one of the Hollywood myths. He carefully details how he has learned about life, real life, during the adventure of his youth, and how the telling of it now is real and truthful. He begins by showing truth in small things, such as the junkyard dog, which the boys had thought was the most vicious canine on the planet. When they see him in the flesh, however, the truth is revealed. "I ... got my first look at the famous Chopper—and my first lesson in the vast difference between myth and reality" (346). The dog is, in reality, rather pathetic, "a medium-sized mongrel dog that was a perfectly common black and white."

By contrast, at the beginning of the story the boys are still living life the way it is expected in the movies. When they cross the railroad trestle, they don't do it the sensible and safe way, on all fours, but walked "firmly upright": "If the Saturday matinee movies down to the Gem had taught us anything, it was that Only Losers Crawl. It was one of the central tenants of the Gospel According to Hollywood" (358). Once the train approaches, however, and Gordie hears its horn, reality sets in, "making everything you ever saw in a movie or a comic book or one of your own daydreams fly apart, letting you know what both the heroes and the cowards really heard when death flew at them" (361).

The narrator also shows that he has learned the truth about adults and the abusive parents of Castle Rock. As Magistrale has noted, one of the major themes of this novel is that of child abuse. Vern Tesso suffers from beatings by his brother, which his parents ignore; Teddy Ducamp has been mutilated and nearly killed by an insane father and seems to suffer from post-traumatic stress disorder himself; and Chris Chambers is the son of an abusive alcoholic father who beats him mercilessly. Gordie is ignored by his parents and relates to Ralph Ellison's *The Invisible Man* because "no one ever notices him at all unless he fucks up" (*Different Seasons* 310). Each of the four families is dysfunctional in its own way, and the children suffer for it. "It is most often King's children who must accept the consequences of adult moral lapses" (Magistrale, *Landscape* 72).

While Gordie recognizes that something is wrong with these families, he doesn't really put all of the pieces together until he becomes an adult, and then, of course, he reveals these truths in the first-person story he narrates. "Chris was home because his father had beaten the shit out of him.... It never occurred to me to question this set of priorities until about twenty years later" (*Different Seasons* 307). Part of the truth that King reveals through Gordie's eyes is the role of love and friendship and the sad fact that is usually doesn't last. Towards the end of the story we learn that Gordie is the only one of the four who is still alive—the others have suffered violent deaths. Going into the adventure, Gordie thought that the four boys would be friends for life: "I never had friends later on like the ones I had when I was twelve. Jesus, did you?" he asks the reader (341). The sad truth that King reveals is that most readers would admit that they didn't, that at that moment, the true nature of friendship was revealed as "for just one moment we looked in each other's eyes and saw some of the things that made us friends" (338).

However, Chris, the realist, knows better: "by next June, we'll all be quits," he predicts (380), and he goes on to reveal how they will all go their separate ways. It is a difficult lesson, and here Chris debates whether to tell Gordie the truth, which he knows will be painful. Finally, he tells Gordie about how friends can "drag you down" (382), that if Gordie lets them he won't ever become a writer and will end up just like his character in "Stud City."

> Chris Chambers was twelve when he said all that to me. But while he was saying it his face crumpled and folded into something older, almost ageless. He spoke tonelessly, colorlessly, but nevertheless, what he said struck terror into my heart. It was as if he had lived that whole life already [382].

In fact, Vern and Teddy do go their separate ways, but Gordie tries to undo the prediction by lifting Chris up, coaxing him to enroll in the college program and tutoring him until he succeeds and pursues his dream of becoming a lawyer. Even that collapses, though, when Chris is killed trying to intervene in a bar fight, which brings terrible grief to Gordie: "I told my wife I was going out for a milk-shake. I drove out of town, parked, and cried for him. Cried for damn near half an hour, I guess. I couldn't have done it in front of my wife, much as I love her. It would have been pussy" (435).

As Magistale has noted, "King's most memorable and important characters, and the ones to whom we, as readers, grow increasingly attached, are his children" (*Landscape* 73) and it is his characterization of them that also displays truth in his writing. S.T. Joshi, who generally writes unfavorably about King, agrees on this point. "If King has any virtue as a writer, it is his really remarkable sense of identification with adolescence, particularly with teenage boys" (76). In the depiction of the teenagers in "The Body," King is at his best. "His depiction of what it is like to be a boy in the country in 'The Body' is wonderful" (Herron 155).

King's boys are not just cardboard characters, but interesting people going through the process of turning into adults. Through their eyes we see the problems of family, school, social life, and even death. While Joshi feels that the story is "deeply flawed" by its attempt to "depict the Evolution of a Writer" (84), I must respectfully disagree. Showing the young adult world through the eyes of a perceptive boy who will grow up to become a writer creates a detailed, focused picture of this world, an alien world to most adults. Through the persona of Gordie, King tells the story simply, honestly, and truthfully, even when the picture isn't always pretty. "We were all crazy to see that kid's body—I can't put it more simply or honestly than that" (394), Gordie says, when speaking of the narrative he is telling. He tells about the beauty of childhood when he describes his encounter with the deer, relates the brutality of adolescent social structure, when the boys are beaten by members of an older gang, and relates the terrifying and painful process of growing up.

Only a writer could describe the perfect encounter with the deer in the forest, and King knows that if he had made Gordie a future mathematician, or astronaut, or even a biologist, the description just wouldn't ring true. Only a writer or a poet could capture the moment, and only an artistic individual would have even tried:

> Her eyes weren't brown but a dark, dusty black—the kind of velvet you see in backgrounding jewelry displays. Her small ears were scuffed suede. She looked serenely at me, head slightly lowered in what I took for curiosity, seeing a kid with his hair in a sleep-scarecrow of whirls and many-tined cowlicks, wearing jeans with cuffs and a brown khaki shirt with the elbows mended and the collar turned up in the hoody tradition of the day. What I was seeing was some sort of gift, something given with a carelessness that was appalling [393].

It is with this meticulous attention to detail, detail that only a writer can capture, that the entire story is told, and since it is told in first-person point of view, the narrator must have this talent and ability if the story is to be believed. The description uses prosaic devices such as consonance as he repeats the soft "s" sounds, giving the moment a quiet, gentle tone.

As we have seen, Gordie has observed these perfect moments as well as the not-so-perfect memories of child abuse and suffering; he retains these memories and later, as an adult writer, synthesizes them and makes sense of this adolescent world, serving as a translator from youth to adult. He is in a unique position to see both places and to see the passageway between them as Gordie grows up and becomes an adult during that trip along the railroad tracks. "There's a high ritual to all fundamental events, the rites of passage, the magic corridor where change happens" (402), Gordie explains. Looking back, Gordie knows that finding the body was a pivotal moment in his life, but even as a 12-year-old he understood that this event was important. "Everything was there and around us. We knew exactly who we were and exactly where we were going. It was grand" (339).

As a young writer, Gordie reveals some insightful details of human psychology that most people would overlook. He has a knack for showing the world as it really is and exploring the minds of people. For example, King's narrator understands the ways that we hurt one another, not just physically, but with words. And he, better than most writers, understands the power and violence of words. "Milo had called Teddy a lot of things, but he was able to go back and get the one that had struck home with no trouble at all—since then I have noticed again and again what a genius people have for that ... for finding the LOONY button down inside and not just pressing it but hammering on the fucker" (347).

While "The Body" is not a horror story, even though it deals with death and dying, it does display truth about fear, and, I believe, captures fear more accurately than in most horror stories. "The oldest and strongest emotion of mankind is fear," Lovecraft wrote (*Dagon* 365), and in "The Body," King describes fear as well, if not better, than he does in any of his tales of terror. The passage where Gordie is being chased down by a speeding train as he crosses the railroad bridge makes the fear real. He describes how "his bowels turned to water" and then expounds upon that "moment [that] ... in the subjective timestream ... seemed forever."

> All sensory input became intensified, as if some powersurge had occurred in the electrical flow of my brain, cranking everything up from a hundred and ten volts to two-twenty.... I could see every little splinter and gouge in the crosstie I was squatting on. And out of the corner of my eye I could see the rail itself with my hand still clutched around it, glittering insanely. The vibration from that rail sank so deeply into my hand that when I took it away it still vibrated, the nerve-endings kicking each other over and over again, tingling the way a hand or foot tingles when it has been asleep and is starting to wake up. I could taste my saliva, suddenly all electric and sour and thickened to curds along my gums [359].

King has said, "The good horror tale will dance its way to the center of your life and find the secret door to the room you believed no one but you knew of" (*Danse Macabe* 4). What Gordie is describing is pure terror—in this passage, King hits the mark. Interestingly enough, as he runs from the train, Gordie begins to wonder if he was enjoying this fear (361). "I think I began to understand a little bit that day what makes men become daredevils" (363).

Finally, Gordie learns about the real meaning of death and of its permanence first by his narrow escape from the train and later as the boys discover the body. One of the subplots of the novella was the death of Gordie's brother Dennis in a jeep accident. Gordie's parents understood the loss, but the boy did not. "I cried when I heard, and I cried more at the funeral, and I couldn't believe that Dennis was gone, that anyone that used to knuckle my head or scare me with a rubber spider ... could be dead" (298). But he came to realize that most of the tears he'd cried were for his parents (299) and not for his brother, who, though he was his brother, was "hardly any more than an acquaintance" (298) since his brother was so much older than him.

Once the boys discover the body of Ray Bower, though, everything changes. They saw just his hand but "it told the truth of the whole matter" (406). It was a simple thing that brought it all home for Gordie—"He had been knocked spang out of his Keds. The train had knocked him out of his Keds and had knocked the life out of his body" (408).

> That finally rammed it all the way home for me. The kid was dead. The kid wasn't sick, the kid wasn't sleeping. The kid wasn't going to get up in the morning anymore or get the runs from eating too many apples or catch poison ivy or wear out the eraser of his Ticonderoga No. 2 during a hard math test. The kid was dead; stone dead.... The kid was *can't, don't, won't, never, shouldn't, wouldn't couldn't.* I could go on all day and never get it right about the distance between his bare feet on the ground and his dirty Keds hanging in the bushes [408–409].

While King goes on to describe the dead boy's body in graphic detail, with a beetle coming out of his mouth, the gross-out, the image of the sneaks hanging in the tree, is what inspires terror. Horror comes next, though, when hailstones fill up Ray Brower's eyes, which is what Gordie remembers *"on the nights I wake up from dreams where the hail falls into his open eyes"* (293).

King has been criticized for his use of plain, colloquial language, what Joshi calls "a plain, bland, easy-to-read style with just the right number of scatological and sexual profanities to titillate his middle-class audience" (63). In this story, and in much of his fiction, this style effectively captures the world and the people that King writes about. As I have pointed out in my study *Out of the Shadows*, H.P. Lovecraft, the master of horrors, writes about scholars, academics, scientists and professors, who are, for the most part, living in the past, and, therefore, his antiquated 18th century prose style perfectly captures these characters in his use of archaic terms and formal, adjective-laden prose (150). Stephen King's characters are quite different, though, and require a different, modern, and more informal style. Even when his characters are "professors," as in "Secret Window, Secret Garden," they are modern professors who teach modern writing, and, as we have seen, many of his characters are adolescents who speak and think in informal, colloquial, and even crude language. To anyone who grew up in the 1960s or 70s, the language is colorful and course at times, but accurate. The boys "can say anything about another kid, you could rank him to the dogs and back, but you couldn't say a bad word *ever* about his mom or dad. That was the Fabled Automatic" (381). The boys experiment with cigarettes and "dirty" words, acting the part of rebellious teenagers.

The use of language brings us back to King's use of metalanguage— the voice of the writer created by a writer tells us about truth. Yet it must entertain us at the same time. The irony of the metalinguistic theme is that writing, especially popular writing, is more about entertainment than truth. Vern and Teddy represent this audience that just wants to be entertained.

"You could have made it so he shot his father and ran away and joined the Texas Rangers," Teddy says. And then the boys request a new "Le Dio" story, the childhood equivalent of popular fiction. Later, on page 387, Gordie does make up a new Le Dio story, which ends up "as most of my Le Dio stories did" with a predictable but unrealistic ending.

For Gordie, though, writing is serious business, and he, like any writer, must constantly balance the needs of the audience with the needs of a "true" story, the needs of making a living by the written word with the desire to create something that might be considered art. "And now I sit here trying to look through an IBM keyboard and see that time, trying to recall the best and the worst of that green and brown summer" (342). Gordie, and presumably Stephen King himself, manage to "parlay all those childhood fears and night-sweats into about a million dollars" (353).

King reminds us that while writing might be lucrative, if the writer is talented and lucky, the profession doesn't come without demons of its own. The writer, depicted by Gordie, is more observant, more sensitive, and more vulnerable.

> My wife, my kids, my friends—they all think that having an imagination like mine must be quite nice.... But every now and then it turns around and bites the shit out of you with these long teeth, teeth that have been filed to points like the teeth of a cannibal. You see things you'd just as soon not see, things that keep you awake until first light [408].

The narrator also reminds us that writing is a private thing, a lonely thing, the type of activity that readers may not be able to understand. "The act of writing itself is done in secret, like masturbation" (364), he reminds us, and then tells of one writer friend of his who writes stories in bookstore windows (presumably Harlan Ellison, who wrote in bookstores and on radio talk shows in the 1970s as part of his marketing campaign) and who was "crazy with courage" to do this.

In the end, though, writers, even best-selling authors, question themselves: "I wonder if there is really any point to what I'm doing, or what I'm supposed to make of a world where a man can get rich playing 'let's pretend.'" King senses the irony in making money by telling stories, but ultimately sees it as the only way to find truth and understand life. It isn't about the money, Gordie says, and we can sense the enjoyment he gets from entertaining others and sharing his make-believe worlds with them. As he begins to tell the story of "Lard Ass Hogan," a gross and silly story at best, we can sense his delight. "I had them now. They were leaning forward. I felt the intoxicating sense of power" (368).

"The only reason anyone writes stories is so they can understand the

past and get ready for some future mortality; that's why all the verbs in stories have -ed endings" (398), King says. His stories might be entertaining, might be "the equivalent of a Big Mac and a large fry," as he says, but even in telling these fast food stories, he is both enjoying himself immensely, while also suffering from the truth of the words, the truth revealed in all stories. "The word is the harm.... If those wounds dry up, the words die with them. Take it from me. I've made my life from the words, and I know it is so" (426).

To summarize, "The Body" fits neatly into Joseph Campbell's formula of the hero's journey. In this case, however, the hero isn't the kind of classical mythic or heroic figure we are used to seeing. Gordie is no Ulysses, at least not in Homeric terms. But, according to King, the writer is a mythic hero who must set out on a journey, overcome obstacles, and achieve a coming of age if he hopes to tell stories that are "true." Gordie achieves this goal by going on the adventure to find the body, and in doing so, he is finally able to understand the beauty of the world, as he has his spiritual moment with the doe, and he is also able to finally comprehend the reality and meaning of death, when he finds the dead boy. This gives him the maturity and courage to stand up for himself, and, ultimately, to write stories (creative lies, if you will) that capture the truth. Indeed, when Stephen King is at his best, as is the case with "The Body," there is more to the story than what appears on the surface. "You always know the truth, because when you cut yourself or someone else with it, there's always a bloody show" (327).

CHAPTER 10

"The Ballad of the Flexible Bullet" and "Dedication": Nature, Nurture and the Writer's Psyche

In this chapter I will examine two short stories about writing and writers, "The Ballad of the Flexible Bullet," from *Skeleton Crew*, and "Dedication," from *Nightmares and Dreamscapes*. While neither of these stories are even remotely considered among King's best, they do shed light on writers and writing and where stories come from. The first delves directly into the writer's mind and the creative process. The second one looks at the difference between the writer as a person and the writer as an author or public figure. It speculates on whether successful writers are created or just the result of genetics.

"The Ballad of the Flexible Bullet" was written in November 1983 and first appeared in *The Magazine of Fantasy & Science Fiction* in 1984 before being collected in *Skeleton Crew*, King's second short story collection. While the story is certainly not one of his best pieces—the characters are wooden, and the story is overwritten—it does contain some interesting imagery about a writer's breakdown and the fear that creative people have that they may lose their ability to create. If writing equates to life in *Misery*, it stands for sanity in this story.

"Flexible Bullet" is not just about a writer, but contains a cast of writers, their wives, editors and an agent, and is really a story within a story.

The tale opens at a barbeque, which has just ended, and the five characters settle down for some quiet talk and to enjoy drinks, all but the editor, a recovering alcoholic who only drinks Fresca. The characters begin discussing madness and "writers who had made their marks early and then had committed suicide" (*Skeleton Crew* 485). Then the editor tells the extended story within the story of Reg Thorpe, a young writer he had worked with who went mad and killed a young boy and himself. As the tale progresses, we learn that the madness was contagious and the editor also suffered from it and nearly died from it as well.

The artist suffering from madness is, sadly, almost a cliché in modern culture. There have certainly been enough historical examples, from Vincent Van Gogh to Silvia Plath, to fuel the popular imagination. In this story, the editor's madness is also fueled by alcohol, and it is no secret that Stephen King has also battled alcohol and drug use throughout his life and at the time when he was writing this story (*On Writing* 96). So in many ways this story, like a number of others by King, document his personal struggle with addiction.

"The Ballad of the Flexible Bullet" is not only the title of the Stephen King story, but also the title of Reg Thorpe's last unpublished story, which was destroyed when his editor crashed his car into the Jackson River (544). The "flexible bullet" is also a metaphor for madness in this tale. Based upon Marianne Moore's description of "some car or other," the editor claims "madness is a kind of flexible bullet to the brain" (496). And while the stereotype depicts writers as addicts, King, himself, is realistic: "Hemingway and Fitzgerald didn't drink because they were creative, alienated, or morally weak. They drank because it's what alkies do" (*On Writing* 98). However, King was afraid that if he stopped his addictive behavior, he wouldn't be able to write.

The story contains two writers, the unnamed young writer whose "first novel had been well-reviewed and had sold a lot of copies" (*Skeleton Crew* 495), and Reg Thorpe, whose one and only novel, *Underworld Figures*, was both a critical and commercial success. Thorpe's new story documents a writer going insane, as he himself did; the subtext is that the young writer who listens to his editor's story might suffer from the same fate and could be one of "those who have gone mad because of success" (496). His wife doesn't want to talk about madness and suicide, and the editor says, "I'm telling you a story I have no idea if you want to hear" (498). Despite his wife's reluctance to hear the story, though, the young writer wants to hear it, and the editor tells it for the first time. "Perhaps I never had the correct listeners," he says (498). In a twist of irony, the editor says that "the one thing the American public doesn't need foisted on them is another story about Going Mad Stylishly in America" (500), yet not only is Thorpe's fictional story alluded to, but Thorpe's own story of madness is told, both by the editor to his listeners, and by Stephen King to his "Constant Reader."

Writer's block is one of the major themes of "Ballad of the Flexible Bullet" and how writer's block can affect an author. As Tabitha King noted, "if I don't do it, I go crazy. Steve used to say he'd commit suicide if he couldn't write" (qtd. in Beahm, *Stephen King Story* 136). The plot of Thorpe's story is "about a young man losing his struggle to cope with success. It's better left vague. A detailed plot synopsis would only be boring. They always are" (*Skeleton* 501).

Many (if not most) writers harbor superstitions, especially about their writing. Hemingway kept three buffalo horns nearby because "during the acquiring of them things went badly in the bush, yet ultimately turned out well" (Plimpton), novelist Charles Baxter is superstitious about spilling salt (Charney), and James Joyce was "fanatically superstitions" (Spender). Stephen King claims to be "afraid of everything" (Rogak 1): "I don't walk under ladders; I'll get seven years bad luck if I break a mirror; I try to stay home cowering under the covers on Friday the thirteenth.... I have a thing about the number thirteen in general.... When I'm writing, I'll never stop work if the page number is 13 or a multiple of 13" (Underwood, *Bare Bones* 37).

This leads to the question of where ideas come from. Jung has proposed that stories come from images that are imbedded in the mind, the subconscious, that these images are "the psychic residua of innumerable experiences" (817) of the human species. Joseph Campbell also suggests that stories are part of the collective unconsciousness and that authors don't really create them but find them from the signs and symbols buried in the subconscious. "The symbols cannot be ordered, invented, or permanently suppressed. They are spontaneous productions of the psyche, and each bears with it, undamaged, the germ power of its source" (*Hero* 1–2). Levi-Strauss and Propp attempted to categorize the ideas of mythology using the structuralist approach, believing that symbols and signs are created not just as single words but as images and ideas that reoccur throughout various cultures. As Jameson says, "the arbitrariness of the sign eliminates the myth of a natural language ... now what distinguished human beings is no longer that relatively specialized skill or endowment which is the power to speak, but rather the more general power to create signs; and with this, the royal road from linguistics to anthropology is thrown open " (31). In "The Flexible Bullet," King explores these ideas of story generation and if they are part of the creative mind and perhaps a by-product of madness.

The fictional Thorpe's superstitions begin to consume him and he begins to believe that radium in his watch will kill him and that electric current is destroying his mind. Then he comes to believe that a creature lives in his typewriter and if it dies he won't be able to write. "The Fornits. They were luck-elves, and he thought one of them lived in his typewriter" (502). He feeds the Fornit, which he names Rackne, by leaving food on the typewriter keys. "He had disconnected his talent from his mentality to such a degree that he could believe there was an elf living in his type-writer" (505). Then the editor, in an attempt to humor him, claims to have a Fornit too, and then he becomes paranoid about the radium in watches and electricity as well, a paranoia that is fueled by his own problem with alcohol, which results in blackouts and other irrational behavior.

The Fornits, then, are symbolic of that collective unconscious, and may be thought of as the method the unconscious mind uses to create stories. "The unconscious sends all sorts of vapors, odd beings, terrors, and deluding images up into the mind—whether in dream, broad daylight, or insanity," Campbell says (*Hero* 5). Whether or not the Fornit creatures exist in reality or not is almost irrelevant. They obviously exist in the minds of both Thorpe and the editor and through their subconscious minds create stories. Jung speaks about writers whose works "come as it were fully arrayed into the world, as Pallas Athene spring from the head of Zeus. These works positively force themselves upon the author; his hand is seized, his pen writes things that his mind contemplates with amazement" (813). He claims that the creative process is a "living thing implanted in the human psyche ... which leads a life of its own outside the hierarchy of consciousness" (814–15). Thorpe begins to see this "living thing" as a real creature, a self-invented myth that does his writing for him, rather than recognizing it as part of his own mind and his own creative process, which, of course, leads to his madness. The interesting part of "The Ballad of the Flexible Bullet" lies in King's insight into the mind itself and how it is attracted towards madness and irrational behavior, much like Poe's con-cept of the "Spirit of the Perverse." "Madness has to start *somewhere*. If this story's *about* anything—if events in one's own life can ever be said to be *about* anything—then this story is about the genius of insanity" (519).

The agent says that "trying to understand the flexible bullet is like trying to understand how a Mobius strip can have only one side" (501). Yet he goes on to explain it in rich detail as the story progresses. "Forced to define 'irrational subconscious.' I would say that it is a small padded room inside all of us, where the only furnishing is a small card table, and the only thing on that card table is a revolver loaded with flexible bullets" (511). Thorpe's short story, though vaguely told, is a metaphor for madness. "'Flexible Bullet' was funny, and on the surface it was easy to follow ... but below that surface it was surprisingly complex" (530). But the story of the editor's increasing madness really tells the plot of Thorpe's "funny, energetic look at the mechanics of going crazy" (504). However, not only are we attracted to our own madness, but we are fascinated by insanity in general, even that of others. The unnamed young writer in "Flexible Bullet" steers the conversation towards suicide and madness at the very beginning of the story. He "not only liked to talk about these things so he could joke about them, and he wanted to joke about them because he thought about them too much" (496). The writer's wife finds the topic disturbing and needs to get another drink in order to listen. But the editor is encouraged to tell his story and as he does, the audience becomes more and more interested. "The agent's wife ... had grown more and more fascinated with the tale, and was now leaning over her not inconsiderable belly in a posture that reminded the writer's wife of Snoopy standing on his doghouse and pretending to be a vulture" (508). According to the subtext of this story, we are all on the very edge of madness, hanging on the brink, if you will, and just waiting to go over the edge.

> That rational voice was right to be frightened. There's something in us that is very much attracted to madness. Everyone who looks off the edge of a tall building has felt at least a faint, morbid urge to jump ... even the most well-adjusted person is holding on to his or her own sanity by a greased rope [512].

As we have seen, many of King's protagonists hover on the edge of insanity and spill over—Jack Torrance, Carrie White, and Morton Rainey, to name just a few. It is no accident that most of them are writers. "You have to be a little nuts to be a writer because you have to imagine worlds that aren't there" (qtd. in Rogak 4).

In previous Stephen King novels, we have seen how writing can keep his characters alive and help them to triumph (*Misery*, *The Dark Half*, and *'Salem's Lot*, for example) and how the inability to write leads to destruction (*The Shining* and "Secret Window, Secret Garden"). Stephen King has asserted his own addiction to writing and admits that writing keeps his own fears in check (qtd. in Rogak 1–2). This is also true for Thorpe. The writing is the only thing that keeps him sane: "The story held him together for awhile, but now the story was done" (509). Once he is assured by his editor that the elf in his typewriter is real, and is safe, he begins to write again (524) and returns to a relatively normal life, even if his paranoia has forced him to have the electricity turned off. He completes the first three chapters of a new novel that his wife finds "quite marvelous" and begins to socialize with people, though he does suffer from "dreadful nightmares" (525).

Although the editor is not a writer *per se*, he does work with words and with writers and his "great joy" is "the great story or novel you didn't expect, landing on your desk like a Christmas present" (504). While he might complain that he was "editing mass-market stories," his own madness and paranoia are fueled by the knowledge that his magazine is in financial difficulty and that he, too, is on the brink of losing the ability to do his work. As his situation gets worse, his drinking and his madness accelerate. "The convenient thing about stories that are true is that you only need to say *this is what happened* and let people worry for themselves about the why. Generally, nobody ever knows why things happen anyway ... particularly the ones who say they do" (525).

As in "Secret Window, Secret Garden," "The Ballad of the Flexible Bullet" rests between two of Todorov's genres, the uncanny and the marvelous. Again, most of the story appears to have a rational explanation in Thorpe's madness and the editor's drunkenness and madness. Thorpe's writing is rational enough that it almost seems believable:

> Some writers possess a very rare gift for cooling their prose the more passionately they feel their subject. Steinbeck had it, so did Hemingway. When you entered his world, everything began to seem very logical. You began to think it very likely, once you accepted the basic Fornit premise, that the paperboy *did* have a silenced .38 in his bag of papers [510].

Throughout most of the story, the editor makes it clear that the narrative is about madness. But things change on page 531 when he says: "We have reached the inexplicable" (531). Then he relates how he himself saw his elf down inside his typewriter composing a letter on a piece of fallen wallpaper. "I saw a hand come out of the typewriter. An incredibly tiny hand. It came out from between the keys B and N in the bottom row, curled itself into a fist, and hammered down on the space bar" (534). King makes an unrealistic event seem realistic by using such specific details that the reader is forced to actually see the Fornit reaching from the machine. But the editor didn't say that it really happened, just that he thought it did— "I don't say that what I'm about to tell you really happened; I only say I still *believe* it happened" (532). This was the part that he had to recant, and he did recant because he wanted to get out of the psych ward. So the reality of the event is still undecided.

Referring to an earlier observation only complicates the matter further, though. The editor did figure out that it was his own fingers that were doing the typing when the first letter was written, because he recognized his own mistakes and misspellings, his "literary fingerprints." Yet these "fingerprints" also call reality into question as they type a term that the editor didn't know the meaning of. "The subconscious leaves its fingerprints, but there's a stranger down there too. A hell of a weird guy who knows a hell of a lot. I'd never seen that phrase 'co-drawer' in my life, to the best of my knowledge ... but there it was, and it was a good one, and I found out some time later that banks actually use it" (522). These "literary fingerprints" work on a metalinguistic level as well and raise the question of whether the author knows more than he thinks when creating a text—does he put in meanings and symbols and subtexts that he is not even aware of, giving the text multiple layers that were never consciously intended? Most critics would answer that question in the affirmative. In fact, discourse analysis studies have shown that "even in the most scripted, controlled discourse situations ... people sound different" (Johnstone 158). In fact, the relatively new study of forensic linguistics is used as a tool to match writing styles to the authors of texts and documents and in 2016 was used by critics to reveal the hand of Christopher Marlowe in Shakespeare's Henry VI plays (Alberge).

The story ends on a very interesting note that once again leaves the reader wondering about the fine line between reality and madness, between the real and the imagined. At the end, the wife asks the writer if there are any Fornits in his typewriter. "And the writer, who had sometimes—often—wondered exactly where the words *did* come from, said bravely: 'Absolutely not'" (545). One would presume that he is hoping to convince not just his wife but also himself that the Fornits do not exist.

"Dedication," the second story I will examine in this chapter, while certainly not one of King's best-known or best stories, does concern writing and writers, and attempts to answer Stephen King's question about "why some enormously talented people turn out to be such utter shits in person" and is loosely based upon a "now dead famous writer." While King admits that the story fails to answer the question, it does shed some light on writing and the writing process, which merits some brief discussion in examining metalanguage and metafiction in his works.

Originally published in Douglas Winter's *Night Visions V* anthology, "Dedication" was collected in *Nightmares and Dreamscapes* and is not, according to King's story notes, a "politically correct story" (*Nightmares* 803). King does expect—even hopes—that some readers will be outraged by it, but says that "the horror story is supposed to be a kind of evil-tempered junkyard dog that will bite you if you get too close. This one bites, I think."

According to Wiater *et al*, this story falls into the "gross out" category (373). The protagonist, an African-American maid named Martha Rose-wall, has married and become pregnant by a shiftless, criminal husband who is killed during a robbery, and she is asked by a witch to choose a "natural father" for the child. She immediately thinks of a rich, white writer who regularly stays at the hotel where she works, and who has a habit of masturbating and leaving the deposits behind on the sheets. Under the witch's spell, she swallows his semen, and her son Peter grows up to be an author whose first novel strongly resembles the work of his "natural father." The son dedicates his first novel to his mother. The irony of the dedication: "*I couldn't have done it without you. And that's no lie...*" is, of course, revealed at the end of the story when we understand the "magic spell" that has been put on Peter by his mother and his "natural father."

The interesting thing about this story is the way the mother reveals the secret, that her son has somehow "inherited" what Spignesi calls the "genetic soul" (521) of Peter Jefferies, the famous novelist. Instead of keeping the story secret, she confides in a co-worker, Darcy Sagamore: "After all these years I have to tell someone—now more'n ever, now that he's published his book and broken through after all those years of getting ready for it to happen" (*Nightmares* 220). But Martha doesn't just tell the secret—she narrates the story, a story so long and complex that it can't be finished at work, and so she invites her friend home so she can "hear the rest."

> "Honey, I think I *got* to hear the rest," Darcy said, and laughed a little nervously.
> "And I think I've got to tell it," Martha replied [231].

While Martha might come across as uneducated and slow, the typical stereotyped African American maid, she is anything but. She is well read—has, in fact, read the novels of Peter Jefferies, much to his surprise—and tells the story masterfully, leading her listener along and carefully building suspense. She uses colorful language, rich in metaphor and detail. If her husband found out she had taken his drugs "he would have plowed me like a pea field" (224), she says. And she remembers meeting the witch and conveys concrete details that create a vivid picture: "Even now, twenty-six years later, I can smell those old burned candles and kerosene from the kitchen and the sour smell of dried wallpaper, like old cheese" (226).

Martha also has a keen insight into people, an important trait for an author or a storyteller. She has lived a harsh life and understands people's characters. "He belonged to the son-of-a-bitch tribe, and that particular bunch comes in all skin-colors" (230), she says of Jefferies. When he leaves her a generous tip, she understands his motivation. "He was following a custom. Custom's important for people like him" (234). She also understands the character of the witch woman—"if you want to be *known* as a *bruja* woman, you have to *act* like a *bruja* woman" (225).

Her real understanding, though, is revealed in how she related Jefferies and his books. "The books were beautiful and the man who made them was ugly as sin…. His *books* were his dreams, where he let himself believe in the world he laughed at and sneered at when he was awake" (241). When her friend questions his character, though, she explains, "he *did* have that something you could call 'quality' without a smirk on your face, although it only came out completely in the things he wrote" (237).

Martha serves as the voice of Stephen King when she reflects about the personality of the writer and how it could be so different from his books:

> I started to wonder about *why* he was a famous writer … how he *could* be a famous writer. I wanted to know what it was the critics saw in him, but I was a lot more interested in what ordinary folks like me saw in him—the people who made his books best-sellers as soon as they came out [239].

She is curious and fascinated that he can be what King calls "an utter shit" and still write such wonderful books. "I didn't know how a man who was so boring when you had to listen to him could write so you didn't never want to close the book, or see it end, either. How a nasty, cold-hearted man like him could make up characters so real you wanted to cry over 'em when they died" (240).

Although King claims that the story doesn't answer his question, it does provide some understanding. Martha seems to have lived a difficult life, enduring discrimination, poverty, an abusive husband, and hard work. Her son served in Vietnam, where the war obviously affected him enough for him to write about it. Peter Jefferies also went to war, and, as Martha says, "all they did was drink and talk about the war" (234), who got killed and what they saw that they couldn't tell their wives. These experiences undoubtedly shaped his writing, made him cynical and bitter, and made him a better writer. "If he'd been a nice man, I probably never would have read even one of [his books]. And I'll tell you an even funnier one: if he'd been a nice man, I don't think they would have been as good as they were" (238).

The only real conversation Martha has with Jefferies is when he had an idea that he needed to share with her. "He talked to me because he *had* to" just as Martha *has* to tell her story to her friend. He shares his idea with her, about the possibility of twin brothers fighting against one another during World War II, and Martha gives him useful advice. First she tells him it couldn't happen in the Pacific, to which he agrees, and then she says, "*Everyone* likes stories about brothers that don't know they're brothers" (250). In fact, modern linguists agree that humans speak because it is programmed into our DNA, that we do *have to* speak, have to communicate, "it is an instinctive tendency to speak" (Pinker 6). In authors, this instinct is translated into the written form, which is why so many writers write because they are compelled to, not because it is a lucrative career with lots of job openings.

Although Martha credits the "magic spell" with her son's success, it is obvious to the reader that she is an expert storyteller and knows what makes a story work. She is a perceptive critic. "There's a feel to them every now and then that's the same ... something you seem to almost catch around corners. It's that sunshine I told you about—that feeling that the world is mostly a lot better than it looks, especially better than it looks to those who are too smart to be kind" (259). Although her son's book—and his handwriting—resemble that of his "natural father," one must suppose that his mother had an influence on his choice of careers as well. She nurtured his talent, worked hard to pay for his education, provided books for him to read, and, no doubt, told him interesting, colorful stories. Thus the dedication—"*I couldn't have done it without you*"—really is true, even without the magic spell.

To summarize, the two stories analyzed in this chapter both look at writing and the creative process. "The Ballad of the Flexible Bullet" examines the psychological realms of language, writing, and the creative process. Despite the fantasy of Thorpe and his editor, it seems that stories come from the author's mind, not from some outside force such as a Forbit, although when the writing is going well, authors sometimes feel as if they are merely conduits and that an outside force is dictating the words, creating the story, and they are merely transcribing the text. While that feeling may be true, psychologists, linguists, and literary critics alike agree that the stories come from within, even if they are not always visible on the conscious level. The "Forbits" are really products of the subconscious mind, perhaps even the collective unconsciousness of the human race, which has collected and stored myths and narratives almost at the molecular level (hence the "language instinct" that Pinker and other linguists theorize). The story also shows how writers and creative people often exist on the fringes of sanity, often walking a thing tightrope between normalcy and madness. Perhaps it has something to do with being in such close contact with the subconscious mind or perhaps it is the fact that creative individuals poke and probe into areas that more "normal" people avoid. That is a question better left to the psychologists than the critics.

"Dedication," while seemingly a "throwaway" story, and probably not worthy of a lengthy critical analysis, does raise interesting questions about the author as a "public" figure, seen and understood through his writing, and as a private individual. There are authors who have or have had private beliefs that we condemn and despise—H.P. Lovecraft's racism is such an example. However, does that negate the work? As Martha Rosewall points out, if Jeffies had been a "nice man" his books wouldn't have been as good. If Lovecraft hadn't been as uncomfortable with outsiders, would he have been able to pen "The Dunwich Horror"? And if Salinger hadn't been a recluse, could he have written *A Catcher in the Rye*? Once again, that may be a question for the psychologists to answer, but it does force us, as readers, to consider the difference between the author and the work and consider which one we are evaluating, the narrative or the person who created it.

Finally, "Dedication" also brings in the age-old question of nature versus nurture. Is creativity a genetic trait, or is it learned, or both? Can great writers be created, or must there be some natural talent embedded in the individual's genetic code? As a practical question, have Stephen King's sons, Joe Hill and Owen King, received their talent from their parents? Or did it result from growing up in a home where their parents wrote, encouraged them to read, and inspired their creativity? I would suspect it is probably some of both. In "Dedication," Martha's son has the advantage of both the pedigree and the nurturing environment, which, in this story at least, results in his success. Perhaps more importantly, it seems that he has not only inherited his mother's penchant for storytelling, but he seems to have received her likeable personality as well.

CHAPTER 11

The Running Man:
Simulacra and Simulation

According to Jean Baudrillard, reality has undergone a fundamental change once we entered the electronic age. "Simulation is no longer that of a territory, a referential being, or a substance. It is the generation by models of a real without origin or reality: a hyperreal" (*Simulacra* 1). He claims that "the real is produced from miniaturized cells … and it can be reproduced an infinite number of times from these" (2) until it becomes the "simulacra." Where "simulation envelops the whole edifice of representation itself as a simulacra" (6). In other words, the copy without an original becomes the reality, as for example in Disneyland and other theme parks (12), political narratives (14), and in American reality television (27), all of which have, in effect, replaced a "true" reality with a fictitious one. This blurring of reality has created a metafiction that has, in effect, supplanted reality. As Bellipanni points out:

> Because of the crossover success of constructing reality, the techniques of metafiction have grown out of their place as a side-show cultural experiment over the past thirty years and into mainstream culture. The genre of creative nonfiction is not the only popular medium to have adopted many of the techniques; the so-called reality television shows mimic metafiction in their elaborate and self-conscious constructions of what is then self-reflexivity presented as spontaneous reality [13].

Urban legends and conspiracy theories are often accepted as being more real than reality, and when Hollywood "fictionalizes" a historic event, it is the film version that is believed and adopted into popular culture, not the actual facts about what happened.

This brings us to Stephen King's *The Running Man*, a nasty dystopia where government-run televised game shows have become the bread and circus of the masses. This novel, originally written in 1971 and published under the Richard Bachman pen name in 1982, foreshadowed the reality televisions shows *COPS* and *America's Most Wanted,* shows that have led to the current reality show craze that dominates American television. Furthermore, reality shows such as the survival shows *Alone* and *Naked and Afraid* are, in fact, becoming increasingly dangerous; this voyeurism has even evolved to a live police ride along show (*Live P.D.*) in 2016, where anything can happen, and 2016's *The Runner*, resurrected from an earlier concept that was shelved after 9/11. As Mastrale has noted, this book "anticipates the so-called reality-television phenomenon that will emerge fifteen years later in programs such as *Survivor*, where contestants are required to endure intense physical torment at the same time as they engage in game show competition" (*Hollywood* 159). The novel, and the 1987 film that was based upon it, starring Arnold Schwarzenegger, have also been the precursor for a new generation of dystopias, ranging from *The Hunger Games*, to *Divergent*, to *The Maze Runners*, as well as HBO's surrealistic theme park, *Westworld.*

In *The Running Man*, the government-run television network and its brutal reality shows, reminiscent of the Roman Coliseum, become a metafictional text that creates a new reality. The inhabitants of this world become so engrossed in the games—and in what little hope of salvation they may offer them—that they forget their own problems and their own misery. "*The Running Man* very accurately predicts the dreamworld to be created by the media in the (as it turned out) not-at-all distant future where ever-present urban-bred criminals from the South Side, North Philadelphia, Watts, and Harlem, lurk at every turn and need to be hunted down by police with the willing help of the American Public" (Texter 51).

The first thing we notice about the novel is its construction. The chapters are numbered in reverse, beginning with "...Minus 100 and COUNTING..." until the novel ends with "000." Metalinguistically, this countdown signifies that something is going to happen and points to a liftoff, a blastoff, or the triggering of a bomb. Chuck Palahniuk used this same technique in his 1999 novel *Survivor*, where the last living member of the terrorist cult has hijacked a plane and released all of the passengers; the clock is running down until it crashes. Ray Bradbury also uses this countdown technique in his short story "Zero Hour," about an alien invasion of the earth. This technique can is an obvious fit into Roland Barthes "hermeneutic code," where "an enigma can be distinguished, suggested, formulated, held in suspense, and finally disclosed" (Barthes, *S/Z* 19). This hermeneutic code is especially strong in all of King's works since his fiction is consciously designed to create and maintain suspense, but in this case the code of reverse chapter numbering can be considered metafictional determinism since it calls obvious attention to itself and the story's impending conclusion, exposing the author's hermeneutic trick, if you will. In a traditional novel, the reader is not aware of how many chapters remain without looking at the end and counting backwards. But King's blatant countdown lets us know that we are getting closer and closer to something big.

The countdown is also emblematic of a simulation, which is usually preceded by a countdown, and, in fact, the premise of the novel is based upon the idea of simulation and simulacra. A simulacrum is defined by *The New Shorter Oxford English Dictionary* as "an image without the substance or qualities of the original"; Jameson sees this concept in postmodern art, film, video and television and "finds in them only a superficial cutting and pasting of ready-made images and styles ... abstracted from their true origins and reused in meaningless new combinations in the trivial, commercialized space created by mass culture" (Ward 86). These become Baudrillard's copies that have been recopied so many times that the original no longer exists. Philip K. Dick's 1964 novel about a fraudulent government is titled *The Simulacra*, a symbol of falsehood and forgery.

The science fiction world of *The Running Man* is a simulacrum under all of these previous definitions. It is a world without substance where the wealthy live superficial, commercialized lives under a government that is hiding behind the smoke and mirrors of "The Network." The government run "Free-Vee" is a simulacra of the real world that is accepted as reality by the masses.

The Games Building is the ultimate symbol of the simulacra: "The highest of them all was the Network Games Building, one hundred stories, the top half buried in cloud and smog cover." As Ben Richards walks towards it "the Games Building grew taller, more and more improbable" (536). Once he enters the building, the simulation begins: "They were like rats in a huge upward-tending maze: an American maze, Richards reflected" (545). The first floor is ordinary and sterile and populated with ordinary, robotic people: "the woman sitting at the rumbling plastipunch looked tired and cruel and impersonal. She looked at him and saw no one" and the lobby itself "was an echoing, rebounding tomb of sound" (537). His next stop, the examination room, "looked like an assembly line" (541), and once he passes the physical tests they assign him to a dorm where "rows and rows of narrow iron-and-canvas cots seemed to stretch out to infinity" (544). Once Richards makes it to the sixth floor, the scenery becomes noticeably better: "The auditorium was luxurious, done in great quantities of red plush" (553). The entire building is designed as a simulacrum of the American Dream, of course, where a poor "maggot" from the wrong side of the canal can become successful and wealthy with talent and hard work. The entire Games Building symbolizes "the fiction of upward mobility which started in the grimy street-level lobby [and] ended here on the tenth floor" where the broadcast facility was located (564).

This simulacrum of the American Dream appears even in the fictional works, in the bad novel that Richards is given when he requests to have "thick novels sent up" (561) to keep him busy. He is looking for something real: "'Books. You know. Read. Words. Moveable press.'" The largest novel sent up, and the longest, is "a huge tome written three years earlier called *The Pleasure of Serving*." Richards summarizes the plot:

> Poor boy makes good in General Atomics. Rises from engine wiper to gear tradesman. Takes night courses (on what? Richards wondered. Monopoly money?). Falls in love with beautiful girl (apparently syphilis hadn't taken her nose off yet) at a block orgy. Promoted to junior techno following dazzling aptitude scores. Three-year marriage contract follows and—[562].

Richards throws the book, symbolizing his awareness and disgust of the simulation, and instead reads the other two older novels, presumably written in a time when books were more real. The fact that these books still exist is probably the reason that "books were regarded with suspicion at best, especially when carried by someone from south of the Canal. Pervert magazines were safer" (540).

The "pervert magazines" represent another simulation, on several levels: they simulate sex; they portray fantasies rather than reality; and they offer pleasure than cannot be achieved. It is ironic in this world that scientific knowledge is censored—the populace is not allowed to know how bad the air quality is—but explicit sex is not only not censored, but is encouraged, since it keeps people's minds off of the real problems. Elections are also part of the simulation—"voting booths had been done away with by computer election eleven years ago" (542)—and even the food is "oddly bland, as if some vampire chef in the kitchen had sucked all of the taste out of it and left only brute nutrients" (545).

The games themselves, of course, are the ultimate tools of the government-run simulacra. Their titles are meant to stimulate: *Dig Your Grave*; *Swim the Crocodiles*; *Run for Your Guns*; and *Treadmill to Bucks* all give the illusion that a player can overcome overwhelming odds and win the American Dream. In the dystopia of Ben Richards, victory is an illusion, since no one actually wins in the games. Ironically, Stephen King's prediction has become true in contemporary America, where the term "reality TV star" (oxymoron though it is) has become reality. The simulacra of American television has created characters such as "Snooki" (*Jersey Shores*), Kim Kardashian, and Honey Boo-Boo, "stars" that lack the ambition or talent to succeed, but which were artificially created by the medium on simulation. As Baudrillard has said, "the cold light of television … no longer carries any imaginary" (*Simulacra* 51).

In King's novel, the ultimate game, the "big-money" assignment is *The Running Man*, a dystopian version of the child's game "Manhunt" (which I played as a youth) where one kid would be given a head start, and then the rest of the group, carrying toy guns, chased him down until he was "killed." In Ben Richards' world, the "big money" games are simulations taken to the extreme, however. They are "the ones that do more than just land you in the hospital with a stroke or put out an eye or cut off an arm or two. The ones where they kill you. Prime time, baby" (555). *The Running Man* is "the biggest thing going on Free-Vee. It's filled with chances for viewer participation, both vicarious and actual" (558). In its six-year history, the program has had no survivors, no winners.

In this world, the game becomes reality, becomes the news itself— "we've been known to interrupt scheduled broadcasting" Killian tells Richards (558). The media creates the reality that the masses believe, and they televise it every night during prime time. "What else do the media dream of besides creating the event simply by their presence?" Baudrillard asks (*Simulacra* 55). "Everyone decries it, but everyone is secretly fascinated by this eventuality."

The Free-Vee program is its own simulacrum as it creates the storyline that it wants its viewers to believe. While the reality is that "the program is one of the surest ways the Network has of getting rid of embryo troublemakers" (558), it is scripted so that the audience believes the runner is a criminal, will watch to see him caught and killed "the more messier the better," and will assist in the capture. When Richards observes, "you're running a crooked table" (558), Killian reminds him that he is "an anachronism" and that no one will be rooting for him to get away.

Richards is "created" by the media as a reality TV star who is doomed to fail. He is given a role: "you're a contestant only for the masses. Actually, you are a working man and should view your role in that light" and he is allowed to act. "Feel free to express yourself as colorfully as you please. It's all good theater" (565). The media retouches his photo so that he looks more dangerous and depicts his wife as unflatteringly as possible—"the airbrush had been at work again, this time wielded with a heavier hand" (567). The studio audience is packed with people who scream for Richards' death and speculates that they have been paid to try to rush the stage to kill him themselves. But when Richards taunts them, they rush at him again, and "this time the rush for the stage was by no stretch of the imagination simulated" (568). This leads us to consider Baudrillard's question: "Is it the media that induce fascination in the masses, or is it the masses who direct the media into the spectacle?" (*Simulacra* 84).

The final simulacrum in King's novel is Ben Richards himself, the character that is created by the media and is admired by Killian, in his own way. "I wish you could be preserved—collected, if you please—just as my Asian cave paintings have been collected and preserved," Killian says (569). This concept mirrors Baudrillard's observation about the Lascaux caves, where visitors were forbidden to enter, so as not to damage the valuable artifact. Instead, an exact replica was created for people to visit, while looking at the original through a peephole (*Simulacra* 9). Richards challenges Killian to create his own simulation—"Grab a copy of my brain waves, you bastard. They're on record" (569).

As the novel progresses, Ben Richards is, indeed, transformed into Baudrillard's "hyperreal" as he defeats the network at its own game, blowing up the YMCA building, eluding them, and even taking a wealthy hostage. He becomes so successful that Killian makes his proposition of collecting him real, and offers Richards a job, that of taking McCone's place because "you're the best runner we've ever had" and "the Network is always in the market for new talent" (678). The plan is to fake Richard's death, and then the Network, the media, will recreate him as a new simulacrum, a government Hunter. While Richards initially agrees to the terms, he changes his mind after learning that his wife and daughter have been killed by prowlers in a "horrible accident ... the story sounded too much like a lie not to be the truth" (678–9), and so he has nothing to live for. Refusing to be recreated in a new simulation, he crashes the plane into the Network Games Building, destroying Killian as the countdown reaches 000.

King's dystopian novel is another illustration of Campbell's mythic hero and fits into that structuralist formula. Ben Richards departs from his family in the very first chapter, answering the call to adventure in an attempt to earn enough money to pay for a doctor for his daughter, who is dying from the flu. In the minus 96 chapter he considers refusing the call and turning back, but ultimately continues into the network headquarters, where he crosses the threshold and begins his initiation by passing the physical, mental, and psychological tests and is cast as a reality star in the hit show, The Running Man. Most of the novel depicts his road of trials as he moves from one city to another eluding pursuit, making allies, and killing those who are trying to catch him. In chapter minus 15 he "meets the goddess" Amelia Williams, a wealthy and attractive socialite, whom he takes hostage. He is briefly tempted by this woman in minus 42, when he has a sudden urge to defile and rape her, but later, in minus 34, he sees her as "almost goddess-like." His atonement with the father comes when Killian asks him to take McCone's place as the Chief Hunter and he accepts. The apotheosis occurs soon after, as he changes his mind, takes over the plane, and decides on his final course of action. His "magic flight" is taken care of by the plane's autopilot, which brings him to Harding City and towards the Games Building "seemingly held up by the hand of God." In the finale, the jet hits the Games Building, in a scene that eerily fore-shadowed the attack on the Twin Towers in 2011, 40 years after the book's publication. Although Richards dies in the end, he dies grinning, and the destruction of the Games Building gives him freedom to live on in myth and legend, since this strike at the corrupt government will, we suspect, be the beginning of the uprising that was so badly needed in this world.

The Running Man is atypical of King's best known work and didn't attract notice when published under the Bachman penname. Although it contains graphically horrible scenes, it is more science fiction than horror. Douglas Texter has observed that "despite some scholarship hinting that *The Running Man* has dystopian qualities, no critic has yet fully articulated the kinds of dystopian maneuvers that King made" (43), and because of King's popular success and his being branded as a horror writer, this novel has largely been overlooked. "Once the King brand name was affixed to *The Running Man*, the chances of the book being dealt with in terms of its own merits dropped to practically nil" (Texter 64). The initial publication under the Bachman pseudonym probably hasn't helped its reputation either.

As Texter has pointed out, once the 1987 film version was released "*The Running Man* was now something quite different from what it used to be" (68). According to him, the film's "plot and politics ... don't take readers anywhere very interesting ... ignored the dystopian conventions" and the film "guts the content of the book" (67). The film, while enter-taining in its own way, turns the story into a Hollywood spectacle within a spectacle, where the characters, resembling wrestling superstars, offer entertainment and not serious social criticism. The major difference is that Richards is "drafted" into playing the game in the film, while in the novel he enters the game willingly in order to save his daughter's life, thus becoming a true hero figure. Ironically, the film version is remembered because of its A-list Hollywood stars, and thus becomes the reality that displaces the novel; just as Baudrillard claims that the electronic age creates its own reality, that reality has become a simulacra, a copy of a copy.

Perhaps the ultimate simulacrum of *The Running Man* was the one that did not occur, the broadcasting of the reality television game show called "The Runner" that was scheduled to be aired in 2001, but was cancelled due to the terrorist attacks of 911. "The idea for 'The Runner' called for one person to set out cross country, accomplishing a series of assignments, all of which he or she would have to perform without being spotted and identified. Every viewer could have potentially captured the runner, winning whatever prize money had been accumulated to that point" (Carter). Although the idea was never officially attributed to the Stephen King novel, the resemblance is obvious, with the only difference being that the runner wouldn't actually be killed. The show, "produced by the actors Ben Affleck and Matt Damon that ABC had confidently forecast would be the next phenomenon in the reality trend" (Carter), would have not only changed King's version of *The Running Man*, but would have contradicted and neutralized it, according to Texter (70). "*The Running Man* is satire. 'The Runner' was to be played straight" (69).

Ethan Campbell has noted not only the resemblance of the show to King's creation, but the complexities "how, for instance, can the network prevent fans from harming the fugitive physically, or the contestant from harming fans in his desperation to escape" (qtd. in Texter 69). At any rate, the show never aired, and plans for such an interactive and potentially violent game show have not been revived. "The series, which had always loomed as a logistical challenge to produce, faced a much steeper fight for public acceptance in the wake of the events on Sept. 11. As one senior network executive put it, 'Would people want to watch someone trying to escape capture after what this country has been through?'" (Carter).

In a case of reality imitating fiction, *The Runner* was reinvented in July 2016, for Verizon. In this show a runner must make it across the country to win a prize, while being chased by a team of "chasers" and mobile phone users who provide clues as to the contestant's whereabouts (Maglio). In similar show, *Hunted*, civilian teams of two attempt to elude professional hunters to win a $250,000 prize.

As Magistrale has noted, "Even as *The Running Man* is a droll commentary on America's fascination with celebrities and televised violent sport, it is also a highly politicized narrative of helplessness born of poverty and social anomie" and "accurately approximates current living conditions for many inner-city Americans" (*Hollywood* 158). In pointing out this reality, a reality from where King himself came from, as a member of the lower-middle-class in his childhood, and of the working class until the publication of *Carrie*, he creates an elaborate simulation within a simulacrum. It is only by telling the story by using a fantastic alternate world, a world that could, potentially, become reality in the future, that he is able to unveil the truth about class warfare, government deception, and the failure of the American dream for many people who are trapped in a world without hope. For these people, the only way out is to play the lottery, so to speak, a game where the odds are stacked against the poor.

In conclusion, *The Running Man* stands as an excellent metaphor for Baudrillard's ideas about how the modern world has become more of a simulation than a reality and how the postmodern world has become more interested in the reproduction than in the real thing. This novel did a remarkable job of predicting the emergence of reality television before it was even invented and shows the hold that the media has over the populace. Written before the advent of 24-hour cable news, before survivalist television shows, the book, as science fiction, has been amazingly accurate in its predictions. While reality television hasn't reached the point of killing off its contestants (at least not at the time of this writing), it, and the media in general, has become increasingly violent and graphic, as news helicopters hover over murder sites and follow high-speed police chases and where beheadings and other atrocities are filmed and shown on social media. *The Running Man* points ahead to a society that can only enjoy an experience if it is video-taped—audiences are too busy videotaping to enjoy the real show, and the mark of having been somewhere is demonstrated by a selfie posted to a social media site.

In the wake of *The Running Man*, a new generation of dystopian films has arisen, led by the highly successful *Hunger Games* franchise, which also features a future world where the government uses violent reality shows to control its people. It is interesting to note that these novels were written for a young adult audience but have attracted followers of all ages. Each of these films seem to follow a similar pattern, that of Campbell's the mythic hero, though the modern trend has successfully transformed the hero into a heroine, a Katniss Everdeen who follows the call to adventure and transforms the world.

CHAPTER 12

IT: The Unnamable Horror

Originally published in 1986, *It* is King's second longest novel (second only to the uncut version of *The Stand*) and the film version, a two-part television series, aired in 1990. When it was published King claimed "it is the summation of everything I have learned and done in my whole life to this point.... It's like a monster rally—everything is in this book, every monster you could think of" (Winter 153). Yet from the wide array of monsters, everything from the Creature from the Black Lagoon, to werewolves, to Rodan, one evil creature dominates them all—Pennywise the Clown. The novel was voted number two in a *Rolling Stone* poll on the top ten favorite Stephen King novels, and Greene says, "*It* has caused more people to fear clowns than perhaps any movie, book, or TV show in history" (Reader's Poll). And the Halloween season of 2016 was plagued by scary clowns playing nasty pranks; the problem became so intense that Stephen King himself pleaded with people to stop the clown craze (Flood).

Yet clowns were scary long before the novel or the film, and King was able to tap into this subconscious fear and magnify it for his own ends. According to *Smithsonian*, clowns in one form or another have been around since 2500 BCE in Egypt, were part of ancient imperial China, and were even part of Hopi Native American culture (McRobbie). According to Andrew McConnell Stott, Charles Dickens was the creator of the modern scary clown when he used a corrupt, alcoholic clown as a character in *The Pickwick Papers*. This evil clown character was, according to Stott, inspired by the life of Joseph Grimaldi, who could be considered the father of modern clowns, who died in 1837 (qtd. in McBobbie). The evil clown myth was further perpetuated by the life of Jean-Gaspard Deburau's

Pierrot, "a clown with white face paint punctuated by red lips and black eyebrows whose silent gesticulations delighted French audiences" (McRobbie). Deburau killed a boy with his cane in 1936, after the youth insulted him, and thus became part of sinister clown history. And, of course, John Wayne Gacy, the serial killer, was a registered clown. Even the director of talent for Ringling Bros., David Kisner, admits that clowns have a dark side: "the clown has always had an impish spirit," he says (qtd. in McRobbie).

Today, clowns are more disliked than ever. "In 2008, *Nursing Standard* magazine and BBC reported the results of a University of Sheffield study: kids hate clowns. Researchers surveyed over 250 children, aged four to 16, and found clowns to be 'universally disliked' by all ages said Penny Curtis, 'Some found the clown images to be quite frightening and unknowable'" (qtd. in Lewis). According to Lewis, clowns are scary for some very good psychological reasons: "The clown insists that we laugh. We may not want to laugh. The situation becomes, at best, awkward, and at worst—combined with the unsettling colorful familiarity—terrifying."

The horror genre used a clown doll that comes to life in the 1982 film *Poltergeist* and King took the idea to new places in *It*. "Of course, it's difficult to say whether there has been a real rise in the number of people who have clown phobias since Gacy and *It*," says McRobbie. At any rate, it seems obvious that King's novel hasn't helped make clowns likeable and that he tapped into a societal fear and dislike of clowns that was already present.

The title of the novel, simply *It*, raises a linguistic question: why wasn't the monster living in the sewers named, instead of referring to it in generic form, especially when King's trademark is to use brand names and trademarks to describe things as concisely as possible? One clue can be found in the work of H.P. Lovecraft, and in many ways, *It* is a Lovecraftian tale of cosmic horror, despite the Hollywood and boogieman masks that the alien entity wears. In some stories such as "The Unnamable," Lovecraft refers to nameless things, and in others, such as "The Call of Cthulhu," the names of his creatures are virtually unpronounceable by human speech. The idea of naming is the foundation for modern linguistics, which recognizes the close connection between language and thought. As de Saussure has noted, "linguistic units are dual in nature, comprising two elements.... A linguistic is not a link between a thing and a name, but between a concept and a sound pattern" (66). The linguistic sign, according to de Saussure, is this two-sided entity. Since the concept and the sound pattern are so intimately connected, one must be able to conceptualize something in order to give it a sound pattern, which, in language, eventually becomes a word or a name. As Searle has said, "whatever can be meant, can be said" (88).

Lovecraft understood this connection and, by refusing to name things, or give them comprehensible sound patterns, he made them more alien, more mysterious. One cannot effectively name or even articulate what one cannot fully understand or comprehend. If one cannot mean, then one cannot say. Thus, many of Lovecraft's cosmic beings cannot be captured by a single word in English. The complexity and vastness of the universe makes human language totally ineffective in understanding it.

Furthermore, naming something gives one power over it. Once named, an object can be controlled, a monster destroyed. A vampire is killed by a wooden stake through the heart, a werewolf by a silver bullet. An entity with no name doesn't fit the formula and is therefore difficult, perhaps impossible to destroy, as it is difficult or impossible to name.

Searle has shown that while proper names don't necessarily have descriptive content, as Frege suggested, they do have "sense," which is linguistically defined as "a meaning being distinct from its referent" (Matthews 362). According to Searle, proper names "enable us to refer publically to objects.... They function not as descriptions, but as pegs on which to hang descriptions" (172). Naming the creature "It," an indefinite pronoun that grammatically has no description, limits the function of the proper name "to perform the speech act of identifying reference" (Searle 174), and nothing more. Since it lacks this intrinsic description, "It" is merely a referent to the creature that cannot be imagined or described.

Stephen King's monster, "It," is an amalgamation of every monster ever imagined—but it is more. It is a cosmic monster that cannot be imagined. It can only be approximated. While each of the children think it is a specific monster—a creature, a werewolf, a zombie, depending on their point of view—it is really a cosmic thing that cannot be imagined except in images captured from mythology or the movies.

When Bill finally does see it in its "final" shape, he cannot quite comprehend it. It appears spider-like but *"not a spider either, not really, but this shape isn't one It picked out of our minds; it's just the closest our minds can come to ... whatever it really is"* (1004). The attempted description of the entity hints of Lovecraftian prose: "Its eyes were bright malevolent rubies, bulging from sockets filled with some chromium-colored fluid. Its jagged mandibles opened and closed, opened and closed, dripping ribbons of foam. Frozen in an ecstasy of horror, tottering on the brink of utter lunacy" (1004). Then Ben sees the creature: "and for an instant he *did* see the shape behind the shape: saw lights, saw an endless, crawling hairy thing which was made of light and nothing else, orange light, dead light that mocked life" (1005). These descriptions attempt to be specific, but ultimately, the thing cannot be specifically named as anything other than "It." As they enter It's lair, the children also see a symbol over the door, a symbol that is not a known letter, but is seen by each of them as something different—a paper boat, a phoenix, a pair of spectacles (989). As Waiter et al. have suggested, the Yog Sothoth from Lovecraft's "The Dunwich Horror" is a spiderlike creature from beyond, something very similar to the description of It (107). In order to destroy It, the boys have to comprehend what they're dealing with. Finally, Bill, the writer, is able to attach a word to it: *"Duh-Duh-Derry* is It," he stutters (931), and they realize that the alien thing has become one with the town.

As the boys travel towards the macroverse and past the "real" world, the text, again, is at a loss for specific words: "It was a barrier, something of a strange, non-geometrical shape that his mind could not grasp, instead his mind translated it as best as it could, as it had translated the shape of It into a Spider, allowing Richie to think of it as a colossal gray wall made of fossilized wooden stakes" (1020). Much like the unnamable color in Lovecraft's "A Colour Out of Space," the non-geometrical shape is impossible to describe and defies the known natural laws of the universe. Since we are no longer dealing with Euclidian geometry, this must be a world of multiple dimensions, something out of string theory, perhaps, that cannot be comprehended by creatures living in a three-dimensional reality.

And there is a being even greater than It, the Final Other. "This Other was a force beyond the universe, a power beyond all other power, the author of all that was" (1009). This other, "God," if you will, is not the creator, but the author. This is a common motif in mythology, that the "creator" is the author and creates the universe with words. The Christian Bible says that "in the beginning was the Word, and the Word was with God, and the Word was God" (John 1.1). The Bambara people of Mali believe the word Yo created the gods, who then created the world. The Taoist creation myth features the interaction of the named and the nameless (Thury 140): "Nameless, it is the origin of the heaven and the earth; Namable, it is the mother of all things." The Mayans, also, consider words and language part of their creation myth. According to the *Popol Vuh*, the "Maker" spoke with the "Plumed Serpent" and they "joined their words" to create the world and everything in it (qtd. in Thury 165). The point of all this is the importance that all people have placed on language, on the word. It is words that create life, whether they come from nothingness, or they are uttered by God or the gods as a command—"Let there be light."

As we have also seen in the King canon, language and writing equal life, and this Other, the ultimate author, brings everything to life with words and language. This theme is taken to the extreme in the Gunslinger books, where the author becomes a god-like character in his own book.

One of the major themes of *It* involves the blurring of reality, of understanding what is real and what belongs in the realm of the imagination. In Stephen King's world, reality is a moving target, and children are more capable of understanding it than adults. Only the children, with their limitless imagination, can see the faces of It and are willing to believe that It exists. Each of the children has a talent that keeps their imagination active until adulthood. Bill, the writer, is the leader because he has the strongest imagination. As an author, he creates a macroverse of his own, a canon of novels and stories composed of characters and nightmares that he has created with language, even as the Other has authored everything in its multiverse. Richie, the man with the voices, is an adult-child that has never grown up, and has managed to use his talents as a D.J. and comedian. Ben uses his imagination to create architectural marvels, and, as a child, wrote a haiku for Beverly. Beverly is a talented fashion designer, and Mike is a writer, though unpublished, as he chronicles the history of the strange things that have happened in Derry. Eddie uses his natural navigating skills as a limo driver and creates a business out of his talent. Stan, the accountant, is the least creative. Unable to regain his childhood imagination, he commits suicide and doesn't return to Derry with the others.

As we have seen, King favors protagonists who are writers, and he uses these protagonists to talk about writing and the psychology of writers. *It* is no exception. As a child, "Bill was good at reading and writing, but even at *his* age George was wise enough to know that wasn't the only reason why Bill got all A's on his report cards.... *Telling* was only part of it. Bill was good at *seeing*" (5). Writers aren't just good with words but are perceptive enough to see things that others might overlook, and this is what gives Bill his power, both as a child, and 27 years later as an adult when he returns to Derry to destroy It for good. In fact, Bill's talent at "telling" is severely impaired when he develops a stutter after his brother's death. The stutter doesn't affect his writing ability, though, and it doesn't affect his ability to see the truth in the world, to perceive the reality that others overlook. He manages to overcome his stutter as he grows into an adult, and it only returns once It has made its reappearance. But even with his "telling" voice impaired, Bill is still strong enough to defeat It, with the help of his friends. He is still considered the leader, and It targets him first, knowing that if he is destroyed, the others will fall. *"The writer was the strongest, the one who had somehow trained his mind for this confrontation over all the years, and when the writer was dead ... the others would be Its quickly"* (975).

The alien being that is It was created to feed, and it feeds on imagination. When it first came to earth *"It had discovered a depth of imagination here that was* almost *new,* almost *of concern. This quality of imagination made the food very rich"* (965). Children, of course, were It's best food, since they have the power to imagine. Very few adults are able to keep this imaginative power. Bill has nurtured his imagination by writing horror novels derived, subconsciously, from the events of his childhood battle with It. For example, when he sends his friends one after another into an underground pipe, the image of clowns coming out of a little car crosses his mind, and "years later he would use that same image in a book called *The Black Rapids*. It muses that when It kills Bill, *"It would feed well"* (975).

The alien being does make one fatal mistake though—it fails to recognize the imaginative powers of the others, especially Richie, who has, in many ways, refused to grow up. He still does his childish voices, only he has now perfected them to the point of being able to make a living with his voice as a successful radio personality. Even as an adult, he says inappropriate things and the others continually silence him with their own childish saying "BEEP BEEP, Richie." "'You're impossible, Richie,' Beverly said coldly. 'You ought to grow up'" (489). And Ben, also, has retained the imagination he had when he wrote the haiku for Beverly and has used this talent to create artistic works of his own, such a building based upon the glass bridge connecting the children's and adult library in Derry. By concentrating It's efforts only on Bill, It allowed Richie and Ben to attack and destroy It.

Like most of King's fiction, *It* contains a strong symbolic code of reality and imagination; however, in this novel, the binary opposition becomes especially blurry. Waiter et al. have posited that all of Stephen King's stories are connected together like spokes in a wheel, with the *Dark Tower* series being the hub, and in *The Complete Stephen King Universe*, they have made a compelling case. *It* is just one of a number of stories about the town of Derry, of course, but "based on the events related in *Insomnia*, it appears as if the city is a cosmic hot spot, a key location in regard to the tale of Roland" from the *Dark Tower* series (Wiater 106). In terms of reality, then, Derry and It are part of a much larger picture that can only be seen from the outside by the reader who is familiar with all of King's works, familiar with his "multiverse," if you will. Bill and the protagonists of *It* see just one part of this multiverse, their own universe, while the reader can put together the larger picture.

Linguistically, the question of reality is an interesting one; philosophers have been trying to define reality and "being" for centuries. Postmodern writers such as Baudrillard claim that reality no longer exists but has been supplanted by simulations and has become "hyperreality": "everywhere the hyperrealism of simulation is translated by the hallucinatory resemblance of the real to itself" (*Simulacra* 23). In other words, modern technology has created a new reality where "the real is produced from miniaturized cells, matrices, and memory banks" (2). According to Eco, "The American imagination demands the real thing and, to attain it, must fabricate the absolute fake, where the boundaries between game and illusion are blurred" (*Travels* 8). Eco cites museums such as Ripley's Museum where "everything looks real and therefore is real; in any case, the fact that it seems real is real, and the thing is real even if, like Alice in Wonderland, it never existed" (16). According to Eco, Disneyland is the perfect example of this hyperreality: "Disneyland makes it clear that within its magic enclosure it is fantasy that is absolutely reproduced" (Eco 43), and the theme park "not only produces illusion, but—in confessing it—stimulates the desire for it.... Disneyland tells us that technology can give us more reality than nature can" (44).

Stephen King's fiction, in its own way, creates a hyperreality of its own, which might account for the popularity of his work. The "plot" of *It* could probably be told in just 300 pages, yet King expands the work to more than one thousand. King himself has joked that he suffers from "a permanent case of *literary elephantiasis*" (Rogak 154). Yet, if we consider that readers want—in fact, demand—this hyperreality, his detailed prose makes perfect sense.

In *It*, perhaps even more than in his previous novels, the reader is given layers upon layers of detail, so much so that we know virtually everything about the town of Derry and its inhabitants. Derry becomes a horror version Disneyland; the reader knows more about this town than he could know about his own hometown, even. We are given glimpses into the thoughts of everyone from the main characters themselves to the most minor characters. We know the intimate history of Stan's wife, who "simply *adored* Richard Dawson" and *Family Feud* (39), the mental illness of Patrick Hoskstetter, who thought he was the only person in the world who was real (788), and even the funeral plans for Bill's cab driver (461). Digressions include the fictional Bradley Gang massacre (621), Ben getting a new library card from Carole Danner, a library assistant (521), and the history of the Tracker Brothers, who ran a truck depot and liked baseball (526). Although none of these details are essential to the story, they work to create a rich tapestry of Derry, making the town more "real" than a real town, with a complex history and peopled with a telephone book's worth of characters. "The basic groundwork of [King's] stories is their intense realism, rooted in genuine small towns ... and quite average individuals, with all the familiar ingredients of their lives," says Ben Indick in his essay on why Stephen King is scary (9).

This hyperrealism is taken to the extreme in the omniscient point of view report of the storm that destroys downtown Derry (1024–1028). This two-hour time block is described in a single paragraph, with an almost minute by minute account of everything that happened. The narrator gets into the minds of the minor characters in the scene and shares extremely detailed but nonessential facts, such as Kilgaton's son taking a photograph that he would sell for $60, "which he used to buy tires for his motorcycle" (1027). While critics would say that King is being too wordy, I would argue that he is creating a "simulation" that works as a hyperreality in the story, making Derry so real that the reader has to believe in it. As Magistale has observed:

> Like Faulkner's examination of Yoknapatawpha Country, King's elaborate and dark history of Derry Maine chronicles many of the most brutal and inhumane events which have occurred during the past three centuries. And also like Faulkner, King uses specific and interrelated histories of his seven protagonists to detail the horrors that transpire daily in this closed society. Consequently, the creature that inhabits the Derry sewer system seems as much related to the environment of the town itself as Percy Grimm, Sutpen, or Flem Snopes emerge as products of Faulkner's South [*Landscape* 111].

Readers become completely immersed in King's fictional world and find that they have difficulty putting the book down because it is so compelling. Once the place and the people become real, the reader has entered a fictional version of Disneyland where the horror comes from "the self-conscious real and imagined fears of the young (which do not vanish even in adulthood) of inadequacy, physical changes, need for love and attention" (Indick 10). Once in such a hyperreality, "as in certain horror films, detachment is impossible; you are not witnessing another's horror, you are inside the horror through complete synesthesia" (Eco, *Travels* 46). The horror exists on multiple levels, of course.

As Magistrale and other critics have noted, *It* is a novel about the evils of child abuse, bullying, and domestic violence and the supernatural/

alien creature that lives beneath Derry can be thought of as an extended metaphor of that evil. As in other King novels, the theme goes beyond the supernatural horror of a scary clown or mythical beings that populate a multiverse of nightmares. The story is used to bring to light real world problems as well. "*It* is an account of child abuse, about how isolated and vulnerable children are ... a veritable treatise on intolerance and prejudice, dealing with hatred of blacks and gays, virtually anyone who is different" (Wiater et al., *Stephen King Universe* 106). Mike Hanlon is persecuted because he is black, Bill because he stutters, Stan because he is Jewish, Ben because he is overweight, and Richie because he is too smart for his own good. Beverly Marsh goes on to marry an abusive husband, which brings the domestic violence theme into the novel. The boys, unfortunately, must not only battle the supernatural monsters in the story but the real ones as well: the neighborhood bullies, their parents, and their own inner demons and fears. The supernatural *It* serves as a metaphorical representation of these real problems that, like domestic violence, for example, cannot always be "named" by their victims.

Jean Baudrillard has observed that history has been recreated by the media. "Today, the history that is 'given back' to us (precisely because it was taken from us) has no more a relation to a 'historical real' than neofiguration in painting does to the classical figuration of the real" (*Simulacra* 45). This idea appears in *It* when the news media arrive after the crisis to cover the story:

> The network news reporters would bring some version of the truth home to most people; they would make it real although there were those who might have suggested that reality is a highly untrustworthy concept, something perhaps no more solid than a piece of canvas stretched over an interlacing of cables like the strands of a spiderweb [1060].

Indeed, the residents of Derry have no idea what has happened to their town. They need the news media to translate it for them, to create a false reality that they can believe. "Seeing themselves and their neighbors on TV—that would make it real It would give them a place from which to grasp this terrible, ungraspable thing. It had been a FREAK STORM" (1060). Thus, "the media carry meaning and counter-meaning, they manipulate in all directions at once, nothing can control this process, they are the vehicle for the simulation internal to the system, and the simulation that destroys the system" (Baudrillard, *Simulacra* 84).

Once the events are finished, even the protagonists of the novel begin to forget. Mike's journals begin to fade with his memories, and the phone numbers in his address book begin to erase themselves. Bill thinks, "I will write about all of this one day" but knows it is just a "dawn thought" and "after-dreaming thought." Still, one can consider the novel itself a work of metafiction, created by a narrator who knew the truth, perhaps a narrator/author who created the entire multiverse and knows the truths about all of the Stephen King universes and how they are connected. After all, the novel does begin in the first-person point of view, with the very first line: "The terror, which would not end for another twenty-eight years— if it ever did end—began, so far as I know or can tell, with a boat made from a sheet of paper floating down a gutter swollen with rain" (3). Since this is chapter 1 of the novel, and not one of the "Interludes" written by Mike Hanlon, the "I" of the story can only be the voice of Stephen King, the "Other" who has authored the multiverse.

It is a very complex and complicated book with seven major characters, a plot that spans two distinct time periods, and a horror subplot that works on multiple levels. With perhaps the exception of *The Stand*, it was Stephen King's most ambitious project at the time, combining monsters and fairy tale into his multiverse that stretches into the Gunslinger universe as well as future novels (*Insomnia* and *11/22/63* are also built around the small town of Derry). It is the book that, in our universe, at least, brings together all of the elements of the multiverse and is the place where characters from our universe can travel to this other place where everything seems to come together. It is a creation myth in its own right, a modern one that, using a somewhat multicultural group of kids, transcends race and religion in its description. This creation myth includes not only "gods" from the multiverse, but all of the legends and horror stories from the contemporary world as well, including The Creature form the Black Lagoon and other movie monsters, werewolves, and, yes, even clowns.

It is the book that has made an entire generation (or two) afraid of clowns, while at the same time making this horror of them virtually "unnamable" by turning the pronoun "it" into a proper name that even creates a grammatical curmudgeon when it becomes possessive—is "It's" possessive or is it "It is" as a form of being or both at the same time? Or is It the title of a novel? Whatever the answer(s), Stephen King seems to be having fun at the linguist's expense. Yet at a linguistic level, the novel does make a statement about the difficulty of naming the impossible, a trick right out of H.P. Lovecraft's playbook. Until the monster can be named, it cannot be destroyed; even as language gives life (in both creation stories and in the Stephen King world), so does it have the potential to kill, destroy, and change, a theme we have examined in "The Word Processor of the Gods" and which King explores more deeply in "Obits," a short story collected in *The Bazaar of Bad Dreams*. And once again King explores the power of creativity and how it is best channeled in the mind of a child—or in the mind of an adult who is still open to the imagination of a child. *It* seems to be a turning point in King's career, the book where he has finally had his say about horror in an almost metafictional retelling of all horror stories. This, I believe, allows him to move on to tell stories that are more of a combination of mainstream fiction and horror, stories like *Bag of Bones*, *Lisey's Story*, and *Joyland*, where the element of horror may still be present but takes a backstage to the more realistic problems that people face in the world.

CHAPTER 13

Needful Things: The Linguistics of Brand Names

Stephen King has often been criticized for his use of brand names and, ironically enough, has become a brand name himself. Yet King isn't the first to use brands in his stories. In the well-known story *A&P*, included in nearly every college intro to literature textbook, Updike not only uses the brand name of the grocery store where his protagonist works but also mentions "Hi-Ho" crackers, "Diet Delight" peaches, "Kingfish Fancy Herring Snacks" and "Schlitz" beer. Interestingly enough, King uses the same "Ho-Ho" crackers in *Needful Things* as well (207). *Needful Things*, billed as "The Last Castle Rock Story," offers an excellent opportunity to discuss King's use of brand names (even Castle Rock has become a brand name, the name of a film and television production company) and the theme of consumerism and "need."

Published in 1991, *Needful Things* is "both a drama and a satire, a critique of American consumerism and greed, and of small-town life in general" (Wiater 166). The story begins with an introduction, where a gossipy narrator, an old-time resident of the town, addresses the reader directly, advising that *"real* trouble is on the way" and asking the reader to "stick around town for awhile" to see what happens, "because it might just be as well if there was a witness" (*Needful* 9). This is classic Stephen King metafictional determinism using what Barthes terms the "hermeneutic code" as it "articulates a question" (*S/Z* 17)—in this case, what real trouble is going to happen?—in order to build up suspense. Addressing the reader directly creates an intimate relationship with the audience, inviting him or her to, in effect, become part of the story and become a direct witness of the events that are about to occur. Steven King's "constant reader" knows that something bad is about to go down, and the author has provided a front-row seat to witness the chaos firsthand.

The plot of *Needful Things* is similar to that of *'Salem's Lot* in many ways. In both books a small Maine town is invaded by an outside force of evil. The evil that comes to Castle Rock isn't vampires, however, but instead feeds upon the human lust for money and possessions. Leland Gaunt, the proprietor of the new store in town, Needful Things, is "the catalyst that brings out the devil, so the speak, in the townsfolk" (Beahm, *A to Z* 146). Gaunt is an ancient evil creature who steals souls in return for the "needful thing" that they just must have, be it an autographed vintage Sandy Koufax baseball card or an antique toy that can predict the winners in today's horse race. Instead of sucking people's blood, Gaunt sucks out their humanity and replaces it with an obsession with things and objects, giving them, in essence, their hearts' desires, but at a very great price. In return for their secret desires and needs, the town residents are manipulated into destroying one another and ultimately the town itself in a spectacular explosion. Only Alan Pangborn, the town's sheriff, is able to see through Gaunt's façade and ultimately defeat him. Pangborn is, of course, the same sheriff who handled the Thad Beaumont case in *The Dark Half*.

Since *Needful Things* contains an obvious subtext of consumerism, possessions, and money, examining this novel through the perspective of the Marxist critics proves to be a productive strategy. The early work of Jean Baudrillard, in particular, offers some insight into this book. In both *The System of Objects* and *The Consumer Society*, Baudrillard levels harsh criticism of capitalist society and the compulsion of people to buy, consume, and collect. In Baudrillard's world, need has come to mean more than the basic needs for food, clothing, and shelter. On a linguistic level, consumption is, in fact, a form of communication, a language of its own. "Commodities are no longer defined by their use, but rather what they signify," says George Ritzer in the Introduction to *The Consumer Society* (7). To illustrate this theory, the owner of an expensive sports car is communicating to the world his wealth, status, and power while the owner of a hybrid or other eco-friendly vehicle is communicating a belief in saving the planet, so to speak. Our possessions, our "objects" become a linguistic code that tells the world exactly who we are. "This code offers a *universal* system of decipherable signs for the first time in history" (Baudrillard, *System* 212).

In a world where millions of men and women pass another every day without being acquainted, the code of "status" fulfils an essential social function by addressing people's vital need for knowledge of others. The fact is, however, that this universalization and this effectiveness are achieved only at the cost of a radical simplification, an impoverishment and a well-nigh definitive regression of the "language" of value: "Individuals define themselves through their objects" [214].

Stephen King's novel offers a fictionalized view of this theory of consumerism as language. In the novel, Gaunt says, "The world is full of needy people who don't understand that everything, *everything*, is for sale ... if you're willing to pay the price" (77). The characters in Castle Rock are willing to pay Gaunt's price. The consumers in the novel fall into three categories. Some, like Polly Chambers, really do "need" what Gaunt has. He offers her a cure for her intolerable arthritis pain. Others, like the first selectman, "Buster" Keaton, need what Gaunt has in order to satiate their hunger, in this case, his addiction to gambling. Finally, others like Brian Rusk and Nettie Cobb are simply mesmerized by objects that appear magical to them, the Sandy Koufx baseball card, and a carnival grass lampshade, respectively. I will examine each of these consumers individually.

The first type, Polly Chambers, actually does "need" something that would be considered basic on Maslow's hierarchy of needs—relief from excruciating pain. Her arthritis gets worse when Gaunt comes to town, and like all sufferers of chronic pain, she will do just about anything to stop her suffering and lead a normal life. "*Oh I would give anything to be free of this,* she thought. *I would give anything, anything, anything at all*" (68). Polly is, essentially, a good person who has been dealt a bad hand and must play it as best as she can. When Gaunt offers her relief, she gratefully takes it, and who could fault her for giving in to this need?

The second type of consumer is driven by greed and obsession. Danforth "Buster" Keaton is a perfect example of this. He isn't a very nice person to begin with. He's overly ambitious and willing to do anything to get to the top, which leads to him going to the Lewiston race track in the first place in an attempt to gain the favor of the first selectman, whose job he aspires to. Once there, he falls under the spell of money and power, but even more so the excitement of the game. "It wasn't the money, not really; the money was just the symbol you took away with you, something that said you had been there, that you had been, however briefly, part of the big show" (197). The harness race track has its own "private language," which Keaton quickly learns, and his addiction builds to the point where he is embezzling the town's money to fuel it. By the time he comes to Gaunt, he is in very bad shape, about to be audited by the State Attorney

General and possibly sent to jail when the story is uncovered. "You're a man who needs a Winning Ticket quite badly, aren't you, Danforth?" Gaunt asks him. Keaton is an unlikeable, corrupt man who only gets worse with time, a perfect soldier in Gaunt's plans.

Finally, there are those in the middle, more or less average people who are simply mesmerized by objects that they think that must possess, objects that they "need." As Baudrillard says, "We may, admittedly, say that it is, then, our fantasies which come to be signified in the image and consumed in it" (*Consumer* 33). These characters, Brian Rusk and Nettie Cobb and others, are, according to Baudrillard, the victims of our consumer society. "The consumer society needs its objects in order to be" (*Consumer* 47), and in this society "there are no limits to consumption" (223). These characters are not evil, and not even greedy in the way that Keaton is. They merely become infatuated by objects that human nature tells them that they need. "The everyday passion for private property is often stronger than all the others.... Objects ... become mental precincts over which I hold sway, they become things of which I am the meaning, they become my property and my passion" (*System* 91).

Brian Rusk is the first victim of this passion when he finds a 1956 Sandy Koufax baseball card in Needful Things. This type of object is a "pure object" according to Baudrillard because, unlike a refrigerator or an automobile, it has no practical function. "The pure object, devoid of any function or completely abstracted from its use, takes on a strictly subjective status: it becomes part of a collection" (92). The single object itself, Baudrillard explains, is no longer enough but becomes part of the quest to complete the collection. Gaunt, of course, understands this concept, and uses it to his advantage when accumulating "stock" in his shop: "how many of the items they needed to fill their respective collections were here" (*Needful Things* 51). As the last and rarest item in Brian's collection, "a card like this was worth practically anything" (36) to the boy. Baudrillard notes that "for children, collecting is a rudimentary way of mastering the outside world, or arranging, classifying, and manipulating" (*System* 93). So to Brian, obtaining this card holds the extra significance of allowing him to complete and master at least one small part of his world, an important accomplishment for an 11-year-old boy.

Nettie Cobb is another example of an everyday person who falls under the spell of an object that she needs to possess. Nettie also has a "little collection of carnival glass" and when she sees the pieces of glass in Needful Things she remarks that they are "like things must look in heaven" (51). Nettie Cobb has a backstory of "being married to a brute who abused her in every way a man can abuse a woman" (65). She finally killed her husband by stabbing him with a meat-fork while he slept and was committed to a mental institution for five years before being released and returning to Castle Rock. Now Nettie finds solace and meaning in her little dog, Raider, and in the carnival glass lampshade she purchases from Needful Things. "Nettie ... looked at the lampshade with the soft eyes of a woman who is in love" (88). Her husband had broken a similar one years before, the tipping point that caused her to kill him. Now the lampshade was replaced; "It was a *beautiful* thing, the sort of thing she had always wanted, the only thing she needed to complete her modest collection" (89). For a mentally unstable woman who feels that the world is out of her control, obtaining this item is an empowering act, and Gaunt knows it.

Most people assume that buying and obtaining objects brings pleasure—in fact Publix, a very successful Florida supermarket, was built on the slogan "Where Shopping Is a Pleasure" (Hacker). According to Baudrillard, however, consumerism has a more complex explanation:

> Consumer behavior, which is apparently focused on, and oriented towards, objects and enjoyment [*jouissanse*]. In fact conduces to quite other goals: that of the metaphorical or displaced expression of desire, that of production, through differential signs, of a social code of values [*Consumer* 78].

Thus, Baudrillard claims, the purpose of consumption is not to create individual happiness but to produce collective happiness. Society, particularly a capitalist one, needs consumption.

Gaunt claims to sell happiness—"to place objects with people who love them and need them ... what I *really* sell is happiness" (88). Yet Baudrillard posits, and the residents of Castle Rock discover, that acquiring things does not bring happiness but only a desire for more, or a paranoia for losing what they have obtained.

> If we pin the need down to a particular spot, if, that is, we *satisfy* it by taking it literally, by taking it ... as the need for a *particular* object, then we make the same mistake as we would in applying a traditional remedy to an organ where the symptom is located. As soon as it is cured at this one point, it will resurface at another [77].

In other words, as soon as we have the object of our desire, we immediately crave a new possession. Brian cannot show his baseball card to anyone for fear that it will be taken away. Nettie cannot enjoy her lampshade but must hide it and lock it up so that Wilma Jerzyck won't destroy it. "It deserves to be in a better place and I know it.... But at least it's *safe*, and that's the important thing" (*Needful Things* 150). These "sequestered objects" are the result of a "jealous complex" according to Baudrillard. This "jealous complex" is "a powerful anal-sadistic impulse [that] produces the urge to sequester beauty so as to be the only one to enjoy it" (*System* 105). While the owners believe the objects will bring them happiness, they are mistaken. "'Affluence' is, in effect, the mere accumulation of the *signs* of happiness" (Baudrillard, *Consumer* 31); unfortunately, the characters in *Needful Things* are unable to flaunt their possessions so, being unable to display these signs, they cannot share in the linguistics of consumerism nor benefit from its perceived happiness.

One of the things that has annoyed critics the most, perhaps, is Stephen King's use of brand names, and it seems that this criticism hasn't ended. In a review of *Mr. Mercedes* one reviewer complained that "whatever mystery and velocity this game of cat-and-mouse generates is hampered by King's exhaustive establishment of his fictional world. This basically means endless brand names, overlong explanations of everything from reality television to modern car-locks" (Kidd). King has been addressing this issue for years, however, and uses brand names as a conscious fictional device. As he said in an interview published in 2006:

> I always knew people would have a problem with that [using brand names]. But I also knew that I was never going to stop doing it, and nobody was ever going to convince me that I was wrong to do it. Because every time I did it, what I felt inside was this little bang! like I nailed it dead square—like Michael Jordan on a fade-away jump shot. Sometimes the brand name is the perfect word, and it will crystallize a scene for me. When Jack Torrance is pumping down that Excedrin in The Shining, you know just what that is. I always want to ask these critics—some are novelists, some of them college literature professors—What the fuck do you do? Open your medicine cabinet and see empty gray bottles? Do you see generic shampoo, generic aspirin? When you go to the store and you get a six-pack, does it just say beer? When you go down and you open your garage door, what's parked in there? A car? Just a car? [qtd. in Lehmann-Haupt and Rich].

Other critics agree that the device is effective. "The brand name dropping, thought to be a sign of King's anti-intellectualism, is part of a heuristic gloss that runs throughout his fiction.... It contrasts with academic post-modernists who delight in burying their themes in arcane codes and allusions that are, in the end, self-referential" (Badley 120).

From a linguistic point of view, a name is a unique type of word. According to Kripke, "*names* are rigid designators" (48), that is to say they embody essential properties that are true of them in any case where they would have existed. Kripke goes on to assert that proper names are also rigid designators, for, to use his example, Einstein would still be Einstein even in a world where he never discovered the theory of relativity. While Kripke doesn't mention brand names, specifically, as proper names they would also fall under the category of rigid designators. Unlike proper names associated with people and places, however, brand names differ because their properties do not develop as a result of their "history" but are artificially manufactured and written by the corporation that produces them. Therefore, brand names such as "Diet Coke" (*Needful Things* 16), "Devil Dogs" (17) and "Corning Ware" (45) evoke the same meaning and connotations in Stephen King's Castle Rock as they do in contemporary America.

According to Baudrillard, brand names are part of the mythology of America and of the consumer society, where "the truth of objects and products is their *brand name*" (*Consumer Society* 116). It is impossible, then, to truly understand our modern society without using the brand names that define it. So, in effect, King is right—"sometimes the brand name is the perfect word."

One of the uses of brand names in King's fiction is to define character. For example, Cora Rusk is immediately defined as a woman who watches soap operas (*Santa Barbara*), eats Little Debbie Cream Pies while ironically washing them down with Diet Coke. (16) The portrait of this urban housewife, a minor character at best, is painted swiftly by defining what she consumes. "The concept of 'brand,' which is advertising's prime concept, sums up the prospectus for a 'language' of consumption rather well" (Baudrillard, *System* 209). Shelia Brigham reading *People* magazine (60), Lester Pratt's blue Mustang (19), and Norris Ridgewick's empty cans of "Jolt" cola (94)—"All the sugar, twice the Caffeine," according to inthe80s.com (not to mention my own personal experience in graduate school)—effectively tell the reader detailed information about their characters. The brands serve as significations that convey style, education, status, and social class. "All men are equal before objects as use-value, but they are by no means equal before objects as signs and differences, which are profoundly hierarchical" (Baudrillard, *Consumer* 90). Thus, the "Rolex" watch signifies the wealth of its owner, while the "Timex" signifies practicality. A rich person might own either, but the reverse is not likely to be true.

While it has been argued that writers date themselves when using brand names, this device hasn't seemed to hurt Stephen King in that respect. If anything, reading King's older work is like a journey back into nostalgia or history, depending upon the reader's age, a world of "IBM electric typewriters" (60), Polaroid cameras (44), and Princess telephones (17). For the Baby Boomer generation, this is a walk down memory lane, almost as good as the time travel motif he uses in *11/22/63*.

King manipulates this brand name language and, perhaps, even spoofs himself by inventing brand names of his own, such as the Bazun fishing rod that Norris Ridgewick covets, "not a well-known brand, but well-regarded among serious fishermen" (140). Of course, the rod is later exposed as junk and Norris destroys it, recognizing it as a fake.

King might also be poking fun at himself when Alan Pangborn grabs a bottle of generic aspirin to relieve his headache and "found himself wondering why generic aspirin always produced more dust than brand-name aspirin" (61). As Russell has noted, "Many characters interact in *Needful Things*, but only a few are fully developed. Most of the people in Castle Rock are defined by their needful things and what they are willing to do to get them" (130). The heavy use of familiar brand names helps the reader to connect to the characters and their needs in King's fiction. In effect, these trademarks are building and defining the characters in the novel.

In *Needful Things*, King's fictional world expands beyond just the single novel and includes previous work, *The Dead Zone*, *Cujo*, and *The Dark Half*, as well as a number of shorter works such as "The Body." Alan Pangborn is, of course, the Sheriff from *The Dark Half* who was present when Thad Beaumont destroyed his pseudonym George Stark. While King's characters often make cameo appearances or are mentioned in other works, Pangborn's "backstory" in *The Dark Half* is significant in *Needful Things* since it mentally prepares him for the events that unfold in Castle Rock by allowing him to accept the possibility of the supernatural and strengthen his ability to use "white magic" to defeat it. Pangborn is mentioned again in *Bag of Bones*; apparently he and Polly were married and moved to New Hampshire. Ace Merrill, one of the bullies from "The Body," also becomes Gaunt's chief henchman in *Needful Things*. Not surprisingly, he dies violently in the novel.

Needful Things, while certainly not King's greatest fictional achievement, marked an emotional turning point for him since it was "the first book he wrote while completely sober" (Rogak 166). Originally conceived as a satire on the 1980s King says:

> When I finished the book, I thought, I've finally written something that's really funny. I thought that I'd written a satire of Reaganomics in America in the eighties. You know, people will buy anything and sell anything, even their souls. I always saw Leland Gaunt, the shop owner who buys souls, as the archetypal Ronald Reagan: charismatic, a little bit elderly, selling nothing but junk but it looks bright and shiny [qtd. in Lehmann-Haupt and Rich].

The book was not seen as satire but instead was considered another typical King horror novel, one where he used many of the same ideas as he'd used in past novels (the "outsider," as in *'Salem's Lot*, the purging with fire as in

The Shining, and the destruction of a small Maine town, as in *It*). Yet despite some of the horror clichés, *Needful Things* isn't a terrible book— it would fit more into the class of what King calls "entertainment" than serious fiction—and it did clear the way for him to write more character-driven stories, including *Gerald's Game, Delores Clairborne*, and, later, *Lisey's Story*, which many critics (and King himself) consider to be his best novel.

In summary, despite its flaws, *Needful Things* lends itself perfectly to a Marxist analysis, which tells us some things about consumerism, greed, and the American obsession with objects. In the time when it was written, King saw Reaganomics as a symptom of a defective society where people cared only about their own wants and needs and not about the greater good. The fact that the book was *not* seen as a satire only shows how accurately the book did define its era. In 1991, the year this book was published, a credit union crisis in the state of Rhode Island wiped out people's life savings and retirement funds because of greed—and, regrettably, foreshadowed the bank collapses that followed in 2008. It was also the year that Starbuck's, the company that is now famous for selling coffee to consumers who are willing to pay more for the brand name product, was founded. *Needful Things* is also a product of this time, but its attempt to make fun of this consumerism failed, and now the culture gap between the rich and the poor is wider than ever. Stephen King, who grew up poor and earned his money through honest hard work and talent, has never been one to flaunt his money or prestige. In fact, he is well-known and well-respected for his philanthropy. It is no surprise, then, that he puts this consumer society under the magnifying glass and shows its decay. And it is even less surprising that this town full of needful people destroys itself from the inside out.

CHAPTER 14

The Green Mile:
Remembrance of Things Past

The Green Mile was originally published as a six-part monthly serial novel, with the first installment, *The Two Dead Girls*, appearing in March 1996, and the concluding section, *Coffey on the Mile*, published in August of that year. The book was subsequently released in a single volume in 1997 and adapted as a very successful film in 1999. The screenplay, written by Frank Darabont (who also wrote the screenplay for King's *The Shawshank Redemption*), was published by Scribner in 1999.

The serialization concept was King's attempt to try to replicate the old serial novels that had made Charles Dickens famous, and judging by both sales and critical reviews of the book, the experiment was a success, though not one that King has wished to repeat since. The book series was aggressively marketed, and even included "The Green Mile Contest," where readers answered a thought question about the book in a 50 word essay. Six winners were chosen for each installment to win an autographed manuscript of *The Green Mile*, 36 in all. On a personal note, my essay was chosen as one of the lucky winners for answering the question posed in book two and I still have my prize, complete with King's signature and some hand-written edits, and, no, it is not for sale.

As King has described in the afterword to *Coffey on the Mile*, serialized novels have special advantages and challenges. He enjoyed the formula because "the end of each episode made the reader an almost equal partner with the writer" (*Two* ix), which is right out of Roland Barthes' "death of the author" concept, and King liked the fact that the reader

136

couldn't "flip ahead and see how matters turn out" (x). But the format created problems, as well. "The format demanded that I wrote it in a hurry," he explains in the afterword (*Coffey* 135), and, since the books were released a month apart and could be easily read in an evening, he had to solve the problem of refreshing the reader's memory of what came before each time the new installment was published. Sharon Russell does a very effective job of describing the techniques he used to accomplish this (*Revisiting*), but I will summarize them here. King basically employed a framework where the narrator, Paul Edgecombe, is writing his memoirs, so to speak, many years after the events of the story took place. This framework allows him to begin each of the monthly books with a section set in his narrative present and tell about his writing process, and remind readers of where he left off in the last section, and even offer some analysis as he looks back on the events. He also ends each book with a question or cliffhanger (Roland Barthes hermeneutic code of enigmas) that won't be resolved until the next month's release. This, of course, builds suspense and has the reader anxiously waiting for the new installment. Because of this device, all six of the books were bestsellers at once (Dyson 43).

The novel is set in a prison in Louisiana in 1932. The protagonist, Paul Edgecombe, is in charge of E Block, the death row of its time, with its "Green Mile" corridor leading to "Old Sparky," the electric chair. The story begins when John Coffey, a gigantic black inmate who was found guilty of raping and killing two young white girls, is brought into the cell block as a "dead man walking." Coffee seems to have a feeble mind, but we soon learn that he possesses a miraculous power to heal, and we later learn that he didn't kill the girls; when he was found holding their dead bodies, he had been trying to heal them. Innocent or not, however, a black man at this time in the South would not have received a fair trial and would not get any appeals. We see that justice, such as it was, worked swiftly, if not always effectively.

The Green Mile is written in a first-person point of view that uses a reliable narrator to tell about unbelievable events that would be classified as miracles. Paul Edgecombe's veracity is established immediately as he describes E Block, the Green Mile, and the electric chair in the meticulous detail of someone who has been there. The fact that he presided over 78 executions gives him instant credibility as a reliable witness as he describes the reactions of the death row inmates in their final hour and effortlessly rattles off names and dates with the accuracy of a historian. Although he sometimes questions his timeline in telling the story, it is obvious to the reader that his memory is sharp, and he is able to recreate what happened in a believable way.

There is also never a question about Paul's honesty. He does not exaggerate details, nor does he slant the story to make himself look good. He doesn't try to hide events he'd be ashamed of, like being bullied by Brad Dolan, or not seeing what Percy was up to before it was too late. He doesn't sugarcoat Delacroix's execution but describes it in painfully graphic detail. He is obviously concerned with the truth and wants to convey this truth to the best of his abilities. "If I can tell the truth about the rest, I guess I can tell the truth about this" (61), he says, in describing his feelings about Mr. Jingles, the mouse. Since Paul is relating the story of a miracle, "an enigma wrapped in a mystery" (186), it is vitally important that he be believed and that he preserve the story of Coffey faithfully: "I want you to see him there, looking up at the ceiling of his cell, wiping his silent tears" (118). At the end of the book, when he gives his memoirs to Elaine Connelly, we realize that he is trying to convince her, a friend, of the truth of the story, and since she is the only friend he has left, he very much wants to be believed. Although she questions his age and the timeline, she does believe his story, and he offers further proof by taking her to the shed to see Mr. Jingles for herself.

The Green Mile was undoubtedly influenced by the Robert Burns poem "To a Mouse," which, in turn, inspired Steinbeck's novel *Of Mice and Men.* In the Burns poem, the narrator's plow destroys the home of a field mouse, which leads Burns to observe:

> The best laid schemes o' Mice an' Men
>   Gang aft agley,
> An' lea'e us nought but grief an' pain,
>   For promis'd joy!

In the Steinbeck novel, Lennie Small, a mentally challenged man, accidentally breaks a woman's neck and, in the end, is mercifully shot by his best friend in order to save him from being lynched by an angry mob. *The Green Mile* takes a number of parallels from these sources.

One of the most important "characters" in the novel is Mr. Jingles, a "genius" mouse that becomes the pet of Edward Delacroix, one of the inmates sentenced to walk the Green Mile and be executed. The mouse has his home uprooted several times, is mortally wounded by the sadistic guard Percy, brought back to life by Coffey, and, when Delacroix is finally killed, is uprooted again and leaves the prison forever. The mouse is symbolic of the best laid plans of everyone going astray: the warden's wife develops cancer; the execution of Delacroix goes all wrong; Coffey's attempt to save two little girls fails and puts him on death row; Wharton, a psychopathic inmate, is brought into the cell block and nearly kills one of the guards; and, worst of all, Coffey, though innocent, is executed and no one can do anything to stop it. The novel is almost a statement that "no good deed goes unpunished" except for the fact that the ultimate deed, saving Melinda's life, succeeds.

Mr. Jingles represents naturalism and the fact that things will go wrong, bad things will happen to good people, and there will not be a divine intervention to fix them. Coffey, with his healing powers, is the only one who can do anything, and even his powers are limited; in the end, he is put to death as well. The mouse also plays a role in the theme of life and death in the novel—it is near death when Coffey reanimates it, and it goes on to live for decades after Coffey touches it.

Coffey, who is also mentally challenged (or at least it seems so at first), is reminiscent of Lenny from the Steinbeck novel. They are both drifters, are unable to function in society, and though both are good people, they are branded as killers and destroyed in the name of justice. When discussing the danger of magic, the narrator reminds us of this connection "as a man who knew John Coffey and saw what he could do—to mice and the men—I feel qualified to say that" (336). Both Coffey and Lenny are "innocents." Lenny, however, doesn't know his own strength and kills a mouse while trying to pet it, then later accidentally kills a puppy, and finally kills a woman, also accidentally. In *The Green Mile*, Coffey is the counter to Lenny—he brings a mouse back to life, cures a urinary tract infection, then restores life to a terminally ill woman. Both Steinbeck and Stephen King portray a cruel world, one that is even crueler for the poor, the mentally challenged, and for blacks. And while Coffey has the power of life, this power really turns into a curse for him.

Coffey seems to be a religious figure, Christ-like in both his actions and his initials, but the question of where his powers come from is never answered. Coffey himself has no idea. "I don't understand," he says, several times. If his ability is divinely inspired, he is unaware of it and makes no attempt to preach or even embrace religion. As Magistrale has pointed out, Coffey "refuses the counsel of clergy on the eve of his execution, but is not averse to others saying 'a little prayer' for him" (*Hollywood* 137). We have seen that some of King's protagonists are plagued by what Poe calls "the spirit of the perverse," and this is true in *The Green Mile* as well. To Paul this spirit is "a kind of demon of discord" (399) but it is offset by Coffey, who embodies the "other spirit ... that opposes it" (401). If his healing ability has been given to him by God, it is a private God of spirituality, and not the product of any specific church or faith. Regardless of whether his powers are a "gift of God" or not, they are a curse to him. Coffey can feel the emotions and pain of those around him, and, no doubt, his mental deficiency is a result of him trying to shut down these stimuli. "It feels like pieces of glass in my head" (491), he tells Paul. Perhaps Coffey's last words, just before he is executed, summarize his predicament: "I'm sorry for what I am" (507).

Paul admits that he uses "electrical metaphors" to describe Coffey's powers, a "strange galvanizing current" (39), which raises the possibility that the big man's healing is based on some sort of science rather than the supernatural. King tackles this theme more fully in *Revival*, as we will see in chapter 21, where he proposes a "*secret* electricity ... that binds the very universe into one harmonic whole" (*Revival* 142), a force that also cures and heals, but at a great price. *Revival* explores the concept of miracles as the result of science, but for Paul, miracles belong in the province of God and religion, even if he can't understand His mechanics.

The theme of life and death is central to this novel, and the "Green Mile" is symbolic of the fact that all life has its DOE, date of execution. The inmates on the Green Mile have been sentenced to death and are obviously living on borrowed time. Georgia Pines, the nursing home where Paul is living, is also a death row: "in its way it's as much of a killing bottle as E Block at Cold Mountain ever was" (79). When he visits the room of the terminally ill Melinda, Paul sees it as "just another version of the Green Mile" (220). Death is the only certainty in this novel.

King also makes the point that death isn't always fair. Before John Coffey enters his life, Paul is a rather pragmatic man. He isn't really bothered by his job as an executioner because he believes that the inmates on death row are criminals and he is merely carrying out justice. He tries to do this in the most humane way possible. He believes in talking to the prisoners and making them as comfortable and calm as possible, both for their own good and for his safety and the safety of his men. "I'm not trying to say anything about right and wrong here, but only to tell how it was" (287). Ironically, a left turn on the cell block means life, and a right turn leads to the execution chamber, the "right" course of action in 1932 (and perhaps King is playing with left and right wing politics here as well?). After Coffey's death, though, Paul undergoes a change in his thinking, and he leaves his job because he can no longer carry out executions. "We'd been part of a monstrous act" (329). He has come to understand that justice is complicated and much of it depends upon a person's race, income, and connections. "John Coffey was black, like most of the men who came to stay for awhile on E Block before dying on Old Sparky's lap" (10). Henry tells him that "the Chief burned and the President walked" (120). "He got commuted because he was white" (121). Ironically, Melinda, a white woman, metaphorically has her sentence commuted by Coffey, a black man. But Coffey, a "gift of God," won't be able to get a new trial or even a stay of execution (478).

Racism and homophobia play an important role in this novel as well. It is obvious that Coffey would never get a fair trial in the South or ever find a jury of his peers. Hammersmith, the journalist who claims to be "as enlightened as the next man," goes on to say, "your negro will bite if he gets a chance, just like a mongrel dog" (206). As Deputy McGee says, "in Trapingus County we're awful particular about giving new trials to negroes" (466). Percy exhibits homophobia when he thinks that Delacroix is trying to touch him and that immediately makes that inmate his target.

In his time on the Green Mile, Paul also sees the nature of good and evil, another one of the novel's major themes. Fictional evil is often stereotyped as ugly and deformed (think zombies, Darth Vader, The Joker), or brutal and animal-like (werewolves, bug-eyed-monsters, barbarians). In *The Green Mile*, evil can be portrayed as attractive. Percy, the sadistic guard, is constantly combing his hair, as is Brad Dolan, the sadistic orderly at Georgia Pines. According to Russell, "both men show how the supernatural may not be as frightening as the evil that exists in ordinary people" (70). Wild Bill Wharton is described as scrawny and harmless, but he turns out to be the worst of them all. When the guards bring him in E Block, they think he has been drugged and isn't a threat, and then he almost kills one of them. We also learn that he is the monster who raped and killed the nine-year-old girls.

John Coffey, on the other hand, provokes instant fear because of his size, and the guards are afraid to let Paul in the cell with him. He resembles Goliath, not the hero David. He is deformed by scars, presumably received when he was beaten as a child. When he is discovered holding the bodies of the two dead girls, he is instantly assumed to be a monster. He turns out to be the innocent man after all. Brutus, nicknamed "Brutal," is also a large, scary-looking man, but he is well-read (he quotes from *The Merchant of Venice* on page 368), merciful, and compassionate.

As we have seen at the beginning of the novel, Paul saw a clear line between good and evil, as symbolized by the two paths at the end of the Green Mile. There was innocence and guilt, and he seems to have faith in both God and the justice system. As he learns about Coffey's power and his innocence, he begins to question both, and he wonders why bad things happen to good people. Russel posits that "his limited understanding of good and evil may be the cause of his ultimate lack of faith and his inability at the end of the novel to distinguish between salvation and damnation" (69). I don't think it was a lack of understanding so much as a confusion. If anything, I believe that Paul has a better understanding of good and evil after Coffey's execution. It is no longer black and white, but is now gray, and the great questions of life (good and bad, right and wrong) no longer have definitive answers. He now questions capital punishment, for example, and even questions the ethics of doctors who conduct executions using lethal injections: "maybe back then they had a clearer idea of what was right for a doctor to be doing" (506). As a man who was forced to kill others as part of his job, and who oversaw 78 executions, Paul Edgecombe seems to have a better understanding of good and evil than most people. "In the movies, salvation is cheap. So is innocence. You pay your quarter, and a quarter's worth is what you get. Real life costs more, and most of the answers are different" (100). His uncertainty is, in fact, an understanding, and that, I believe, is what King is trying to tell us. There are no easy answers. There is no instruction manual. We must find our way along the path of uncertainty as best we can.

Of course, the death penalty debate plays a major role in this novel, and the most interesting part of the debate is the fact that the story is told by the executioner. As I have said, Paul seems to change his mind about the death penalty after witnessing the executions of Delacroix and Coffey. Yet even before Delacroix's bad death, he treated even convicted murderers with compassion and humanity. Paul shows that the true cruelty of the death penalty isn't necessarily in the execution itself but in the time leading up to it, particularly in the hours just before. "The inmates make jokes about the chair, the way people always make jokes about things that frighten them" (3), Paul says. Even when he realizes that Coffey has had enough and, in fact, wants to die, he understands that "a man can simultaneously want to go and still be terrified of the trip" (507). Paul instinctively knows that talking to the inmates and allowing them to unburden themselves will make their deaths more humane. He believes the guards act as the inmates' psychiatrists: "without the talk, men facing Old Sparky had a nasty habit of going insane" (49). As we have seen in previous chapters on *Misery*, *The Dark Half*, and other books, writing and storytelling can equate to life and sometimes to sanity. Therefore, Paul gives them the opportunity to tell their stories and make their peace in whatever way they can. They might be hated criminals in the outside world, but in the Green Mile they are under Paul's care, no matter who they are, and he sees his job as making their passing as comfortable as possible. As he is strapping Delacroix into the electric chair, Paul worries about pinching him with the clamps. "The fact that he had killed a half dozen people seemed at that moment the least important thing about him" (287). Although Delacroix was a self-confessed killer, he was still a human being.

To Percy and others in the novel, life isn't about being humane. It's about power. Both Percy in E Block and Dolan in Georgia Pines use their positions of authority to hurt and bully others. Wild Bill Wharton uses power to rape and murder little girls and to try to bully the guards. Interestingly enough, these men who think they have power only use it on the weak. When Percy should use his power to subdue Wharton, he freezes and can't hit him, but he has no reservations about hitting Delacroix with his baton or crushing Mr. Jingles with his boot. The guards understand that they have no power over the prisoners since they are on death row with no hope of survival and therefore have nothing to lose. Instead of physical force, the guards prefer to keep the inmates calm and will only resort to force when it is necessary. Coffey likewise has immense power but prefers to use it for good, "to help," as he calls it. He could easily have overpowered the guards on a number of occasions and chose not to. He uses his power to heal—and to exact justice on both Percy and Wharton at the book's conclusion.

One interesting image in the novel is the color green, which is supposed to be a symbol of spring, growth, rebirth, and harmony, at least in traditional fiction. Ironically, it is the color of the floor that leads to the death chamber, the color of "tired old limes" (6). This is not the green of grass or growth but of old linoleum that had probably seen better days. There was no hope on this mile, only death, for unlike in the movies, the call from the governor for a pardon never came, the phone "never rang during all my years on E Block, never once" (100). It was the green of deterioration and rot, which leads to death.

As we have seen in *Pet Sematary*, sometimes there are things worse than death. When Paul expresses guilt for having to execute Coffey, the big man speaks to him in a moment of lucidity and clarity as he tells Paul that he wants to die. "I'm rightly tired of the pain I hear and feel, boss.... If I could end it, I would. But I can't" (491). It's the longest speech he's ever made, and Paul finally understood. We have no way of knowing how old Coffey is, either. If Paul lives to be 104 just from Coffey's touch and Mr. Jingles lives to be at least 64, might not Coffey be hundreds of years old? In a novel that examines life and death—and aging—as such an important subject, it is possible, and that, coupled with Coffey's constant bombardment of pain and loneliness and people being ugly to each other might be the reason that he can't remember his past, where he got his scars, or much else about himself except how to spell his name.

While both Mr. Jingles and Paul suffer no ill effects from their miraculous gift of extended life—they don't come back as zombies but are actually sharper than ever and immune to common diseases and ailments—even this long life becomes a curse. At 104 years old, Paul has watched almost everyone he has known and loved die—his wife, his children, his friends on E Block, and, in the novel's conclusion, even Mr. Jingles and Elaine. Even his grandchildren are old, and since they convinced him to go into a nursing home "for his own good" where "time is like a weak acid that erases first memory and then the desire to go on living," he has nothing left to look forward to. Writing his memoir about his time on E Block has given him a purpose—in King's world, writing is life—but now that the project is complete, this purpose will also end, and he finds himself wishing for death (534): "we each owe a death ... but sometimes, oh God, the Green Mile is so long" (536).

Although he isn't a writer *per se*, writing becomes important to Paul Edgecombe and, once again, introduces a metalinguistic element into the novel. Paul has a diary in order to keep track of the time in Georgia Pines. More importantly, he has used writing before in order to court his wife. He wrote her a long letter that he thinks she will find foolish, but instead she treasures it and it wins him the love of his life (117). Now, as he passes the time in a nursing home, he uses writing to give him a greater purpose, to help him accept and perhaps understand the events that happened to him so many years ago on the Green Mile. As a reliable narrator, it is important for him to tell the story truthfully, even if the truth takes him into dangerous territory. As Russel has noted, "there is a dangerous magic in writing. Both Paul and King have come to terms with the good as well as the bad that must be described, as in the presentation of the death of Delacroix" (72).

When Paul begins writing his memoir, he seems to be writing it for himself, in order to answer his own questions: "There was only one time I ever had a question about the nature of my job. That, I reckon, is why I'm writing this" (6). He thinks it will be relatively easy, a way to pass the time and, perhaps, unburden his soul. He doesn't understand how difficult the journey will be. "If I'd known the story was going to go on this long, I might never have started. What I didn't realize was how many doors the act of writing unlocks" (118). The act of writing forces him to confront very difficult metaphysical questions that have no real answers and forces him to confront difficult truths about both himself and the world. "Writing is a special and rather terrifying form of remembrance.... I believe that the combination of pencil and memory creates a kind of practical magic, and magic is dangerous" (336). This causes him to question why he was chosen to be a recipient of this magic, which is also a curse to him, and to wonder what he will say to God about his role in killing one of his miracles. As Magistrale has noted, Paul is on his own death row awaiting his date of execution and carrying his own "worldly burden of guilt and sin" (*Hollywood* 144).

In another metalinguistic message, *The Green Mile* also demonstrates the deconstructionists' theory of the inadequacy of words and language to convey meaning and the ease with which language can be misinterpreted, the slippage between the sign, signified, and signifier. This is most evident in Coffey's "confession" where he says, "I tried to take it back, but it was too late" (20). Once the entire story is revealed, these words make perfect sense—Coffey was trying to bring the little girls back to life but couldn't. However, these words, judged by a white audience that already believes he is guilty, mean something totally different. To them Coffey is little more than an animal, a mongrel dog that will bite, as Hammersmith believes. Not even Paul understands Coffey's words until he does some investigation and gets to know the man better.

The Green Mile is not a typical Stephen King novel with ghosts, ghouls, and killer clowns: in fact, unless told, many people not familiar with the horror genre have only watched the film and are not aware that it is a very accurate rendition of a Stephen King novel. While there is a supernatural element to the book, it is a positive force, not the usual evil that we are accustomed to. The real evil in the book comes from two distinct places: the "normal" people who possess no supernatural power, such as Percy, Dolan, and Wharton, and society itself, which is filled with racism and hatred and often forces even good men like Paul Edgecombe to do things that conflict with their own personal ethics.

As we have seen, the novel addresses a number of complex themes and moral dilemmas but in a subtle, non-preachy way. King uses a reliable and likeable narrator to present these themes and uses both the Robert Burns poem and the John Steinbeck novel to place them in a larger context. He examines religion, the nature of evil, and questions of life and death as well as contemporary issues such as racism and the morality of the death penalty. Rather than using the traditional methods of storytelling found in literary fiction, he once again explores the supernatural as a vehicle to take us to places where realism cannot go. It seems that the best way to explore the idea of miracles is to actually show them, using an authentic narrator. In a Stephen King novel, the reader is willing to suspend disbelief and go for the ride. Once these gates are open, the Constant Reader is willing to continue on the journey into real-life issues that face contemporary society, issues like the death penalty and racism that are difficult to face.

From a metalinguistic point of view, *The Green Mile* dramatically shows that good writing, true writing, must confront and delve into difficult issues if it is going to endure. While much of genre fiction is written purely for entertainment—and there is nothing wrong with that—this doesn't mean that it can't handle more difficult subjects and, in fact, the supernatural is often the most appropriate way to face realistic issues. Shakespeare knew this when he created witches, ghosts, and fairies, and Stephen King knows it too. King also knows that confronting these truths is a difficult task, as Paul realizes when he tells the story of Delacroix's botched execution, the writing of which he called a "dirty job" (336). But it had to be done. As always, writing is the force that brings life, searches for truth, and, sometimes, changes people's minds, for better or worse. *The Green Mile*, though, does end with some hope. Coffey has changed Paul for the better, and Paul has carried part of Coffey with him for many years. The memoir that he writes keeps whatever spirit that opposes the demonic one (401) alive and helps the world to remember the character of John Coffey in detail, just as the narrator wanted us to.

CHAPTER 15

Bag of Bones:
King's Horror Matures

Bag of Bones, published in 1998, won a Stoker award for best novel that year and a British Fantasy Award in 1999. King calls *Bag of Bones* "a grown-up novel ... with a real arc" (Minzesheimer). It was his first book written for Scribner, his new publisher, and it was billed as "a haunted love story" on the book's back cover. "Although not a happy book, King's new one is a powerful, moving novel," according to Charles de Lint's review in *The Magazine of Fantasy & Science Fiction*. Beahn says that King has "deliberately written a mainstream novel that will appeal to a greater audience.... The treatment of [supernatural elements] caters not to horror fans per se but to mainstream readers that want a good story that coincidentally has horrific elements" (*A to Z* 11).

The story revolves around the protagonist Mike Noonan, a best-selling novelist who suffers from writer's block when his wife and unborn son die unexpectedly and moves to his vacation home near Castle Rock in order to try to recapture his creativity and be able to write again. Once he returns to his home, named "Sara Laughs" after an African American singer who lived in the original structure in the early 1900s, he becomes involved in a child custody case when he rescues a three-year-old girl, Ki, who was wandering in the middle of a busy road. He's caught between Ki's mother, Mattie, whose husband has also died unexpectedly, and her multimillionaire father-in-law, William Devore. The plot becomes more complicated when Mike learns that his wife had been writing a history of the area before her death and had unearthed secrets about the "TR" that

147

have haunted the area and the families living there for generations. He learns that Sara Laughs and her family were killed as victims of racism and their spirits have cursed the area, inspiring the inhabitants to give their children names beginning with the letter K and then killing them in sacrifice.

Although Stephen King claims to never suffer from writer's block, his protagonist seems to have a terminal case of it in this novel. After finishing the book he was working on when his wife died, he is unable to write another for four years and is only able to publish by pulling out old work that he has kept in storage. King's descriptions of writer's block are as frightening as his ghosts and monsters: "I was in the worst sort of trouble a writer can get into, barring Alzheimer's or a cataclysmic stroke" (*Bag of Bones* 28). "I was tempted to tell him [his agent] *I can't write two paragraphs without going into total mental and physical doglock—my heartbeat doubles, then triples, I get short of breath, and then start to pant, my eyes feel like they're going to pop out of my head and hang there on my cheeks*" (27). "I was now having heart palpitations—yes, I mean this literally— almost every time I opened the Word Six program on my computer and looked at the blank screen and flashing cursor" (30). As time goes on, it gets worse when he looks at the computer and can't breathe, vomits, and bangs his head so hard he knocks himself out (45). At this point he realizes that the writer's block might be permanent and that his career might be over. "I thought I would sell my soul to be able to write a story again" (47).

As Collings has said, a writer's struggle with writer's block "makes it increasingly difficult for readers to empathize with characters" (*A to Z* 13), especially when the writer is wealthy and successful. For Noonan, though, writing isn't just a way of making a living, it is a way of living. "Without my wife *and* my work, I was a superfluous man living alone in a big house that was all paid for, doing nothing but the newspaper crossword over lunch" (32). We have seen that writing equals life in *Misery*, and we will see that writing helps maintain one's sanity in *Revival*. In *Bag of Bones*, writing represents something more mundane, if not less important—a person's self-worth. Without his writing, Noonan seems to just drift from one day to another. He is unable to establish a relationship, has no friends to speak of, and doesn't even bother much with family. When his brother-in-law Frank tries to befriend him, he is hesitant and agrees to visit, more on a whim than anything. And, later, when he meets Frank for lunch, Frank chides him "like a Jewish mother" (75) for not getting on with his life. "You look like someone who's caught on something and can't get loose," he tells Noonan (76). The writing isn't about the money or the fame for Noonan—since his wife's death, it's his only purpose in life, and he is lost without it. Writing is, in fact, like a drug to him:

> Work had always been my drug of choice, even better than booze or the Mellaril I still kept in the bathroom medicine cabinet. Or maybe work was the delivery system, the hypo with all the dreamy dreams inside it. Maybe the real drug was the zone. Being in the zone. Feeling it, you sometimes hear the basketball players say. I was in the zone and I was really feeling it [381].

While he refers to it as "work," writing is described more like a drug-induced high. "When I write I pretty much trance out," he says (10), and "I'd been hypnotized by the fantasies in my head" (352). Once he breaks his writers block he describes it as "That old magic, so strange and wonderful. It never really felt like work to me, though I called it that; it felt like some weird kind of mental trampoline I bounced on. Those were the springs that took away all the weight of the world for awhile" (276). Not even Mattie and the prospect of a sexual affair can tear him from his writing, once he is back in the zone. "Go on back to work. It's what you want to do, isn't it?" (227). Noonan recalls how his wife used to say, "You'll have to call him back.... Michael is currently in the Land of Big Make-Believe" (361).

Through the persona of Noonan, King tries to describe the process of creativity and the way a writer's mind works using a metaphor of moving into a house: "It was a special kind of thinking, the sort I've always done when I was getting close to writing a book":

> It's like some guys with a big truck have pulled in your driveway and are moving things into your basement. I can't explain it any better than that. You can't see what these things are because they're all wrapped up in padded quilts, but you don't need to see them. It's furniture, everything you need to make your house a home, make it right, just the way you want it.
> When the guys have hopped back into their truck and driven away, you go down to the basement and walk around.... Everything is here, the movers didn't forget a thing, and although you'll have to get it all upstairs yourself (straining your poor old back in the process, more often than not), that's okay The important thing is that the delivery was complete [60].

Noonan refers to an Oscar Wilde quote when he explains that a writer's mind isn't "normal": "a writer is a man who had taught his mind to misbehave" (20). "I am a man who has trained his mind to misbehave, and I can imagine too many things waiting for me inside" (40). "I hear voices in my head, and have for as long as I can remember. I don't know if that's part of the necessary equipment for being a writer or not; I never asked one" (89). The writer is invaded by images of sight as well as sound—"I see things, that's all. Write enough stories and every shadow on the floor looks like a footprint, every line of dirt like a secret message" (125). In a statement that sounds remarkably like that of Derrida and the deconstructionists, King's protagonist expresses the difficulty of capturing things and ideas and conveying them to readers. "Things conceived by minds and made by hands can never be the same, even when they try their best to be identical, because we're never the same from day to day or even moment to moment" (79). These images show that writing, "the work," is more than work but is an integral part of him, and this does make the reader, who is presumably not a writer (and most-probably not a best-selling novelist), sympathize with Noonan at a level that anyone can understand—being unable to pursue one's passion, whether it be a writer with writer's block, a runner with a knee injury, a surgeon who has developed tremors, or even a reader who might be going blind.

The writing theme plays a role in a much larger truth in the novel, however. Noonan's journey and ultimate discovery is that of Melville's Barteby, that there is more to life than just work. The irony of his situation is lost on Noonan when he explains the theme of the Melville story to Mattie: "Barteby begins to question work, the god of middle-class American males" (204). Until the end of the novel, Noonan has never questioned the importance of his work, has considered it a necessary part of him and has felt like part of him was missing when he suffered from the prolonged writer's block. His wife's death makes him begin to realize the importance of love and relationships. Mattie's death and his adoption of her daughter cements this insight. The mythic journey of the novel is Noonan's discovery that writing and storytelling, while important, are not *the* most important things. They do help him to feel whole and productive, which is why he writes the "Memoir," as he calls it, which "came out with nary a gasp or missed a heartbeat" (527), in an attempt to make sense out of everything that had happened. But love is more important than writing. He knew this in the beginning, and when his wife and love died, writing was all he had. But now he has Ki, and so has "put down my scrivener's pen" (529).

It is interesting to note that Noonan's new book, the one he never finishes, was a "major" book (260)—this symbolizes the direction King is taking in *Bag of Bones*, which is a more mature work for a new publisher (qtd. in Beahm, *A to Z*). In another ironic twist, Noonan's publisher tells him that older books, the ones he had written years before and kept in storage, are "a new direction for you" and show "a kind of maturity" (47).

According to Roland Barthes, "the mythical is present everywhere *sentences are turned, stories told*, (in all sense of the two expressions): from inner speech to conversation, from newspaper article to political sermon, from novel ... to advertising image" ("Change" 169). The mythical, the folktale are, indeed, a part of *Bag of Bones*, which draws on the "Damsel in Distress Versus the Wicked Stepfather" (*Bag of Bones* 121) tale and references are made to the Brothers Grimm throughout the novel. "Little Red Riding Hood" is referred to on page 196, "Hansel and Gretel" on 343, and "Cinderella" with the evil stepsisters recast as "Tammy Faye and Vanna" on 181. Noonan thinks of his situation with Mattie as "a melodramatic situation, a fairy tale where there's good and bad and a lot of repressed sex running under both" (201). He retells "Once upon a time stories" to Kyra, modernizing them with references to current events and modern objects and brand names. "The recurrent brand names place the fairy tale in the present, and the contrast between the mythical past and the modern age aids reader identification with the story" (Strengell 116). Joseph Campbell has claimed that there are, essentially, two kinds of fairy tales, those told for entertainment, and those that "have to do with the serious matter of living life" (*Power* 168). *Bag of Bones* is really a hybrid of both types in that it is entertaining yet it also examines serious issues such as racism and the theme that "monsters live inside ordinary people" (Strengell 92). One track of the story is the mystery behind Sara Laughs, the ghost story and the curse, and putting an end to the evil, the more traditional fairy tale. The other track involves Max Devore and the real world problems of child custody, violence, and power, the world where the damsel in distress does not marry the charming prince and does not live happily ever after but dies a violent and senseless death. The two tales both run parallel and intertwine at the same time. In this novel, Stephen King has turned the corner from the traditional horror story that he has trademarked into a new type of more literary fiction that uses horror elements as one of its tools.

Stephen King has been criticized (unfairly, I believe) for his lack of characterization in his novels. He addresses his critics almost directly when Noonan's creative writing teacher attributed a quote to Thomas Hardy: "Compared to the dullest human being actually walking about on the face of the earth and casting his shadow there, Hardy supposedly said, 'the most brilliantly drawn character in a novel is but a bag of bones'" (33). Noonan thinks, correctly, that his professor "made it up himself and attributed it to Hardy in order to give it more weight." Ironically, he adds, "It's a ploy I have used myself from time to time, I'm ashamed to say," as, indeed, Stephen King is doing in a metalinguistic way in this novel. However, the invented quote does support Derrida and the deconstructionists in their thinking that language cannot fully capture truth and reality because of the slippage in meaning between the sign, the signifier, and the signified. This slippage is "trace, that which does not let itself be summed up in the simplicity of the present" (Derrida 66). As Jameson says, "meaning is in its very structure always a *trace*, an already-happened" (175). One may extrapolate that if words, descriptions, and events are a "trace," then characters, infinitely complex, must lose even more meaning in their description and development, not only because of the complexity of their lives and the inability of language to define them, but from the fact that people are dynamic, growing, changing, and living even as their story is being told. This is the dilemma of the novelist—how to create characters that are more than just a "bag of bones"; Stephen King admits that the task is impossible.

The problem of the trace also appears in the attempt to show truth and reality, and once again King addresses this issue in a subtext. Speaking through the first person voice of Noonan, he says, "When you make your daily bread in the land of make-believe, the line between what is and what seems to be is much finer" (21). In much of King's work, we find that reality is thin, both in place and time. "It was a sense that reality was thin. I think it is thin, you know, thin as lake ice after a thaw, and we fill our lives with noise and light and motion to hide that thinness from ourselves" (78). This is most true, of course, in the Dark Tower series of novels, a subject for a book-length study of its own, but it pervades the novels set in the "real" world as well, as we have seen in *It* and other books. Noonan finds himself wandering in dreams that seem more alternate realities than nightmares, where he is able to move in time and space and loses track of which is which. "I realized that the line between what I knew was real and what was only my imagination had pretty much disappeared" (87). This concept can be seen as a metaphor for language itself, as we attempt to construct reality from words, which come from the imagination. The space between reality and a writer's attempt at recreating it is the trace that can only attempt to reveal the truth, a truth that can and will be interpreted differently by each reader, each observer.

Bag of Bones is almost an encyclopedia of references to other writers—Christopher Lehmann-Haupt has identified "nearly 40 of them by my rough count"—including classics (Daphne du Maurier, Herman Melville, Thomas Hardy), contemporary best-sellers (Thomas Clancy, V.C. Andrews, Marry Higgins Clark), and even writers King has created in his other novels (William Denbrough from *It* and Thad Beaumont from *The Dark Half*). In the novel King takes aim at publishers who will only release a single book a year and at the tabloids—"America has turned the people who entertain it into weird high-class whores, and the media jeers at any 'celeb' who dares complain about his or her treatment" (304).

Names, naming and identity form a strong subtext in *Bag of Bones*, as Janicker has observed (187). The idea of naming is a basis for much of modern linguistic theory. As de Saussure has noted, "linguistic units are dual in nature, comprising two elements ... a link between ... a concept and a sound pattern" (66). Proper names are among the most powerful sound patterns—Kripke refers to them as "rigid designators" (49)—and even pets recognize the sound of their own name when called. Naming something gives one power, and, thus, names are an important part of society and "have a mythic or magical importance in all cultures" (Leach 781). Parents choose their children's (and pets') names with care.

According to Lyotard, children not only enter into a culture by learning proper names (*Lyotard Reader* 319), but must learn names and be named in order to take part in narratives.

> To be named is to be recounted.... Every story, no matter how anecdotal it may seem, reactivates names and nominal relations. And by repeating that story, the community reassures itself as to the permanence and legitimacy of its world of names thanks to the recurrence of that world in its stories. And certain stories are explicitly about the giving of names [320].

Researchers of historical place names do collect and study folk tales as part of their work and often find that place names come about because of a local story or legend. "Often the legend comes first; and the place, the setting of the legend takes its name from the story. Thus, not only is folklore created from names, but names are created by folklore" (Baker 370). Noonan's summer house comes with the name "Sara Laughs," which is based upon the local stories of a former resident, Sara Tidwell, who was well-known for her rowdy laughter. The ghost of Sara haunts the home and the local region and has been taking out her vengeance on the inhabitants of the area for generations. Noonan's wife, Jo, who has died before the novel begins, is the folktale researcher in this story. "If the place names researcher is interested in names as an index of culture ... then accompanying legends can sometimes be more revealing than the study of official names and hard data," Barker says (371). Once Jo uncovers the truth behind the legends, she is able to successfully pass this information on to her husband so that he can destroy the ghost and the curse once and for all. And the place name does, in the end, reflect the racist culture of the area, a fact that folklorists have often found to be true, according to Barker, and may indeed commemorate the names of people who died there, as is the case of at least one place in Indiana where African American railroad workers drowned in a swimming hole (372).

People's names are also tied to the place and are an important component in *Bag of Bones*. Mattie consults a baby name dictionary to name her child (101) and the Noonans have chosen their child's name before they even conceived. Little do they know that their choice of names is influenced—indeed, haunted—by the presence of Sara. "Sara's legacy has endured through the act of haunting: her lingering presence causing the long-standing community members to name their offspring in memory of her murdered son, Kito" (Janicker 187). This haunting through names ensures that Sara's legacy will not be forgotten. Sara is able to tell her story though her haunting of the names in the TR. This "power of narrative mechanism confers legitimacy ... it ensures a mastery over time, and therefore over life and death" (Lyotard, *Reader* 321). Janicker reminds us that slaves arriving in America were given new names, which they did not understand.

> Inherent in this observation is the idea that inflicting a name upon an individual—or a group of individuals—is tantamount to deconstructing and redesigning their identity.... In the same way that Anglo-American identity became inscribed on the children of African slaves, the African identity of Sara and her family becomes indelibly conferred on TR [189].

The story of Sara and her family, while an "untold" secret in the township, is told over and over again with the death and ritual sacrifice of the children by haunting the space around the lake. "Without the device of the haunted space, the horror and injustice experienced by Sara and her relatives and friends would be relegated to the dusty photographs and newspaper clippings left to disintegrate in the bowels of the log cabin" (Janicker 193).

Bag of Bones is a novel of telling stories and not telling stories. The story of Sara has not been told in the traditional way—when Johanna tries researching the story, she runs into roadblocks from the residents; the caretaker, Bill, also asks her husband not to tell this story. "You wouldn't write about a thing like that, would you Mike? Because there's a lot of people around here that'd feel it bad and take it wrong. I told Jo the same thing" (277). Jo, of course, never did write the story—she never went beyond the note taking stage. On the other hand, Mike is unable to write after his wife's death, suffering from writer's block of his own, but for a different reason. Jo, apparently, wanted him to discover the story of Sara for himself, and she dissolved his writer's block so she could incorporate the clues to the mystery within his manuscript, the novel that would be a "major book." In order for him to "write" the story of Sara (in the memoir that has become the text), Mike must begin an entirely different book.

Once the story of Sara is "written" and the curse is broken, then he has fulfilled his purpose and sees no need to write again.

The epilogue of the novel is especially rich in metalanguage and metafiction, as Noonan tells the story of his writing his memoir and tells of his decision not to write. One reason he has stopped writing is because he has seen the violence in his books played out in real life, just as Stephen King has seen real violence blamed on his novels, as when students in a Kentucky high school were killed by a student with a copy of *Rage* in his locker or when another student in Washington state shot his teacher while quoting a line from the Bachman book (Rogak 194). "To think I might have written such a hellishly convenient death in a book, *ever*, sickens me," Noonan says about his novels (528).

In summary, *Bag of Bones* explores a number of different themes. First, it delves into the mysteries of writer's block, and in doing so explores the importance of work in a person's life. For Noonan, his writing—his work—has been his life. Once his wife dies and he is unable to write, he loses part of his life. It is only at the end of the novel, when he really has lost everything except for Kyra, he finally realizes that work is not the most important thing. He can retire, enjoy his newly-adopted daughter, and not feel the need to write. The book also touches on the difficulty writers face when trying to create believable characters. King is, I think, poking a jab at his critics with his "bag of bones" remark, but he is also admitting the herculean task of creating people out of words. He also delves into the concept of naming, which leads into the real and the make believe and the parallel plot structure of literary realism and horror fiction.

As a number of reviewers and critics have pointed out, *Bag of Bones* marks a turning point for Stephen King, a point where he is using horror in order to create a more mature, realistic story, more like literary fiction, instead of depending on the traditional conventions of the horror genre. With this book, King had signed with a new publisher and says he "wanted to write a story that would please my old friends and perhaps make some new ones as well" (Beahm, *A to Z* 12). For the most part, the novels that follow continue in this vein, where King showcases his talents as a more mainstream writer, exploring the "thinness of reality" in books like *Hearts in Atlantis, Under the Dome,* and *Revival,* for example. While he has not completely given up horror, the character of Mike Noonan expresses it best: "I've lost my taste for spooks" (529).

CHAPTER 16

Cell: The Metalinguistics of Technology

Cell was written in 2006 and squeezed in between drafts of *Lisey's Story*; King would rewrite *Lisey's Story* at night and work on *Cell* during the day. King recalls that "Graham Greene used to talk about books that were novels and books that were entertainments. Cell was an entertainment" (Lehmann-Haupt and Rich). Since the book is short (by Stephen King standards), involves a journey similar to that in *The Running Man* and *The Long Walk*, and describes a dystopian world where technology has caused a catastrophic problem, the novel reads more like a Bachman book than a typical Stephen King novel. The novel was adapted into a film in 2016, staring Samuel L. Jackson and John Cusack; Stephen King and Adam Alleca wrote the screenplay.

The novel begins on a typical day in Boston Commons where the protagonist, Clay Riddell, a graphic artist, has just signed a lucrative comic book contract. Without warning, a mysterious "pulse" emitted from every cell phone turns every cell phone user into a violent, mindless zombie. Clay unites with two others, Tom and 15-year-old Alice, who don't have cell phones, and they manage to flee the city and search for Clay's wife and son.

Released in the same year as the highly successful film *World War Z*, *Cell* represents part of the development of the zombie subgenre, which began with the voodoo traditions of Haiti and the release of the 1932 film *White Zombie*, which was itself based upon *The Magic Island*, a nonfiction travel book on Haitian voodoo by William Seabrook (Phillips 27). A brief recap of the zombie phenomenon in modern culture will be useful in putting *Cell* into its correct context. According to Bishop and other critics, the zombie phenomenon can be divided into distinct stages of evolution (6). The first stage of development was a direct result of Seabrook's travelogue, the "'real'; zombie ... the 'walking dead' monstrosity created by ... Vodou ritual or magic" (7). This zombie was either a reanimated dead body or a peasant drugged into an eternal stupor and used as a form of slave labor to run the Haitian plantations. This zombie isn't an object of fear so much as an object of pity, according to Bishop; however, this type of zombie soon transformed into a subject of horror as films exploited the fear of being turned into a zombie by an evil sorcerer. This is the subject of *White Zombie* and other films, where it isn't only the Haitians who become victims of voodoo but Americans as well who may happen to be in the country. In Halperin's *White Zombie,* a white woman is transformed into a zombie by the evil Legendre, played by Bela Legoisi, to be a sex slave. These first film zombies created the prototype of slow-moving, mindless, somnambulistic creatures. At this point in their development, though, they are not really a threat to anyone except themselves. This type of zombie, as Bishop has pointed out, taps into the horror of being trapped in a menial assembly line job with no hope in sight.

The next evolution of the zombie was single-handedly brought about by George Romero with his 1969 classic film *Night of the Living Dead.* This is the point where the zombies became cannibalistic, attacked in hordes and turned normal people into the walking dead. Individually, they could be killed or outrun, but it is as a swarm that they became real objects of terror. Romero's first zombie film was set in rural America, and the zombies were fought off by people who fortified themselves and hunkered down. In 1978, Romero moved his zombies into the city in *Dawn of the Dead,* which created urban zombies that invaded shopping malls rather than farmhouses.

Modern zombies, such *The Walking Dead* of Robert Kirkman's graphic novels and television series, or those from the 2006 film *World War Z,* infest the entire planet and the human survivors must migrate from one safe place to another in order to stay alive. These zombies, Bishop suggests, are the direct result of the terrorist attacks of 9/11 and the fear of the apocalypse that has become a new reality (11). It is in this category of zombie that the phone crazies in *Cell* belong. They have deviated from Romero's zombies by the fact that, when "activated," they are not slow and plodding, nor do they eat flesh and turn their victims into zombies by doing so. They are zombified by an outside force, the "pulse," which the characters believe might have been part of a terrorist attack. And the pulse and the phones can create new zombies from the living.

This novel is obviously a statement about the dangers, perhaps even evils, not only of terrorism but of technology, which in the form of urban legends and fiction has become part of our modern mythology. "If you want to find your own mythology, the key is with what society do you associate? Every mythology has grown up in a certain society in a bounded field." (Campbell, *Power* 27). Contemporary society is associated not only with technology in general, but with instant communication through the internet, chat rooms, and, more than ever, cell phones that transmit not just our voices, but text, pictures, and videos. It makes perfect sense for such devices to be incorporated into modern myth.

Since the bio at the back of the book says that Stephen King "does not own a cell phone," the story also reflects the negative attitudes and distrust that those from older generations have of new technology that is embraced by the young. According to the book jacket of *Cell*, "There are one hundred and ninety-three million cell phones in the United States alone." In 2013, the PEW Research Center estimated that 91 percent of American adults used cell phones (Rainie). While the new technology has enabled people to call for help in an emergency and stay connected with loved ones, it has also caused problems with distracted driving, annoying people in public places, and, with the advent of "smart phones," being just general time wasters. But in *Cell*, Stephen King sees something far more sinister in these devices that have the potential to communicate with hundreds of millions of people at once and, metaphorically, at least, turn them into zombies. Reflecting on technology and the modern myth of its destructive potential, Joseph Campbell says, "there comes a time when the machine begins to dictate to you" (*Power* 24).

From a linguistic point of view, cell phones have changed the way that people speak and interact. In the years since *Cell* was published, the technology for texting has become commonplace, and texting has developed a shorthand language of its own. Smartphones have made it possible to have access to information instantly, at virtually any time and place. As Lyotard predicted in 1979, "technological transformations can be expected to have a considerable impact on knowledge.... The miniaturization and commercialization of machines is already changing the way in which learning is acquired, classified, made available, and exploited" (*Postmodern* 4). Lyotard also realized that information could (and would) become political: "In the computer age, the question of knowledge is now more than ever a question of government" (9). We have seen the politics of cell phones played out on social media during the Arab Spring and in the success of social media in organizing protests after the events of Ferguson, Missouri (Tucker).

The cell phone, then, can be a strong force for democracy, for freedom of speech and expression, and for universal education, regardless of social class or position. However, in his discussion of Wittgenstein's "language games," Lyotard posits that knowledge, and its specific languages, have become "compartmentalized and no one can master them all" (*Postmodern* 41). This has the potential for knowledge to be controlled by machines, and access to the "language games" of these machines might reside with just a few.

> Functions of regulation, and therefore reproduction, are being and will be further withdrawn from administrators and entrusted to machines. Increasingly, the central question is becoming who will have access to the information these machines must have in storage to guarantee that the right decisions are made. Access to data is, and will continue to be, the prerogative of experts of all stripes. The ruling class is and will continue to be the class of decision makers [Lyotard, *Postmodern* 14].

This battle, in fact, appeared in a court case with Apple when the United States District Court in Los Angeles ordered the company to assist the FBI in retrieving records from the iPhone used by Syed Rizwan Farook in the deadly San Bernardino shooting in December 2015. Even as Apple fought the order in court, the government experts were able to hack into the phone and retrieve the records, even though the phone was considered hack-proof. This supports Lyotard's fear that the ruling class can access and control information. This fear, in fact, is what the Stephen King novel is all about.

Although King leaves the mystery of who or what caused the pulse unsolved, it is obvious that the problem is created by someone who has mastered the "language games" of technology and computer programing, and then it went out of control. "Some terrorist group—or maybe just a couple of inspired nutcases working in a garage—set this thing off, but no one had any idea it would lead to this" (*Cell* 253). In the aftermath of the 9/11 terrorist attack, America's paranoia was (and has been) high, and experts have warned that cyberattacks on smartphones are imminent. "What will happen is one of these smartphone makers will release a new OS or browser, and there will be a hole," said Alan Wlasuk, the managing partner of WDD, Inc., a software development company. "An attacker will exploit that. That's going to happen for sure," (Goldman). The United States Computer Alerts Readiness Team warned that "from 2009 to 2010, the number of new vulnerabilities in mobile operating systems jumped

42 percent. The number and sophistication of attacks on mobile phones is increasing, and countermeasures are slow to catch up" (Ruggiero and Foote). Finally, according to Hilburn, "the so-called Islamic State (IS) group has displayed prowess on the battlefield, sophistication in their propaganda and savvy use of social media and, according to a recent report, there is 'plausible' reason to believe the militant group may be branching into cyber warfare." The idea of a pulse, which reads like science fiction in Stephen King's novel, may not be so far-fetched, especially if hackers or terrorists were to infect the global network with the type of "worm" described in the novel. "By using cell phones, which have become the dominant form of communication in our daily lives, you simultaneously turn the populace into your own conscript army" (*Cell* 84). In King's tale, the "phone-crazies" have a "new form of communication, available to only one group" (254). What makes cell phone terror so frightening is the popularity and accessibility of the technology. "There's now as many cell phones in mainland China as there are people in America," Mr. Ricardi recalls reading in *Inc* magazine. And "who can resist a ringing phone?" Tom asks (*Cell* 123).

As we have already seen in the work of Austin, speech acts are used not only to describe and explain, but as performatives, to do things. Writers use speech acts to create worlds and characters and leaders use them to command followers to act. After the initial "pulse," the "phone-crazies" are mindless and violent, and they are unable to communicate but are "speaking in tongues" (18). As time goes by, they begin to form a hive mind through telepathy, but "still think mostly in words" (287). The disconnect, however, and the phone-crazies' downfall, is their inability to use speech acts to share information or give commands. As Dan observes, "I don't think they can talk. They can *vocalize* ... but I don't think they can actually speak words" (254). Once Clay and his group decide to destroy the flock by driving a truck full of explosives into their midst, the phone people are powerless. According to Lyotard, the "capacity to articulate what used to be separate can be called imagination.... What extra performativity depends on in the final analysis is 'imagination,' which allows one to either make a new move or change the rules of the game" (*Postmodern* 52). It is obvious that Clay and the "normies" have imagination and they do change the game. The phone-crazies, with their lack of language skills, do not. They cannot adapt or even understand what is happening to them until it is too late, and they are like the passenger pigeons alluded to in the novel.

Speaking and language use is one of the defining characteristics of what it is to be human—even those who cannot hear or speak are capable of using sign language fluently. As Chomsky posits, language is not a result of culture or experience but is the product of "millions of years of evolution or ... principles of neural organization that may even be more deeply grounded in physical law" (55). Most linguists today believe that the human language ability is instinctual and that the human mind comes equipped with a universal grammar, which "specifies the form and functioning of human language in general, hence, principles which hold in all languages" (Fromkin 15). According to Chomsky, universal grammar is "the system of principles that specify what it is to be a human language. This system ... is a component of the human mind/brain and ... appears to be unique to humans" ("Language" 679). Linguists and biologists now believe that language is a uniquely human trait that is coded into our DNA and which allowed us to evolve into creatures that are best adept at communication. Noted Harvard psychologist Steven Pinker has called language an instinct: "Language is so tightly woven into the human experience that it is scarcely possible to imagine life without it.... Language is a distinct piece of the biological makeup of our brains" (4).

Since the phone-crazies in *Cell* cannot speak or generate language, they have not only lost their imagination but have also lost their humanity and are evolving into a new species, one without language as we know it. They are, in effect, zombies, able to function but unable to use language and experience the human condition. As Clay speculates, "if left alone, they might eventually have turned out to be better custodians of the earth than the so-called normies" (*Cell* 342). But he realizes that he and his friends had no choice but to destroy them; even if they didn't, their programming was being infected by a "computer virus" of sorts, as evidenced by the fact that they were regaining language skills, and this virus would have led to their destruction anyway, since it seemed to feed off of language.

At first glance, *Cell* is written in a rather traditional point of view, what Fowler refers to as a "Type B," a "third person narration by an 'omniscient' author who claims knowledge of what is going on in the characters' heads, reporting their motives and feelings" (173). This point of view begins on page 4, with the section numbered "2": "Clay's attention was attracted by the tinkle of an ice cream truck." However, if we turn back the page, it is obvious that the narrator is a more distinct individual, an historian, if you will, who is looking back and telling events that happened in the past. "The event known as The Pulse began at 3:03 p.m., eastern standard time, on the afternoon of October 1" (3). The narrator then addresses the reader directly: "Inside the bag, swinging back and forth, was a small round object.

A present, you might have guessed, and you would have been right." This voice continues for the rest of the page, and then the narrator evaporates into the background, leaving the "constant reader" free to read the novel without being directly addressed again. In *Linguistic Criticism,* Fowler labels this a specific type of "dialogic rhetoric, in which the writer puts the opinions of the narrating voice into argument with his presumed *readers* or *narrates* (153). This type of authorial intrusion was a common device of 18th century novels.

One might wonder why Stephen King employs this old device here in a futuristic piece of science fiction/horror. The answer, I believe, lies in the book's ending, which has been criticized as being ambiguous—Is Johnny ok at the end? King doesn't exactly tell us. Yet by addressing the reader directly, he asserts that there is a narrator telling the story in the future, as if the text were history. This means that there must be a future audience reading this history, and, therefore, things must have turned out all right in the end. This answers the question of whether Clay was able to bring his son back to normal. He must have, or his story wouldn't be told, for at the time of the pulse he was just "a young man of no particular importance to history" (3), yet now he is important enough to be written about in a "history" of the pulse and its aftermath. In fact, King himself finally had to clarify the ending:

> I get a lot of angry letters from readers about it. They want to know what happens next. My response now is to tell people, You guys sound like Teddy and Vern in Stand by Me, after Gordie tells them the story about Lardass and the pie-eating contest and how it was the best revenge a kid ever had. Teddy says, "Then what happened?" And Gordie says, "What do you mean, what happened? That's the end." And Teddy says, "Why don't you make it so that Lardass goes and he shoots his father, then he runs away and he joins the Texas Rangers?" Gordie says, "Ah, I don't know." So with Cell, the end is the end. But so many people wrote me about it that I finally had to write on my Web site, "It seems pretty obvious to me that things turned out well for Clay's son, Johnny" [Lehmann-Haupt and Rich].

The 2016 film version of *Cell* has Clay and his son walking off together, both perfectly normal, in search of their friends. Yet, as the credits roll, we see Clay's face in the crowd of phone crazies, walking around and around in a zombie-like state, so perhaps the jury is still out and Clay only thinks he has saved his son. This, however, doesn't negate the novel's telling the story as if it were a historical event.

While critics of King's early work have suggested that his fiction highlights themes of morality, that ethical behavior generally leads to hope and a happy ending, critics of his later work have found the opposite to be true. "His works after 1995 often expose the dark underbelly of humanity and chronicle societal mayhem and cultural fear that are, perhaps, better kept in the closet" (Findley 58). *Cell* does seem to fit this definition as "King ... creates ... a society that must come face to face with a monster of its own creation" (McAleer 173). Yet, while it may appear that this fiction shows no hope, and that both the zombies and the "normal" commit horrendous atrocities, I believe a case can be made for the book's belief in the goodness of humanity. First of all, the "phone-crazies" are no longer human, since they have lost their use of language, and language defines humanity. Therefore, they cannot be accountable for their actions in a moral sense. Like language, ethics seem to be a distinctly human trait. And while the normal people also commit terrible acts of violence against each other, we have seen this dark side of humanity in earlier King novels—the Trashcan Man in *The Stand* serves as an excellent example. As McAleer has pointed out, Ray Huizenga committed a heroic act by sacrificing himself "to keep his plan hidden from his friends and enemies" (181) so that the phone-crazies wouldn't figure it out. But Clay, with his human imagination and persistence, did solve the problem and offer hope for humanity. The fact that humanity does survive, and actually "chronicles" the events, demonstrates the idea that humanity will persist, and that heroic acts like that of Huizenga will offer deliverance.

On a more personal note, cell phones create a major problem for horror writers. With the invention of new technology, many of the old Gothic trappings no longer induce fear—help is at one's fingertips with a 911 call. Writers then must either disable the cell phone, or put their characters in a place where it won't work, and with increased network coverage, those places are few and far between. Perhaps on an unconscious level, Stephen King was destroying the modern implements of technology that have made writing traditional horror stories more problematic.

To summarize, *Cell* works on three different levels and explores three different but interrelated themes. First, King explores our fears of technology and the dangers it presents in a post–9/11 world. This fear is expressly related to the danger of the ruling class holding too much power and in their control of technology. The characters speculate that the pulse was probably the result of experimentation by some government that went out of control. And one of the greatest dangers to our freedom is cyber warfare, including computer hacking and identity theft. Furthermore, the novel echoes the fears of the older generation, in particular, that we are becoming slaves to our technology and gadgets, zombies, if you will, and that our phones are, metaphorically speaking, controlling us. Campbell articulates this in relation to what humankind is seeking in its mythology:

"Man should not submit to the powers from outside but command them. How to do that is the problem" (*Power* 23).

Cell also addresses the idea of what it is to be human and how language and communication are such integral parts of who we are as a species. The latest research points to language being hard-wired into our very DNA: birds have developed complex songs and humans have developed complex languages that all share a universal grammar. The loss of language would render us no longer human. Language is, indeed, the tool of the imagination and the basis for how we think. Without it, we would have no creativity, no knowledge, and no morality. The phone-crazies serve as a metaphor for humans without language—mere zombies going through life without any thoughts of their own.

Finally, King does return to the idea of hope for humanity and our ability to recover from even the most terrible apocalypse. Even as humans are the only species to have created and used language, we are also capable of incredible acts of creativity and bravery. We seem to be able to solve problems just when we need to. Just when American cities were being polluted by horse droppings, we invented the automobile. And now that we are being polluted by carbon emissions, we have invented alternate sources of energy (whether we have the willpower to adopt them or not is a different theme). The normal are able to use their imaginations and problem-solving abilities to escape from the phone-crazies and the novel ends with hope that humanity will once again triumph.

Humans are also capable of incredibly heroic acts where people sacrifice themselves for the greater good. The sacrifice of Ray Huizenga, who at first seems to "have died for a useless phone" (*Cell* 405), ultimately kept the secret knowledge out of the minds of the phone-crazies. Without his sacrifice, all would have been lost. It can be argued that without communication, this concept of utilitarianism would not be possible. Even as words gave life to Paul Sheldon in *Misery*, language gives hope and deliverance to humanity as a whole.

CHAPTER 17

Lisey's Story: Private Language

Stephen King has said that *Lisey's Story* is his best book (Greene 77). Released in October 2006, the novel was nominated for a World Fantasy Award and was praised by reviewers in *The New York Times* (Windolf) and *The Washington Post*, which wrote "with *Lisey's Story*, King has crashed the exclusive party of literary fiction" (Charles).

The novel is told through the point of view of Lisey Landon, the widow of a famous and successful novelist, Scott, who had died three years before the novel begins. The book is really several stories in one. The first is about Lisey's being stalked and almost killed by Dooley, one of Scott's crazed fans. The second story is about Lisey rediscovering the secret world of her husband and finally accepting his death and letting go. And the third story concerns an alternate world, Boo'ya Moon, where Scott was able to travel and where he taught Lisey to travel as well.

Like the novels we have examined so far, *Lisey's Story* contains a metalinguistic subtext about writing, in this case through the persona of Scott Landon. Scott is, perhaps, Stephen King's idea of a fantasy—a writer who is not only a best-selling author but one who has won the National Book Award and the Pulitzer Prize in fiction and who has published horror and fantasy and won the World Fantasy Award. This combination, in the "real" world, is probably less plausible than the idea of vampires invading a small New England town and perhaps shows King's wishful thinking—although the "real" Stephen King probably never expected to be recognized by the National Book Foundation, win an O'Henry Prize, or receive an arts award from President Barack Obama.

Scott Landon is also another example of a King character who was a victim of child abuse. His mentally-ill father cut his sons on a regular basis in an attempt to keep the "bad-gunky" at bay (*Lisey's* 222). Scott finds his escape in his imagination, where "the world is so thin" (326) and discovers an alternate world, Boo'ya Moon, where he can escape and heal himself. This world also provides inspiration for his stories in the form of "the word-pool, the story-pool, the myth-pool" (97). Scott tells Lisey that the pool is where writers go to find stories. "And cast our nets. Sometimes the really brave fisherfolk—the Austens, the Dostoevskys, the Faulkners—even launch boats and go out to where the big ones swim, but that pool is tricky" (224). The imagination is both a dangerous and a beautiful thing, as it is depicted in this novel. "Scott Landon can jaunt off to places like Boo'ya Moon, but such strangeness and beauty were not made for ordinary folk such as she [Lisey] unless it's between the covers of a book or inside the safe dark side of a movie theater" (327). While Stephen King did not have an abusive father, he had an absent one, and he has recounted on numerous occasions how he found escape in science fiction stories and weird tales. In fourth grade, when he suffered from an extended illness, he "read my way through approximately six tons of comic books, [and] progressed to Tom Swift" (*On Writing* 27); his boyhood room in Durham had "a hundred or so paperback books, mostly science fiction" (40). These stories encouraged him to take out his old Royal typewriter and compose his own tales.

Scott's father and brother have gone insane, and he fears that he carries mental illness within his DNA as well. He tells his wife: "I *am* crazy. I have delusions and visions. I write them down, that's all. I write them down and people pay me to read them" (222). When Lisey and he have their first fight, he cuts himself badly as a sort of ritual cleansing, a way to keep insanity away. Unlike his father and his brother, though, Scott leads a productive life, both professionally and emotionally. His imagination allows him to travel to a different world and fish from the story-pool. However, the danger of the story-pool lies in its beauty. Most of those who travel there, like Lisey's sister Amanda, become mesmerized by what they see, staring into the pool for hours that can turn endless and never returning to the real world. Scott manages to walk the tightrope between reality and the imagination, between sanity and madness. "Two things have tied him to the earth and saved him from the long boy. His writing is one. The other is a waist he can put his arms around and an ear into which he can whisper" (350). Writing, as we have seen in previous stories, equals life. In some cases, such as "Secret Window, Secret Garden," it also leads to insanity. In *Lisey's Story*, it actually works to keep the character sane, as a means of channeling demons into a productive reality.

Love is the other key to his remaining sane, the "waist he can put his arms around and an ear into which he can whisper." While the waist and the physical part of love is important, it is the listening ear that really matters, and in Lisey he has found the perfect partner. "He speaks a language she grasped greedily from the beginning" (108). This love is also part of Stephen King's life, which he has found with his wife Tabitha, who shares his love of words, and his children, two of whom have also become successful authors. The shared language that he discusses in *Lisey's Story* is an important tool to building this bond of love between couples and families, as I will discuss later in this chapter. And, in Stephen King's case, it is fair to say that his wife has been an essential part of his career; not only did Tabitha save *Carrie* from the trash bin, but she has been one of King's most trusted critics and advisors in each of his books—as just one example, he thanks her for her "valuable suggestions ... including what turned out to be the right title" in the author's note to *End of Watch* (431).

Wittgenstein said, "*The limits of my language* mean the limits of my world" (88), which led to Lyotard's ideas about private language (Ward 116). According to Lyotard, science and the modern word are dissolving "metanarrative" (the "big" stories), and so the modern world is developing more specialized languages, languages that give power to those who understand them and deny power to those who don't (*Postmodern* xxiv). "Perhaps Lyotards's most provocative idea is that these little narratives should be thought of as highly specific and completely incommensurable language games" (Buchanan 301). Thus, we all have access to "private languages" that are known to those who share specialized knowledge and understanding. When families and couples have strong, intimate bonds, they, according to King, also develop a private language known only to those within the intimate circle. Since Scott is a writer, he is a master of language games, constantly inventing new words, metaphors, and sayings, and he invites his wife into the inner circle so she can play as well. Lisey says that "my husband has a word for just about *everything*" (188). The couple can speak in code words that only they know. "Everything the same.... It had been a part of her marriage's inner language" (7); "their marriage's interior language, like *strap it on* and SOWISA and *smuck* for *fuck*" (64); and "*SOWISA, babyluv—Strap On Whenever It Seems Appropriate*" (95). "They had their code words, of course, and God knew those words floated out of the purple on occasion when she'd been unable to find him" (309).

In this novel, all of the families have a secret language. "In the Debusher family, where there was a saying for everything, urinating was *spending a penny* and moving one's bowels was—odd but true—*burying a Quaker*" (139). The use of these distinct phrases and the "Yankee dialect" helps to bring the reader into the story; according to Alberico, by adding "a touch of the real ... these phrases can also make us feel comfortable with the characters King creates" (186). While he has been criticized for using "common language," I agree with Alberico that using the language of the people (including brand names, slang expressions, and regional dialect) makes his characters more believable and more genuine. Although I admire the prose of H.P. Lovecraft and Clarke Ashton Smith (and Shakespeare, for that matter), no one in the modern world actually speaks like this. By capturing the more authentic speech of real, breathing people, King has made his imaginary worlds much easier for readers to accept and appreciate.

Scott has carried on words from the private language of his family as well, passed down to him and his brother by an insane father. The "bool" is a puzzle or a trick and the "blood-bool" is cutting oneself for atonement. "If you take a bool—especially a blood-bool—then sorry's ok. Daddy said so." And the insanity that seems to run in Scott's family also has its own code word—"the bad-gunky" (115).

The secret language of marriage and families seems to have two sides to it. While Lisey's sisters use euphemisms when speaking of bodily functions or harmless sayings, the secret language of Scott's father camouflages sinister things such as mutilation and madness. The private language of Lisey's marriage contains harmless, entertaining euphemisms ("SOWISA"), words of love and affection ("Babyluv"), and more sinister words, both those from Scott's childhood and those from the alternate reality where he visits ("Boo'ya Moon" and "the long boy"), phrases that help strengthen the couple's bond of love. In fact, as Alberico has observed, some of these phrases are "words of power" (187) that stay with Lisey after her husband's death and, in fact, become a mantra to help her survive. "Everything the same" is an example of a phrase that becomes part of her inner being, reminding her that life is still good and worth living, despite everything. Furthermore, the repetition of interior language helps the reader to understand Lisey's thoughts and emotions.

About *Lisey's Story* King says, "I wanted to talk about two things: One is the secret world that two people build inside a marriage, and the other was that even in that intimate world there's still things we don't know about one another" (Greene 77). Much of this novel is about Lisey's discovery—and then rediscovery—of the things she didn't know about her husband that were revealed in his private language. "Each marriage has two hearts, one light and one dark" (*Lisey's* 50). The light is expressed in the private words of endearment. The dark is expressed in the secrets of Boo'ya Moon, the place where Scott goes to escape from reality, and, importantly, the place where he writes his manuscript version of "Lisey's Story" and leaves it for her to find under the story tree. Although Scott has told her intimate details of his life, told her about the abuse he has suffered, the death of his brother, his fear of ancestral madness, and his trips to a "real" fantasy world, he cannot tell her about the day when he killed his father. She surmises what happened, but he does not tell the details until he writes them down and leaves the story in a place where she will find it after his death, by playing along with him in a "bool" that will also save her life. It seems obvious that Scott knew his wife would need to escape to Boo'ya Moon herself, just as he knew her sister had gone there, but he never revealed either of these secrets to his wife. It is not clear exactly how he knew what would happen, except, perhaps, for the fact that travelling to the alternate world was a movement in both time and space, similar to what characters in the Gunslinger series experience, but it is clear that he has knowledge of what was going to happen in Lisey's future. Perhaps they were just feelings, or instinct or intuition, but both he and Lisey placed a high value on such things. "She had come to believe that the very things the practical world dismissed as ephemera—like songs and moonlight kisses—were sometimes the things that lasted the longest. They might be foolish, but they defied forgetting. And that was good" (461).

Although the novel is "Lisey's Story" and not Scott's, the book does devote much of its time to the process of writing. The first metalinguistic lesson speaks of the world of imagination where writers live. The Boo'ya Moon, while an alternate world, is also a metaphor for creativity and the imagination, and how the imaginations of children evaporate as they grow older, but remain strong in creative people.

> I think most kids have a place they go to when they're scared or lonely or just plain bored. They call it NeverLand or the Shire, Boo'ya Moon if they've got big imaginations and make it up for themselves. Most of them forget. The talented few—like Scott—harness their dreams and turn them into horses [387].

Very creative people can create imaginative worlds and actually turn them into reality. According to King, these imaginative worlds, like J.M. Barrie's "Neverland" or Tolkien's "Shire," become them part of our language, part of our reality. As J.L. Austin has noted, "to say something is in the full normal sense to do something" (94); the act of speaking or writing about make-believe worlds, in essence, creates them. Once the fantasy world is described—a verb that Austin calls an "expositive" (162), a word that is used to express views and clarify references—it exists in both the author's and the reader's mind and becomes part of the shared reality of a society. That is why we have no problem picturing L. Frank Baum's Oz, Mallory's Camelot, or King's magical but frightening world of Boo'ya Moon even though we cannot physically visit those places. As one review has expressed it, "You come away from *Lisey's Story* convinced of the existence of King's fantastic realm" (Windolf).

Yet as real as fictional worlds may seem, King echoes Derrida's frustration with the inadequacy of language to express truth: "No tale can tell how ugly such dying is" (504). As in *The Running Man*, King is critical about the news media's ability to convey truth. When a deranged fan shoots Scott, the news misses the truth and makes the security guard a hero, even though it was Lisey who hit the attacker with the ceremonial shovel. "There were only two people in the whole round world who knew the truth about that afternoon" (25).

The difference between creativity and mental illness is thin, as Amanda tells Lisey: "My imagination was just big enough to get me in trouble.... The Looneybins are full of people like me. *Our* dreams harness *us*" (387). Amanda can create a make-believe world in her mind, but she can't bring it to life, can't "cross over." Creative people can travel into their own imaginations and bring things back, but their lives and reality also shape their creations. In the manuscript he writes to his wife, Scott says, "I think my imagination, febrile as it is, has been exhausted by the many shocks of the long day and longer night, and that I have been reduced to seeing exactly what is there" (500). The horrors of his "real" life have worked with his imagination to shape his books. "I get up thinking *I killed my father* and go to bed thinking it. It has moved like a ghost behind every line I ever wrote in every novel, any story: *I killed my father*" (504).

Lisey's Story contains a metafictional element in the form of the "bool hunt." Initially described as a treasure hunt game that Scott played with his brother Paul, it becomes a metaphor for putting together a sequence of clues and events in order to discover truth. In other words, a bool hunt is a story, a narrative. Scott says that "writing a book was a bool hunt" (418). *Lisey's Story* itself is, in fact, a bool hunt, where Lisey, and the accompanying "gentle reader," must find and interpret a series of clues and puzzles in order to find the meaning of the story, both on a narrative and a thematic level. By solving the puzzle, Lisey not only saves her life (hence the idea that writing and reading equal life, a concept King explores in much of his fiction) but also discovers the truth about Scott's final secret, how and why he killed his father. It is worth noting that Scott is unable to "tell" Lisey the truth about this incident. He can only reveal the details in written form. The "lies" of fiction reveal truth and the fantastic world of Boo'ya Moon that Scott has brought to life mirrors reality, with scary things lurking in the dark, people being mesmerized into inaction by pretty pictures they see in the pool, and beauty in the most unlikely of places. "Maybe when you got right down to where the short hairs grew, truth was a bool, and all it wanted was to come out" (310).

King also makes fun of the difference between fictional reality and actual reality, saying, in effect, the real thing is more difficult to believe. At one point in the story, Lisey remembers her husband being annoyed at an editor asking him to rewrite a scene in his book because "it creaks." He tells her the fantastic but real story of a dog named Ralph that miraculously found his way home after being lost for three years. "Novelists labor under tremendous handicaps. Reality is Ralph, showing up after three years, and no one knows why. But a novelist can't tell that story! Because it *creaks* old boy!" (400).

There is, of course, an alternate meaning of "bool" in Scott's lexicon. In addition to it being a hunt or a riddle, it could also, in certain contexts, mean "a joke or harmless prank" (81). This is illustrated in Scott's posthumous joke on the scholars, when he leaves behind an enormous manuscript with a title, a couple of lines, and reams of blank paper. The "prank" is on the scholars, and one wonders if, perhaps, Stephen King isn't playing a few jokes of his own on the critics.

As in *Misery*, King again turns to the theme of the crazed fan who stalks and kills Scott and shows that fame and success come with a price. "Scott's Deep Space Cowboys ... want to grab Scott by the arm and tell him they understand the secret messages in his books" (34). Although one of the fans "made Lisey very nervous," she never expected him to be violent. Stephen King himself has been the victim of crazed fans, of course, including one who broke into his home in 1991 (Rogak 166). His books have also been linked to violence; a teenager killed two students and a teacher in 1996 while quoting a passage from *Rage* and a another who killed three students and wounded five others in 1997 had a copy of *Rage* in his school locker (194). These acts caused King to stop the book from being sold.

King also mocks the literary scholars who feel compelled to collect every word of every story that an author has written, whether good, bad, or indifferent, in the persona of Joseph Woodbody who wants to collect Scott's papers and deposit them in the Scott Landon Collection in the university library "for the Incunks to drool over" (75), "Incunks," of course, being the nickname given to the academics and scholars who collect and dissect Scott's work.

In summary, *Lisey's Story*, like *Bag of Bones*, is a hybridization of mainstream literary fiction with elements of fantasy and genre fiction, a phenomenon that is happening on a more regular basis in the literary world as literature is seen in terms of popular culture. As Windolf has noted:

> Cormac McCarthy, one of the few living novelists to have met with Bloom's approval, left behind the tangled style of "Blood Meridian" and "Suttree" to update the Western with his Border Trilogy; he has since ventured deeper into genre territory with the one-two punch of "No Country for Old Men" and "The Road." Another of Bloom's pets, Philip Roth, borrowed a conceit from science fiction in using an alternate reality as the jumping-off point for "The Plot Against America."

The novel contains the basic thriller plot of the "damsel in distress" being stalked by the madman, only this damsel, Lisey, is not saved by the cavalry but by messages left behind by her dead husband. While Lisey seems to be the invisible housewife at the beginning of the story, she becomes strong, fierce, and independent by the book's conclusion, and she is finally able to live a life of her own, without Scott.

The novel's major theme concerns writers and writing, like that of so many the novels I have discussed in this work. King shows both the good and bad aspects of writing—how it can grant life and sanity, and how it can also bring about death, through the crazed fan, and madness, since the creative person walks on such a narrow path of mental wellness. The book also dramatically illustrates what the linguists call "private language," that interior language that is known and shared among lovers, families, and like-minded individuals. This private language can be dangerous, according to the Marxist critics, since it divides people, creates barriers, and keeps knowledge secret except to those who possess the code to this interior language. And in *Lisey's Story*, it obscures the truth and hides unpleasant things like child abuse, mental illness, and violence. But the private language can also be a binding force, a glue that holds families and couples together, a force that ultimately saves Lisey's life.

Although King has been criticized for his use of plain language, language that borders on baby talk in some places in this novel, his use of informal diction does create a realistic picture of how average, everyday people speak and behave. While King's characters do not have the complexity of a Stephen Dedalus, they are easier to identify with and much easier to like (personally, the thought of spending much time with one of Joyce's pretentious characters makes me cringe). Even the writers speak in a common language when they're not writing, and King's invitation to join in his characters' private language makes them accessible, almost like we are part of the family. King's ability to make us identify with his char-

acters, I think, is one of his secrets to success and probably one of the reasons he has been able to sell millions of books. Embedded in this intimate
characterization are some interesting themes and observations about life,
which we are receiving from those we are intimate with, from whom we
trust, and not from a preachy scholar who is trying to convince us of some
great truth. In this way, *Lisey's Story* succeeds both as a good story and as
a work of literature that helps to bring to light some truths about life in
21st century America.

CHAPTER 18

"Ur": Textual Reality

"Ur" is an experimental novel written and published exclusively for the Amazon Kindle in 2009 as electronic book platforms became popular and was also released as an audio book. The novella, approximately 53 text pages long, was not available in print format until it was revised and reprinted in *The Bazaar of Bad Dreams* in November 2015. "I decided I would like to write a story for the Kindle, but only if I could do one *about* the Kindle," King wrote in *Entertainment Weekly*. "I didn't do 'Ur' for money. I did it because it was interesting" (qtd. in Trachtenberg). For my analysis, I have chosen to refer to the original version as published by Amazon for the Kindle and have referenced my citations to the Kindle location markers.

Machinery and technology gone wild is a common enough theme in Stephen King's works. As we have seen in "Word Processor of the Gods," new reading and writing technology are not off limits. King says:

> Gadgets fascinate me, particularly if I can think of a way they might get weird. I had previously written about homicidal cars, sinister computers, and brain-destroying mobile phones; at the time the Amazon request came in, I'd been playing with an idea about a guy who starts getting e-mails from the dead. The story I wrote, "Ur," was about an e-reader that can access books and newspapers from alternate worlds ["On the Kindle"].

The protagonist of the novel, Wesley Smith, is an instructor in the English Department of Moore College in Kentucky. A "lover of books" and a wannabe novelist, he calls his girlfriend an "illiterate bitch" (loc 148) when she throws his first edition of *Deliverance* across the room and asks him why he doesn't "read books on the computer like the rest of us."

She breaks up with him and, out of spite, he purchases a Kindle, only instead of receiving the generic white model, he receives a hot pink Kindle with an experimental program called Ur. Smith soon learns that an Ur is an alternate reality and there are almost ten and a half million of these Urs on his device. He can, therefore, read books from alternate Urs where an author might have lived longer and written different books. Enlisting the help of a student, Robbie Henderson, and his colleague, Don Allman, he explores the Urs and learns that his Kindle came from a different reality, and he can access the history of each Ur through its *New York Times*. He also discovers that he can see his own future through the local newspaper included in the pink Kindle. Once he learns that his girlfriend is destined to be killed in a bus accident, he sets out to change the future of his Ur.

At its simplest metalinguistic level, "Ur" is a book about books and about the electronic publishing revolution. While Smith admits that books are his "mistress" (loc 863), he reluctantly purchases the electronic reading device to spite his girlfriend and prove to her that he is "new school." His colleagues call it a gadget, an interesting word choice when we consider Baudrillard's "System of Objects." Baudrillard claims that "automatism ... opens the door to a whole world of functional delusion, to the entire range of manufactured objects in which a role is played by irrational complexity, obsessive detail, eccentric technicity or gratuitous formalism." He defines a "gadget" as a "Functional Aberration" (121) where "*the object answers no need other than the need to function*" (122). Still, even Baudrillard, the hypercritic of capitalism, admits that through its arousal of "delighted fascination ... something that serves no purpose whatsoever may in this sense still serve *us*." Wesley tells his colleagues that he is "experimenting with new technology" (loc 42). Based upon Baudrillard's definition, he would probably consider the Kindle to be a "gadget" as well, and he even calls the Ur function "useless" because he can't actually "do" anything with the novels from the alternate realities. Robbie suggests he could copy them down and publish them under his own name, but publishing them would not only "violate the Paradox Laws" but make him "feel ashamed" (loc 190–95). Robbie would argue that the electronic book does serve a purpose, and in the end of the story when they are able to change the future, the device is proven to be much more than a "gadget."

Another metalinguistic theme of the story is the discussion between Wesley and Robbie about the definition of a book. Wesley says, "There will always be books. Which means there will always be paper and binding. Books are *real objects*. Books are *Friends*" (loc 249). Robbie counters with his definition: "They're also ideas and emotions" (loc 262). Westley thinks of books as having a smell that gets better with time but finds electronic books have their own merit—they are less expensive and will give him a more modern image. Still, when asked by Allman if e-books will ever replace the real thing, he replies that it would never happen—"But he had already begun to wonder" (loc 102). This debate has become part of modern discourse as electronic books and documents have become more common and easily accessible. The traditionalists distrust e-books and express distrust that they aren't "real"; they also worry about the legal aspects of e-books. Not only can they more easily be pirated, but they are, strictly speaking, rented property, while a reader feels a sense of ownership with a hard copy of a book. Of course e-books have their merits as well—they are portable, usually more affordable, easy to navigate, and a huge library of e-books doesn't require bookshelves and storage space, which makes them more valuable to students living in dormitories or people living in small apartments.

"Ur" has constant references to books and mentions a number of authors by name, including James Dickey, Roberto Balano, and Fritz Leiber, to name just a few. The most interesting part of the new "reading gadget," though, is its library of books by great writers that had never been written in the current reality. The first such book Wesley finds is *Cortland's Dogs*, a novel published by Hemingway in a Ur where he had lived until 1964. King speculates on writers and their styles and the uniqueness of each author: "Somewhere—at some college a lot more ambitious than Moore of Kentucky—there was a computer programmed to read books and identify their writers by their stylistic tics and tocks, which are supposed to be as unique as fingerprints or snowflakes" (loc 571). In an example of life imitating fiction, such a computer, using forensic linguistic software, did recently reveal that J.K. Rowling was the author of *The Cuckoo's Calling*, a crime novel she published under the pen name Robert Galbraith (Zax). In a miniaturized work of metafiction, King recreates the first paragraph of this alternate reality novel using lean and terse prose that might have won an imitation Hemingway contest: "A man's life was five dogs long, Courtland believed. The first was the one that taught you. The second was the one you taught. The third and fourth were the ones you worked. The last was the one that outlived you. That was the winter dog" (loc 558). Ironically, Stephen King says, "Hemingway sucks, basically.... If I set out to write that way, what would come out would've been hollow and lifeless because it wasn't me" (qtd. in Greene 74). Yet his Hemingway imitation isn't lifeless at all. If he were to complete the tale, though, I would speculate it would deviate away from Hemingway and turn into a horror story that would have King's trademark all over it.

The subtext of "Ur" is about reality itself, a subject that has been extensively questioned by postmodern critics and physicists alike. "Many of these [postmodern] theories do set out to raise doubts about the relationship between reality and representation. The claim is ... that there is no simple, direct relationship between reality and its supposed expression in words and pictures" (Ward 72). In his stories, Stephen King is using words to create a fictional reality, one that, as Baudrillard has suggested in *Simulation*, blurs the boundaries between the real and the simulation. King is, in essence, creating the "simulation" that Baudrillard claims has substituted signs of the real for the real (*Simulacra* 2). As King himself has said, "I'm aware that between reality and unreality you have to stitch a seam, and I try to make that seam as fine as possible so the reader steps over it. I like the whole illusion of reality" (qtd. in Underwood, *Bare Bones* 83).

The "book reading gadget" in Ur creates over ten million realities, each of them slightly different. "The real is produced from miniaturized cells, matrices, and memory banks, models of control—and it can be reproduced an indefinite number of times from these.... It is a hyperreal, produced from a radiating synthesis of combinatory models in a hyperspace without atmosphere" (Baudrillard, *Simulacra* 2).

Since reality has been produced so many times within the memory banks of the Ur, it is impossible to know which reality is real. At one point as Wesley is debiting large purchases on his credit card from another reality, he vaguely wonders what the Wesley Smith of the other reality will think when he looks at his MasterCard bill. And one must wonder, if his reality is truly real, how is it possible to change it using knowledge gained from the Kindle? Wouldn't that create another new reality?

King took this alternate reality concept to a greater level in *11/22/63*, a novel written in 2010 but which he had originally tried to write in 1972 (*11/22/63*, "Afterword" 846). This book, which runs to more than 800 pages, explores the possible Urs of November 22, 1963, the date that John Kennedy was assassinated. Kennedy's assassination plays a role in "Ur," when Wesley and his friends begin looking up the assassination and its aftermath in different realities. "In some Urs, that day in November had passed with no assassination stories, either attempted or successful" (loc 991). This is, of course, the core plot for *11/22/63*, where Jake Epping (another English teacher) discovers a time portal and attempts to return to the past and to find Lee Harvey Oswald the day before the assassination and stop him from killing the president. "The JFK assassination ... was the seminal event of the twentieth century" ("Ur" loc 975).

Both "Ur" and *11/22/63* highlight the theme of predestiny and speculate on the possibility of changing the past or the future. Jake Epping, like Wesley, also teaches English, and he also finds a gateway through time. Where Wesley changes the future, Jake tackles the problem of changing the past, and he finds that a single minor change in past events can have a major and unpredictable impact on the future. This begs the question of whether, if offered the opportunity, we would travel back in time and change terrible events—smother Adolf Hitler in the crib, stop the Kennedy assassination, or prevent the death of a loved one. According to *11/22/63*, the answer is not as simple as it sounds. In preventing one disaster, we may inadvertently create another. The laws of space and time seem to operate to prevent such intervention, and, in the Stephen King multiverse, *all* of these different possibilities are already playing themselves out.

In "Ur," Wesley's dilemma is more personal, since he is trying to save the life of someone he knows personally and loves, not a famous historical figure. His quest is to change the world on the micro level rather than to change "big history," and he is trying to change the future, not the past. Still, the whole mechanism of space and time seems to be set up to prevent such a change from happening in King's multiverse of Roland, the Dark Tower, and millions of Urs. The miracle in the novella isn't that Wesley finds the mechanism, the "gadget" that gives him access to the multiple Urs, but the fact that he is able to successfully use it to change future reality, despite the Paradox Police, the "low men in yellow" who enforce the laws of the multiverse. The question of whether or not we should change the past or the future is unanswered in "Ur"; perhaps the future where Ellen Silverman's death was prevented by mistakenly giving Wesley a pink Kindle becomes a separate Ur of its own and is added to the fabric of the multiverse. At any rate, the average person faced with this time paradox would most certainly change the future if he or she could.

At a metalinguistic level, the very word "Ur" causes problems, because it doesn't have a meaning. Neither of its accepted meanings, as an ancient city, or as a prefix, seem to work. It also fails to work as an abbreviation—wouldn't "Ar" for alternate reality be more accurate? It is because the word does not have meaning that its meaning is created. Language is reality. Once it's written down, it's real. Language captures reality and is so powerful it even creates alternate realities and solidifies them. Returning for a moment to J.L. Austin's "performatives," King is actually "doing something with words" when he creates the noun "Ur." He "is able to create that which does not [exist] through poetry" (Heidegger, "Language" 1125). Ur is not only the software that creates the multi-universe, but it also represents the different universes themselves, the Urs. Each is numbered, catalogued, and has its own history, its own authors, and its own newspaper clippings. The newspaper story, the symbol of reality, creates these multiple realities with words. The newspaper is the authority, and the *New York Times* ("All the News That's Fit to Print") represents objective truth.

In another case of reality imitating fiction, an MIT computer programmer named Adam Chlipala has created a programming language called Ur, which is used in creating robots: "Ur is a programming language in the tradition of ML and Haskell, but featuring a significantly richer type system. Ur is functional, pure, statically typed, and strict. Ur supports a powerful kind of metaprogramming based on row types" (Chlipala).

As we have seen in "The Word Processor of the Gods," the protagonist, a writer, created his own reality by writing it. Wesley Smith, however, is not a writer, but *hopes* to be a writer, a big difference. "Like all instructors of English, he thought he had a novel in him somewhere and would write it someday" (loc 56). Yet he has only filled one page of a 200-page blank journal, and even that page has just bad novel ideas (loc 186–202), and he realizes that "the novel in him might remain in him, like a wisdom tooth that never comes up, at least avoiding the possibility of rot, infection, and an expensive—not to mention painful—dental process" (loc 129). And when he checks his name in the author index, he "discovered what he feared: although the Urs were lousy with Wesley Smiths ... none seemed to be him" (loc 623).

The fact that he is *not* a writer is important in this story, because Wesley Smith cannot "do things with words," as Austin would say. Since he cannot write his own reality, he must take physical action to create it. Hence he must intervene in the events that are about to happen and stop them, despite the warnings about violating paradox. Jake Epping, the writing teacher in *11/22/63*, must also take action and travel through the time portal because he is also incapable of changing reality with words.

In a final metalinguistic in-joke, Stephen King uses images from his *Dark Tower* books, the picture of a "large, black tower" on the welcome screen of Ur books (loc 440), and the Paradox Police in the "yellow-colored coats" (loc 1618), a reference to the low men in yellow coats who are the enforcers of the Crimson King and who appear again in *Hearts in Atlantis* where they are chasing Ted Brautigan. The rose, a symbol in the Dark Tower books, also appears in "Ur." And when the low men confront Robbie one of them says, "the Tower trembles; the worlds shudder in their courses.

The rose feels a chill as of winter" (loc 1632). These references help to complete the interconnectedness of the Stephen King universe and suggest that all of the Urs are alternate universes tied together with the Dark Tower as the hub.

Stephen King has extensively used—and been criticized for—using brand names in his fiction. As discussed in a previous chapter, this use of branding works as a shortcut form of character development, since we are in modern American society, to a large extent, defined by the brands that we consume. Writing for a specific brand name, Amazon and Kindle, posed challenges of its own. As King said: "I realized I might get trashed in some of the literary blogs, where I would be accused of shilling for Jeff Bezos & Co., but that didn't bother me much; in my career, I have been trashed by experts, and I'm still standing" ("On the Kindle"). Yet the brand name use is effective on a couple of levels in this story.

First, it addresses the theme of consumerism and why people buy things. Wesley doesn't buy the Kindle because it will be useful, or interesting, or even enjoyable. As he admits, he buys it out of spite, to prove to his girlfriend that he fits in to her world. "It has to be recognized that consumption is not ordered around an individual with his personal needs, which are then subsequently indexed, according to demands of prestige or conformity, to a group context" (Baudrillard, *Consumer* 93). In other words, we consume in order to project an image of ourselves, not just for personal needs. Wesley wants to be considered "new school" by his colleagues, and he likes the image of himself using the electronic reading gadget. He imagines his girlfriend seeing him reading it, and, when she does learn that he has purchased the gadget, she finally calls him and leaves a message that they might be able to get back together.

Secondly, "Ur" stands as an example of Stephen King himself "experimenting with technology" and an example of how the technology itself can create the reality, as Baudrillard has suggested. The book did not originally appear in print form because the technology is the thing that helps make it seem more real. When reading the book on a Kindle, the alternate reality of Urs seems more possible than when the story is read in a bound paper and ink copy. Thus, the brand name functions in creating reality for the reader, offering almost a three-dimensional view of the world as the reader actually holds the gadget in his hands.

Although the story seems to be a gimmick designed to promote a gadget, "Ur" is an interesting little novel that collects many of King's themes into one place. By this time in his career, of course, he is consciously aware of the interrelatedness of his fiction and of the multiverse concept he has created in *The Gunslinger* books and which has found its way into the novels he has set in the present Ur of his Constant Reader. The story addresses the contemporary issues of e-book publishing by using the metafictional device of both publishing the story on the Kindle and reading it on one. It also addresses the modern fascination that we have with technology and gadgets, how, it seems, we always have to have the next "best big thing," a trend that has expanded even further since "Ur" was published with tablets and smart phones that cannot only read books but show films and videos as well and that seem to need upgrading at a ridiculously fast rate.

But the book also addresses some larger philosophical themes such as the morality of changing the past or the future. If we were capable of manipulating time, who would decide how it would be done? Would there, indeed, be Paradox Police? Would we be guided by our individual interests or would changes be made for the "greater good"? These questions have no answers, of course, and it is unlikely that we will ever be able to manipulate time anyway or see future events before they happen. Still, as strategic planning and analysis improves, and as science and technology become more sophisticated (and sometimes deadly), we may be able to predict possibilities and make better decisions if we are able to get a handle on not only the strategic issues but the moral dilemmas as well. Novels such as "Ur" and *11/22/63* that force us to think about different scenarios and possibilities may assist us in navigating these difficult philosophical paradoxes of the future.

CHAPTER 19

"1922" and "A Good Marriage": The Secret Collection

In 2010, Stephen King published *Full Dark, No Stars*, a collection of five novellas that are, indeed, dark and bleak, stories King himself found "hard to write" (*Full Dark 365*). These stories are psychological horror rather than supernatural. As King himself admits in the afterword, "these stories are harsh" (365), but he says he wrote the stories "to record what people might do, and how they might behave, under certain circumstances" (366). "Fair Extension," much like *Needful Things*, explores human greed and envy. In "1922" the protagonist is a murderer. In "The Big Driver" the main character is the victim of a psychopath. And in "A Good Marriage" the protagonist is the wife of a serial killer. These stories are all about secrets, people who lead double lives, and all the stories are about revenge and retribution. "1922" is about a man who enlists his son to help him kill his wife and then keeps the secret for eight years. "Big Driver" is told from the point of view of Tess, the victim of an assault and rape, who learns the secret identity of her attacker and seeks revenge. In "Fair Extension" the dying protagonist makes a secret deal with the devil in order to extend his life and exact revenge on his privileged best friend. And in "A Good Marriage," a woman uncovers the secret that she is married to a serial killer. Each of these stories has a theme about the secret person inside of each of us. In this chapter, I will briefly examine two of these stories, "1922" and "A Good Marriage," since they are both about murderers who keep their violence a secret and both stories deal with violence against women.

"1922" is about a Nebraska farmer who kills his wife when she inherits property and plans to leave him, sell the land and move to the city and open a dress shop. He refuses to leave his farm. Set in 1922, just three years after women were granted the right to vote in America, much of the subtext of this story deals with the conflict between men and women and how in rural areas of America women were still considered property of their husbands. While the sheriff says that "if they're [women] gonna vote, they better learn," he follows this wisdom up with "Mine does what I tell her. She better, if she knows what's good for her" (79).

While Wilfred seems meek and appears to give in to his wife's will on most things, he does so out of inertia and not respect. He considers her a "nagging and ungrateful Wife" (4) and doesn't care that she "never took to the farming life (or to being a farmer's wife)" (3). He dismisses her dream of moving to the city and opening a shop as foolish, even as he acknowledges that he spends most of his time working and not with her. To Wilfred, all that matters are a woman's looks, "the honey ... that lure men on to the stinging hive" (6). Although he admits that Arlette was "warm-natured" (7), he has come to hate her and wishes her dead. Once Arlette receives her father's inheritance of 100 acres, her dream of opening a dress shop becomes possible, and she stands up for what she considers fair. To Wilfred, however, and the other men in this rural town, women are simply wives and are not allowed to have dreams.

Wilfred also sees Shannon, his son's girlfriend, only for her looks: "when my boy looks at you, he sees the prettiest girl in all the world. And he's right. Why, if I was his age, I'd spark you myself," he tells the girl (60). It comes as a complete surprise to him when he learns that Shannon is the more gifted student in the class and has a good chance of being the first girl accepted into the teaching college. To him, a woman's intelligence is irrelevant. A wife should be attractive and obedient, nothing more.

The construction and plot of the story are Poesque—sort of a montage of "The Cask of Amontillado" and "The Telltale Heart" with a bit of Lovecraft's "The Rats in the Walls" thrown in for good measure. In the very first line of the story, Wilfred Leland James confesses to the murder of his wife in a letter written "TO WHOM IT MAY CONCERN" (3), and that letter turns out to be a novella-length confession. The audience is whoever finds the manuscript, and that, of course, is King's "Constant Reader." The story also features a classic Poe unreliable narrator, whose spirit of the perverse makes him do the one thing that will bring the most misery upon him. Even worse, he convinces his 14-year-old son to go along with the plan, which brings about his destruction and death as well.

Like Poe's mad narrators, Wilfred claims to be sane, and claims that everything he says is true: "this is my confession, my last words on earth, and I've put nothing in it I don't know to be true" (99). Yet it doesn't take the narrator long to place the blame on "the conniving man," who devised the murder plan. "I believe that there is another man inside of every man, a stranger, a Conniving Man" (4). It is this stranger, a form of Poe's "imp of the perverse," who is responsible for the crime.

The dual nature of Wilfred is especially evident in his description of the murder itself. "Let it be told quickly," he says (17), and then he drags the reader through a graphic two-page description, including the most gory details, followed by several more pages devoted to the disposal of the body. Although he had promised his son that the murder would be painless, he was wrong; he also admits to being wrong when he tells his son that his mother won't "come back" (24).

The horror in the story is that Arlette *does* come back to haunt him and exact revenge on him and the boy. Whether or not she *really* comes back or if the haunting is a product of Wilfred's guilt-ridden mind is open to speculation. Is the narrative a "marvelous" story, according to Todorov's definition, which "suggests the presence of the supernatural" (*Fantastic* 52), or it is "uncanny," where the supernatural elements have a rational explanation?

One might be tempted to say that the wife's return, through the use of a pack of rats as her medium, is nothing more than Wilfred's madness, stirred by his guilt. Just as the heart is not beating underneath the floorboards in Poe's "Tell-tale Heart," neither are the rats coming from his wife's walled up grave to "get" him. There is, indeed, evidence that Wilfred is the only one who sees the rats. When he leaves the bank, he calls attention to a rat running along a rail above the tellers' windows, but all they see is a shadow (123). "On several occasions I called the attention of my co-workers to these vermin. They claimed not to see them" (128) and go on to nickname him "Crazy Wilf" (129). Even Wilfred himself admits that "the mind is a funny thing" (82). By the end of the story, he certainly appears to be losing a grip on reality, and he is seeing rats in the library and in his hotel room. Yet he denies that it is only in his imagination. The very end of the story contains a newspaper account of Wilfred's death, where, according to the reporter, "he had bitten himself all over—arms, legs, ankles, even his toes" and that he had "chewed his own wrists open" and "certainly must have been deranged" (131) In addition, he had apparently even chewed up his own confession "like paper when rats chew it up to make a nest." His death is officially ruled a suicide.

There is also a case to be made for a "real" haunting—after all, Stephen King is a horror writer who uses the supernatural in his stories as part of his trademark. First, it seems as if Wilfred's cow is maimed by a rat (63), and Wilfred is bitten by a rat (93), which leads to an infection so severe that his hand must be amputated. He also claims that his wife comes to him while he's suffering from the rat bite and tells him exactly what will happen to his son and the girl he has run away with. These incidents can, of course, be explained logically—rats do tend to infest farms, especially those that have not been taken care of, and Wilfred has obviously let his property fall into disrepair. And his vision of his wife can be attributed to delirium caused by fever and infection. She tells him the prophetic events about his son, but Wilfred does admit to researching these events himself later on, so the haunting by his wife—her revenge—may very well be part of his own madness and not supernatural at all. Since King is trying to record "what people might do, and how they might behave under certain dire circumstances," my money is on Todorov's "uncanny." I think the guilt of murdering his wife compounded by guilt about his son drove Wilfred mad, and he creates a reality that destroys him. On the other hand, it does seem that Wilfred is a victim of Karma—what goes around, comes around, and he ultimately pays a very heavy price for the work done by the "conniving man" inside him.

One of the ironies of "1922" is embedded in the character of Wilfred, a simple farmer who reads the classics and names his cattle after Greek goddesses. Although not highly educated, he did finish public school and seemed to excel—well enough that one of the other students used to copy his answers to test questions. He is also intelligent enough to fool the sheriff and his wife's lawyer, and, in fact, he did get away with the murder. Only his confession links him to the crime and that, in the end, is chewed to pieces, as if by rats. The story ends with a paradox, however—if the confession is, in fact, destroyed, how have we, the reader, come to possess the manuscript? This, and Wilfred's last words, written, supposedly, while he was being bitten to death, are, I believe, the major flaw in this story and similar to the ending of Lovecraft's "Intruder in the Dark"—if a monstrosity was really coming to get you, wouldn't you run away rather than keep on writing until you are killed? The same can be said of this story; regardless of whether Wilfred is biting himself or is being bitten by rats, how can he continue to write while he is being eaten alive? The story might have been more effective if it ended sooner, and if the manuscript survived for detectives and psychiatrists to analyze and wonder about.

The second story I will analyze, "A Good Marriage," is based upon the BTK (blind, torture, and kill) serial killer who murdered ten people over the course of 16 years without his wife's knowledge (*Full Dark* 368). King also wrote the screenplay for the film version, which was released in 2014. This book, like *Lisey's Story*, is about marriage, but if Lisey's husband, Scott Landon, can be thought of as Thad Beaumont, then Bob Anderson, the villain of "A Good Marriage," is George Stark, the "dark half."

King wrote "A Good Marriage," specifically, "to explore the idea that it's impossible to fully know anyone, even those we love the most" (368), a theme that he visited in a much more optimistic way in *Lisey's Story*. The title is irony at its best. The novella begins with the puzzling line "The one thing nobody asked in casual conversation, Darcy thought in the days after she found what she found in the garage, was this: *How's your marriage?*" The reader, of course, fully expects that the thing she found in the garage was evidence that her husband was cheating on her; however, we soon find that Darcy's discovery was much more sinister.

On one level a "good marriage" is about marriage, but its subtext, of course, is about the secrets that even the most intimate people can keep from each other. As in *Lisey's Story*, this novella speaks about the "private language" that spouses have, about the secrets they share only between themselves. This private, secret language is what makes a marriage work; it is almost like a psychic bond between two people, each of whom knows what the other is thinking. "They had been married so long that they had become almost exquisitely attuned to each other" (*Full Dark* 304). After her discovery of her husband's secret life, Darcy recalls a litany of things that only she knew about him.

> The sight of a crossword book on his knees glimpsed through the half-open bathroom door as he sat on the commode. The smell of cologne on his cheeks, which meant that the Suburban would be gone from the driveway for a day or two and his side of the bed would be empty for a night or two.... His slippers at the end of the bed, one always tucked into another.... The taste of Dentyne on his breath when they kissed. These things and ten thousand others comprised the secret history of marriage [288].

In fact, Bob has some secrets that he didn't know that Darcy knew, such as his trying out various items to regrow his thinning hair (285). Darcy realizes that she doesn't know everything about her husband, nor does he know everything about her, but that doesn't concern her. "There was no knowing everything, but she felt that after twenty-seven years, they knew all the important things" (289).

On the surface, then, it was a "good marriage." She had learned how to make it work, and she believed he had as well. "They agreed. When they didn't agree, they compromised. But mostly they agreed. They saw eye-to-eye" (285). "A successful marriage was a balancing act—that was a thing everyone knew. A successful marriage was also dependent on a high level for irritation—this was a thing *Darcy* knew" (286). She thought that they had mastered the code of private language, and whatever secrets they had, such as her secretly eating too much candy, just made the bond stronger: "ordinary mysteries, she believed (*firmly* believed), were the stuff that validated the partnership" (287).

Once she learns the truth of his double life, everything changes. She lives in the "Darker Bedroom" with the "Darker Husband," slept on the "Darker Bed," and became the "Darker Wife.... Mrs. Brian Delahanty" (333). "This was the Darker Life, where every truth was written backward" (334).

When Darcy finds a bondage magazine in a pile of old catalogues, she is unnerved, but willing to overlook the secret. "A long marriage sometimes contained a few unpleasant relics you would just as soon you hadn't found. But that was no biggie" (295). Like one of H.P. Lovecraft's narrators about to stumble upon a cosmic truth, she doesn't want to know, but she can't help herself from looking. "*I don't want to know*, she told herself, and was pretty sure that thought wasn't coming from the Stupid Zone but from the smart one" (295). But "with a sense of misgiving so strong it almost had texture" (299), she removes his box from the "hidey-hole." Even then she tells herself not to look, but had come "much too far" not to.

Once Bob returns home and confesses his secret, then Darcy has to keep a secret of her own, that she knows he will kill again, and that she will be responsible for any more deaths. She tries to live a double life as the "Dark Wife" and is successful at it, given the situation. "They resumed their old ways, the small habits of a long marriage" (336). While she is now repulsed by him, she also has moments of nostalgia. When he draws a heart around his name in a note he left her, "she felt a wave of love for him" (334). "You could not turn off love—even the rather absent, sometimes taken for granted love of twenty-seven years—the way you'd turn off a faucet" (306).

In all of Stephen King's fiction, Darcy is one of the strongest, most heroic characters. She truly is caught in a dilemma, the proverbial between a rock and a hard place. If she turns him into the police, she will be implicated as well. And if she does nothing, or if she leaves him, she knows he will kill again. So she waits for something to happen, an act of amazing courage, both in keeping the secret and in living with a man who she knows is capable of torturing and killing others. She keeps his secret for unselfish reasons—she doesn't want her children's lives to be ruined by the revelation that their beloved father is a serial killer—but she knows she must do something to keep him from harming others. When Bob decides to celebrate the finding of a rare penny, she finally sees her chance: "the Darker Wife knew that what he thought of as his good luck had really been her own" (341), and she forms a plan to kill him and end her dilemma once and for all.

Perhaps we can never fully know another person, regardless of how intimate the relationship is, as King suggests. But Darcy does obtain that ultimate forbidden knowledge in the end. When she pushes him from the top stair, in that moment where she is about to kill him, she finally sees exactly who her husband is. His guard is down and she sees him truly. "In that moment her understanding of him was complete. He loved nothing, least of all her. Every kindness, caress, boyish grin, and thoughtful gesture—all were nothing but camouflage. He was a shell. There was nothing inside but howling emptiness" (342). Later, the retired detective gives her further details of the murders, and she learns that the child her husband killed did suffer after all (362).

It is noteworthy that Bob Anderson was a coin collector. In his discussion of collections and collectors in *The System of Objects*, Baudrillard says that "the passion for objects ends up as pure jealousy" (105) and "the possession of objects and the passion for them is, shall we say, *a tempered mode of sexual perversion*" and "sexual perversion is founded on the inability to apprehend the other *qua* object of desire in his or her unique totality as a person" (Baudrillard *System* 107). It is obvious that Bob, through the persona of Beadie, looks upon his victims as a sort of collection. He, in fact, takes perverse pleasure in collecting their identification cards, then sending these back to the police as a way of taunting them. Some serial killers collect trinkets or other objects from their victims; in the film adaptation of "A Good Marriage," Bob collects a piece of jewelry from one of his victims and gives it to Darcy. King says that in writing the screenplay, "I wanted another bite of that particular apple.... It also gave me a chance to refine some of the things that were scary in the story" (Murphy). This added detail of the collected jewelry does just that. As Baudrillard concludes, "collectors, for their part, invariably have something impoverished and inhuman about them" (*System* 114).

One of the dominant images of "A Good Marriage" is that of the mirror. The mirror is first seen as a method of self-reflection, when Darcy sees herself in it while sitting on the toilet with her laptop, looking for more information on the Beadie murders. "There was a mirror on the back of the door, and she didn't want to see herself in it. Why was it there, anyway? ... Who wanted to watch themselves sitting on the pot? Even at the best of times, which this certainly wasn't?" (307). In this instance, the mirror shows shame and embarrassment. Baudrillard has noted that "in a general sense ... the mirror is a symbolic object which not only reflects the characteristics of the individual but also echoes in its expansion the historical expansion of individual consciousness" (*System* 21). Apparently the mirror in the bathroom has never bothered Darcy before. But she now suddenly sees herself as a victim, forced into an impossible situation by her husband, and sees herself as stupid and naïve for not knowing about his secret life beforehand. She also sees guilt within the mirror—if she does nothing, she knows other women, eventually, will die because of her inaction. "Did she really think she could condemn more women to horrible deaths just so that her daughter could have a nice June wedding?" (312). It is the dilemma of victims of domestic abuse, who often blame themselves for the crimes of their spouses. As her husband reminds her, "Nobody would believe that you were married to me all these years and never knew ... or at least suspected" (330).

Once Darcy moves past the initial feelings of shame and guilt, however, the mirror takes on a new symbol, the enchanted looking glass of an Alice in Wonderland type world. "She found herself remembering the year in early childhood when she had gone around the house looking in mirrors.... She had been convinced that mirrors were doorways to another world.... It was *similar* on the other side of the glass but not the *same*" (315). The world she sees in the mirror now is a dark one, though, not enchanted so much as haunted:

> What interested her was the idea that there was a whole other world behind the mirrors, and if you could walk through that other house (the Darker House) and out the door, the rest of the world would be waiting.... Now, all these years later, she had found her way through the mirror after all. Only there was no little girl waiting in the Darker House; instead there was a Darker Husband, one who had been living behind the mirror all the time, and doing terrible things there [316].

The mirror, in a strange way, becomes her salvation. Darcy metaphorically enters the mirror and becomes the Dark Wife, beginning a new and secret life of her own: "on this side of the mirror, she could keep secrets, too" (340).

As it turns out, Darcy, the Dark Wife, is as good at leading a hidden life as her husband was. She keeps his secret, kills him, and then keeps that secret as well. She remains hidden behind the mirror until the very end, when the detective Ramsey arrives and tells her what he knows. He tells her, "I see a courageous woman who should be left alone to get after her housework," acknowledging that he knows and approves of what she did.

"Walking him to the door, Darcy realized that she felt on the right side of the mirror for the first time since she had stumbled over that carton in the garage" (363). Once she is absolved, so to speak, she can finally get back to normal and leave the Dark World of the mirror behind.

In *Full Moon, No Stars* we do find stories that are "hard to read in places" and "gets in your face" (365). "1922," "The Big Driver," and "A Good Marriage" are particularly disturbing in their portrayal of violence towards women. The scene in "1922" where Wilfred kills his wife is particularly troubling since it does not go well and he tells the story in graphic detail—his son faints twice because the murder is so horrific. Wilfred seems to have little remorse for killing his wife, though he does regret the bad luck that it causes him afterwards. King has created a believable madman in the finest tradition of Poe. Despite being marred by an ending that lasted too long and perhaps tried to explain too much, the story captured what might be going on inside the mind of a killer that, driven by self-interest and an inability to see women as human, can callously take a life over a hundred acres of land.

"A Good Marriage" is, perhaps, even more disturbing since it is loosely based upon a true story. The narrative asks us to put ourselves into probably the most unnerving situation one could imagine—knowing that a spouse or loved one is a psychopathic killer—and asking us, what would you do? These are not just dime store novels, here, but stories that go for the throat. As King reminds us in the Afterword, "the writer's only responsibility is to look for the truth inside his own heart.... For writers who knowingly lie, for those who substitute unbelievable human behavior for the way people act, I have nothing but contempt" (366). "A Good Marriage" forces the reader to probe into places where we don't want to look, to ask questions that we, perhaps, don't really want answers to.

Wilfred James can perhaps be forgiven for his attitude towards women because of the time and place that he lived. However, Bob, the serial killer in "A Good Marriage," has no such excuse. His "conniving man" is much more dangerous than Wilfred's; he viciously kills women just for fun to turn them into part of his collection. And he manages to do this while maintaining the outward appearance of being a loving father, a dutiful husband, a man admired by others and respected in the community. The dilemma that his wife faces is truly horrific—much more so than vampires in the basement or rats in the walls, even. She is between a rock and a hard place. If she goes to the authorities, she won't be believed and will be seen as an accessory, not to mention the fact that it will ruin her daughter's life. And if she does nothing, she is an accomplice in any of his future murders, with blood on her hands. So she must keep a secret of her own and bide her time until she is able to act, and then she can assert herself as the heroine.

In "1922," "The Big Driver," and "A Good Marriage," Stephen King has empowered his female characters. Arlette avenges her death from the grave by filling Wilfred's mind with guilt and driving him to madness and then suicide. In "The Big Driver" Tess becomes a "real" detective, finds her attacker, and kills him. And in "A Good Marriage" Darcy discovers her husband's secret and delivers justice in her own way. *Full Dark No Stars* is a "harsh" book, but in all of the stories justice is served, each in its own way. The collection of novellas are all about crime and punishment and express the idea that in the long run Karma will prevail and evil will pay its price.

CHAPTER 20

Joyland:
Linguistic Registers

In 2013, Stephen King did a complete 180 from "Ur," published only on the Kindle, and released *Joyland* in print *only* in an effort to bring customers back into bookshops. Whether this experiment will work or not remains to be seen—the print edition can be ordered online without going into a bookstore—but regardless of the marketing efforts, this novel will be successful because of the Stephen King name alone.

Joyland is billed as a mystery, and it is, of sorts, yet it also retains elements of the supernatural that we have seen before, a psychic child with a terminal illness, and a ghost—and, of course, a narrator who is an English major and destined to become a writer: "a twenty-one-year-old virgin with literary aspirations" (12).

Deven Jones, the protagonist, is a more pragmatic writer than previous King narrators. Although he dreams of becoming a fiction writer whose books were "well reviewed" (45), he ends up as a reasonably successful magazine writer who writes for and edits trade journals and makes a living at it: "I never produced the books I dreamed of, those well-reviewed almost-bestsellers, but I do make a pretty good living as a writer, and I count my blessings; thousands are not so lucky. I've moved steadily up the income ladder to where I am now, working at *Commercial Flight*, a periodical you've probably never heard of" (49).

One of the major themes of *Joyland* is speech and storytelling. As a magazine and trade journal writer, Devon's work would be in a third-person journalistic style, just the facts. Apparently, his fictional career never took off, though the narrator doesn't explain why. He does admit, though, that he isn't much of a conversationalist. Tom "possessed the gift of gab I sadly lacked" (55), he says, and telling stories is a sort of talking on paper. Devon's best "acting" is as Howie the Happy Hound—"Don't talk. Howie never talks, just gives hugs and pats 'em on the heads" (76), Devon is told. So his best performances are anonymous, which is probably true of his magazine and trade journal writing, the type of writing where the author stays behind the scenes.

When Devon "tells" his story, however, he does it as a first-person narrative, from the point of view of a 60-year-old man looking back at his life. The story is told in a chatty, conversational style, and it seems that, in this story, at least, the narrator does have the "gift of gab." He addresses the reader directly numerous times, using the technique of author-reader discourse discussed by Fowler (153) that allows him to connect with the audience and make the reader one of the "characters" of the story. When he first "puts on the fur" and has to play the role of Howie without any training, he asks the reader directly ,"Do you know what it felt like just then?" (*Joyland* 74). When he explains about how he saved a little girl from choking, he speaks to the reader directly: "I'm not sure you'll understand how fortunate that was" (102). And when he speaks about his depression and suicidal thoughts after the breakup with his girlfriend, he reminds us "you have to understand I had no scale by which to judge it. They call it being young" (87). This conversation with the reader lends truth to the story, making the reader a confidant, as if an old friend is telling a truth about his past.

According to Lyotard, "there are many different language games—a heterogeneity of elements" (xxiv) and there is, therefore, no one "universal" language game. This postmodern theory believes in "the other" and instead of the melting pot it recognizes differences which should not be ignored. There's also the structure of language in different places, and it doesn't have to be one language. In fact, one language is a controlling device of the powerful. We have different language games at work, with family, at church, etc. The linguistic term "register" is used to describe varieties of language according to use. Distinct from a dialect, which is a variety spoken by an individual user, "the category of 'register' is needed when we want to account for what people do with their language" (Halliday et al. 87). Registers describe different types of styles in writing. "Registers are distinctive varieties of language used in different *situation types* such as church service, lesson, textbook, sports reporting, etc." (Fowler 190). Fowler uses the example of Henry Reed's *Naming of Parts* as an example of a poem that uses two distinct registers for literary effect (198–200), the register of the drill sergeant weapons instructor ("Today we have the naming of parts") mixed with the register or voice of the poet ("Japonica glistens like coral in all of the neighboring gardens"). As a trade journal writer, Devin would be familiar with this specific register, since trade journals use their own type of language. However, as a former English major and aspiring novelist, he is also familiar with the register of storytelling, which he uses to great effect in narrating this tale.

Stephen King is a master of mixing in these different types of registers in order to create what Fowler calls a "defamiliarizing effect," which "in the texts which feature literature courses the mixing is often deliberate and pointed" (204). This defamiliarizing is one of the characteristics that makes literature different from other forms of writing.

Hohne observes this effect in Stephen King's work: "a fine example of its [language's] slippery dual nature is Stephen King's writing, where there is a great deal of tension between the heteroglossic orality that is slang speech, which codifies a knowledge rejected by those in power, and monologic orality, which embodies that power" (93–94). King's texts, then, contain both "official" and "unofficial" language (94); the official language of those in power and the "speech ... full of highly unofficial slang and obscenities" that "is celebrated and accepted as a vital aspect of the narrative of readers' lives" (95). She adds that "King's works provide a paradigm illustrating the tension between official and unofficial languages/ ideologies that exists not only in literature but throughout our society" (101). It is also, I believe, emblematic of the contrast between literary fiction and popular fiction and working class people and intellectuals.

Stephen King uses this concept to bring realism and verisimilitude to the novel, establish Devin's credibility, and to explore the meaning of language itself. "Even in his use of slang King draws attention to language, and this language self-consciousness fits the classic Formalist definition of poetry" (Hohne 98). Perhaps this use of "unofficial" language is most evident in his use of the "carney language." According to Halliday, "At certain times and places we come across special forms of language generated by some kind of anti-society; these we may call 'anti-languages'" (570). Examples of this language might be in the secret slang of prisoners as a sort of code that their guards wouldn't understand. The carney language would fall into this category as well, since it is a secret code that the "rubes" don't know.

This carney anti-language creates the concept of "other" in the novel. We have the carney people, and the rubes. The carney people are the insiders.

"The simplest form taken by an anti-language is that of new words for old" (Halliday 571). Not all words are different, but just those; the differences in vocabulary, according to Halliday, exist "only in certain areas, typically those that are central to the activities of the subculture. So we expect to find new words for types of criminal act, and classes of criminal and victim; for tools of the trade" (571). Their secret "talk" gives the carney people a linguistic power over the "rubes."

In fact, the carney words in *Joyland* fit Halliday's model. In his "Author's Note" at the end of the novel, King acknowledges that "much of what I call 'the Talk' doesn't exist" but "most of the terms here really are carney lingo," which he found in *The Dictionary of Carney, Circus, Sideshow & Vaudeville Lingo* by Wayne N. Keyser. The anti-language is real; for example, a rube is "a scornful term for the outsider to show business" and a "rag" is "a tiny stuffed prize (for example, a small stuffed fruit), usually kept out of sight under the counter. This practice leads customers to believe that the smallest of the prizes on open display above is the smallest prize they stand to win" (Keyser). King uses the Carney anti-language throughout *Joyland* to give veracity to his book. "I learned the Talk; ... I learned how to run a joint, take over a shy, and award plushies to good-looking points" (*Joyland* 70). Some of the "talk is authentic carnie language"—"gone larry" for a broken ride, "bally" for a free show—and some of it is Joyland Lingo that King makes up: "points" for pretty girls, "frumps" for complainers, "hammer squash is a cony (usually a frump) who bitches about having to wait in line" (66). Devin becomes enamored with the world of the theme park and its language: "The cool tunnels under the park were there. So was the Talk, that secret language the other greenies would have forgotten by the time Christmas break rolled around. I didn't want to forget it; it was too rich" (127).

If we might wonder how the editor in chief of *Commercial Flight* has managed to pen such a convincing story as what has occurred at Joyland, we must remember that Devin has learned the registers of literary fiction as an English major. "When it comes to the past, *everyone* writes fiction" (43), Devin says. And that's exactly what he does; he writes the piece as fiction, using lengthy and concise dialogue, recreating complex conversations he couldn't possibly remember. "Writing unfolds like a game that inevitably moves beyond its own rules and finally leaves them behind," observes Foucault. The reliability of King's narrator may come into play, especially since he admits "passing time adds false memories and modifies real ones" (101). As Frye has noted, "one of the most familiar and important features of literature is the absence of a controlling aim of descriptive accuracy.... The apparently unique privilege of ignoring the facts has given the poet his traditional reputation as a licensed liar" (75). This highlights the theme of illusion and reality, a theme we will return to later.

Despite the fact that Devin is telling the story from a future perspective, and telling it using narrative, fictional techniques—King's persona liberally employs flashback, foreshadowing, and other narrative techniques to build suspense and delay the ending to the mystery—the narrator comes across as reliable and believable. This is partly true because he writes for no-nonsense trade journals where writers and editors are not allowed to make things up. And it is also true because Devin has a strong belief in being truthful. He admires the park's owner, Easterbrook, for that very quality and reflects on his speech to Joyland's employees: "It was one of the best speeches I ever heard, because it was truth rather than horseshit" (60).

One of Devin's faults as a fiction writer may be that he can't make things up and fiction is, ultimately, a lie. Devin says he imagines himself "writing novels and the kind of short stories they publish in *The New Yorker*" (26). In other words, his fiction would be truthful, mainstream literary fiction, not ghost stories and mysteries. So when he tells a ghost story with a mystery, we must accept it as true. He's a writer of facts, not fiction, not "horseshit," and therefore the story of what happened to him must be true.

One of the major themes of *Joyland* is the difference between reality and what Devin terms "horseshit" and the carnival itself is the perfect metaphor for this dichotomy. Some of the carnival rides are "real" (like the wheel), but most are "horseshit," a "butcher's game." Ultimately, though, the carnival is real for Devin because they are not selling lies— they are selling fun (59). However, several amazing things happen in the narrative, and Devon is careful to explain them all in a truthful, convincing way that makes us believe. In order to do this, he is careful to separate reality from the supernatural.

First of all, Devin "exposes" the tricks of the Horror House ride. The first stage of the ride "rumbled with machinery that sounded dangerous (it wasn't) and stuttered with strobe lights of conflicting colors" (115). Erin demystifies the ride: "The dungeon part wasn't scary, because all the prisoners were Dobies," and the "bats at the end of the ride, how she knew they were just wind-up toys on wires" (118). And since neither she nor Devin sees the ghost, Tom's seeing it makes it convincing, since Tom is the self-proclaimed skeptic. "'Why me?' Tom asked plaintively" (120). The reality of his vision is explained when he can identify the colors of the dead girl's clothes and the "Alice band" that she wore, details that were not public information. "I'm just telling you what I saw," he tells them, unable to explain why they didn't see it as well. This also makes it clear that the "ghost" wasn't an official part of the ride or they all would have seen her. Tom's claim is rendered even more believable because he never speaks of it again "until about a month before he died, and then only briefly" (120–121).

Devin, the narrator, wants to see the ghost, "I hoped to see her. It would be a great story to tell Wendy" (42), but he doesn't. He goes back into the Horror House after the season has ended, hoping once again: "'Let me see you,' I whispered.... Wanting it to happen, hoping it wouldn't" (144). But "there was no ghost-girl holding her hands out to me" (144). He knows that something is strange because the air turns cold, but he doesn't see what he came to see. If he were truly "telling a story," he could have easily made that up—he is, after all, familiar with the registers of fiction. But he doesn't exaggerate. He also has mastered the registers of journalism and nonfiction as a staff writer at *Cleveland* magazine ten years after the events at Joyland occurred (135). Even when the girl is set free by Mike, the boy asks him if he saw her. "No, not even a little" (240). All Devin sees is her headband.

Devin also deals with the reality of psychic abilities, first with "Madame Fortuna," and later with the psychic child, Mike Ross. The fortuneteller is unmasked as being "Rozzie Gold ... just a Jewish mother," but "Madame Fortuna sees much." The carney fortune teller "act" is exposed in several places, "they are called *mitts* in the Talk, for their palmistry skills—[they] have their ways of picking your brains so that what they say sound like telepathy, but usually it's just close observation" (97). He explains that her crystal ball was "underlit by a small bulb Madame Fortuna could operate with her foot" (122); inside her tip box was "something that looked suspiciously like a punchboard (*not* legal under North Carolina law)" (123), which suggests she was making extra money by running illicit gambling games. And Lane Hardy, while admitting that she "told some people stuff that rocked them on their heels," also admitted that "ninety percent of her predictions are total crap" (108).

However, once the rules of the fortune telling game are exposed, Devin goes on to show that Madame Fortuna does have some psychic talent. She successfully predicts that his girlfriend would not be a lasting part of his life and that he would encounter a girl wearing a red hat and carrying a doll, whom he does save from choking to death on a hot dog. Since she thinks the Horror House is haunted, Devin, Erin and Tom put her to the test, and, as we have seen, Tom, the skeptic, sees the ghost. Devin puts her to one final test, and she knows what he is up to: "Actually, you want to know if I'm a fraud. Isn't that so?" (122). While Madam Fortuna's previous predictions might have been due to luck, insight, or fraud, she proves her abilities to Devin by handing him a printed note that tells him what he is going to do before he does it and how it will turn out. "She was right, I wanted to know if she was a fraud. Here was her answer. And yes, I had made up my mind about what came next in the life of Devin Jones. She had been right about that, too" (124). It is not surprising, then, when her final prediction comes true, that he will meet a boy with a dog and the boy would be an important part of his life.

Mike's grandfather, Buddy Ross, is another example of psychic ability of the Madam Fortuna variety. A wealthy televangelist, "his shows are half miracle healings and half pleas for more lover-offerings," according to Tina Ackerly, the librarian. Erin tells Devin:

> "My gramma listens to that old faker all the time! He pretends to pull goat stomachs out of people and claims they're tumors! Do you know what Pop Allen would say?"
> "Carny-from-carny," I said, grinning [171].

Carny-from-carny is, of course, another word for fake in carney language. And Devin is quick to note that "he didn't have any luck healing his grandson."

Mike, however, sees his grandfather in a different light. "Whatever I have, the special thing, I think it came from him. He heals people, you know. I mean sometimes he fakes it, but sometimes he really does" (186). The boy wishes his grandfather had been there when he freed the dead girl's ghost. "He would have seen her, and heard what she said at the end" (239).

The boy, Mike Ross, proves to be the real psychic, with the true powers of sight.

> What she [Madam Fortuna] had, I believed (and still do, all these years later), was some small but of authentic psychic ability amped up by a shrewd understanding of human nature and then packaged into glittering carney bullshit. Mike's thing was clearer. Simpler. *Purer.* It wasn't like seeing the ghost of Linda Gray, but it was akin to that, okay? It was touching another world [158].

"Sometimes I see things and sometimes I hear things," Mike explains (186). The boy "sees" the clues to uncovering the murderer of Linda Gray. He also knows that he must visit Joyland, not for himself, but for his mother, Devin, and the ghost of the dead girl. "We're going for *her* [his mother]. She'll know it when we get there.... And it's for you, Dev. But mostly it's for the girl. She's been there too long. She wants to leave" (187).

But even with this kind of psychic power, Mike doesn't understand everything. He thinks the girl is the reason he asked his mother to come live in the big house near Joyland. But his premonitions about "it's not white" make no sense to him or to Devin. Mike never suspected Lane Hardy was a killer. Devin asks him if he'd ever had a "vibe" about him and Mike says, "No. I liked him. And I thought he liked me," and Anne tells him that "even people with powerful intuitions can get fooled" (276). Mike did "see" the ghost of Eddie, who told him that his friend was in trouble, though. The power of the supernatural has limitations and not everyone has the ability to use it. Even for those who do, like Mike, there are limits. He was able to save Devin's life, but his grandfather, the faith healer, was unable to save his.

The novel ends with Devin much older and wiser, looking back on the years, and telling the story to us, his unnamed audience. He lists the things that happened to him like things on a list—he got his heart broke, saved a girl's life, and was almost murdered on a Ferris Wheel. He doesn't exaggerate or make himself seem a hero. Mike and Annie are the heroes in the end. He mourns the loss of good people and reflects on the injustice of life. He states it matter-of-factly—"The world has given me a good life since then, I won't deny it, but sometimes I hate the world anyway" (279).

Joyland, then, works on several different metalinguistic levels, all of which come together to show the difference between the truth and the artificial both in stories and in life. King uses a direct first-person narrator to connect with the reader, but unlike the narrator in "1922," Deven Jones is believable and reliable on many different levels. He has demonstrated his truthfulness both in his profession as a nonfiction writer and in his personal stories, where he does not exaggerate or try to make himself look good. The stories he tells ring of honesty. King is also able to show the truth of the story by using different registers, as Devin shows familiarity with the language of the journalist, the storyteller, and the carnival-insider. The use of different registers is much more subtle in this story than, say, in *Carrie*, yet it is less artificial and thus more effective. *Joyland* also dramatically shows the power of language. Knowing "private languages" gives one power over those who don't. This is true of the carney, the prison and the academy, and it is the reason that attorneys even exist. Anti-languages, a form of private language, exist to give power to those who don't have it—which explains why teenagers constantly invent new words each generation to describe, essentially, the same things, and why most of these words disappear and change as soon as the older generations learn their meaning.

From a thematic point of view, *Joyland* is really two parallel stories. The first and most obvious is the coming of age of Devin as he grows up during the time he spends working at Joyland. During these few months he learns about love, sex, human cruelty, and death. He comes to know himself through experiences that remain with him forever. He saves a child's life and someone else saves his.

On a second level, and related to the first, the novel examines the theme of dying as Devin befriends a child who is terminally ill. This theme is important in *The Green Mile*, where Coffey and other inmates await their executions on Death Row, and again in *End of Watch*, where Bill Hodges learns he has pancreatic cancer and his chances of survival are slim. But this theme is particularly poignant in *Joyland* because Mike is a child who knows he is dying and accepts his fate and tries to cherish every moment of his life while he can. This idea of making the most of our lives, no matter how much time we might have, runs throughout much of King's fiction, and Devin himself learns that valuable lesson from his friendship with Mike. As Devin shares his account with the reader, he is older and looking back, confronting his own mortality as, I suspect, everyone does when they reach a certain age of maturity. He has come to an acceptance of death, and he has learned to live life without fear and without regrets. Most of all, Mike has taught him the importance of really living and not just existing; until the very end, Mike's goal was to make people happy and make the world better. In the brief time that he has before his execution in *The Green Mile*, Coffey also makes the world better by curing a dying woman, and in *End of Watch*, Bill Hodges refuses to get treatment for his cancer until he completes the unfinished business of putting a stop to Brady Hartsfield's reign of terror.

The metalinguistic tricks in *Joyland* really add up to a single purpose in the book, and that is to tell a story that is totally believable, despite its fantastic elements. There are critics who look at the weird tale in terms of logic and believe that all the rules must be in place—vampires, for example, cannot tolerate sunlight, or silver bullets are the only way to kill a werewolf. There are some problems with this way of thinking, however. Perhaps most importantly, the rules have changed, as they have with the development of zombie stories from the time of Seabrook's *The Magic Island*, where zombies were the victims of voodoo, to more modern version of zombie pandemics such as Whitehead's *Zone One* (even vampires have undergone a major metamorphosis in Brian Lumley's *Necroscope* novels, where they become aliens rather than products of the supernatural). And some stories, such as Bradbury's *Something Wicked This Way Comes*, make no real attempt to explain the supernatural elements, either in scientific or mythological terms—we must merely suspend our disbelief, and when the story is good enough, we willingly do so. Most of King's horror stories fall into that category. He asks us to suspend our disbelief and, if we are willing to do so, he takes us on a ride through Joyland (or 'Salem's Lot, or Castle Rock, for that matter), and if we hang on, he will show us something about the human condition and perhaps even something about ourselves.

Such is the case with *Joyland*, the coming of age story of Devin, and the lessons he has learned from working at a theme park and meeting a sick child who would play such a major role in his life. King combines two genres in the story—supernatural horror and mystery—but in the end neither of these genre devices are what gives the book its power. We are not asked to explain either the ghost in the park or the psychic power of the child. Through the voice of a reliable narrator, we are simply asked to believe that it happened. *Joyland* is successful because of its insights into human nature, its insight into how we deal with lost love, and how experiences, both bad and good, help us to grow and mature. As he has done in "The Body" and *It*, King once again brings us back to a world where we were younger and looks back on it with mature eyes and an adult sensibility. It is, I believe, his greatest strength, his ability to remind us all about the lessons we have learned from the past.

CHAPTER 21

Revival: Cosmic Horror

Revival was published in November 2014 and was inspired by Arthur Machen's novella *The Great God Pan*, which King, on the dedication page, says has "haunted me all my life." Machen's story, originally published in 1894, like much of his fiction "deals with malign, elemental forces that destroy modern man when he comes in contact with him" (Stern vi). Machen had a major influence on H.P. Lovecraft, who wrote "Machen is a titan—perhaps the greatest living author" (*Selected Letters I* 134), and influenced the concept of cosmic horror that became Lovecraft's trademark. *Revival* picks up Lovecraft's cosmic horror theme and, using typical King modern prose, including brand names, slang, drug addiction, and rock and roll, transports the concept into the 21st century.

Lovecraft wrote that "the basis of all true cosmic horror is *violation of the order of nature*, and the profoundest violations are always the least concrete and describable" (*Selected Letters III* 174). *Revival* puts a twist on a common force of nature, electricity, and proposes an abstract form of energy called "*secret* electricity, that power which binds the very universe into one harmonic whole" (142). Like Coffey's power in *The Green Mile*, it is not clear where this secret electricity comes from—"he had no more idea of what it really was than a toddler has of a gun he finds in Daddy's closet" (170)—until the cosmic horror ending is revealed, and, even then, there is no exact scientific explanation. The power comes from a world of "insane light and colors never meant to be looked upon by mortal creatures" (*Revival* 381).

H.P. Lovecraft uses cosmic horror as a device to show the insignificance of mankind in the universe and at the end of *Revival* man is also shown to be insignificant in the cosmic scheme of things as, after death, we are all doomed to be suffering servants of the Great Ones, which, if they are the same "Great Ones" that exist in the *Dark Tower* series, are the "nastiest demons inhabiting TODASH space" (Furth 131). Yet King's view, dark as it is, is more optimistic than Lovecraft's. As I have shown in my critical study *Out of the Shadows*, Lovecraft's characters are one-dimensional and function mostly to move the plot and reveal man's insignificance to us. These one-dimensional characters work in his case because they are not very unique or interesting—the real character of the story is the cosmos and the powerful alien creatures it harbors.

In King's book, however, the characters are drawn as three-dimensional people with strengths and weaknesses, with distinct personalities and descriptions. The reader is made to like the characters and sympathize with them. Even the reverend who causes all of the chaos is sympathetic; after all, he lost his beloved wife and child in a horrible and senseless accident. The people in King's books matter. Although insignificant in the larger picture, they are *very* significant to each other in human terms. They have times where they show courage, fear, creativity, and weakness. Jamie, for example, makes a difference in the lives of others. He moves them with his music, falls in love and receives love, tries to lead a good life, and, at the very end, even makes time to do volunteer work where he can help others. He doesn't judge others, he accepts his gay brother, and he is tolerant of other religious beliefs. He cares about his family and his friends, and he even cares for the reverend. When he realizes that the pastor's cures have horrible side effects, he takes it upon himself to research the problem and try his best to stop it. Unlike the typical Lovecraft protagonist who is usually a stuffy academic, he is quite likeable. Finally, Jamie is the key element in what finally happens, the opening of the door to another reality. As the reverend tells him at the book's climax, "As for the connection ... it's *you* Jamie. Haven't you even guessed why you're here?" (374).

The dilemma that King proposes is as simple as it is complex: how do we make our lives count and make them meaningful and worthwhile in a universe (perhaps even a multiverse, which seems to be the foundation of Stephen King's fiction) where we are but insignificant specks? Jamie answers this question by wanting "to live as long as possible" (397), trying to be a "do-right daddy" (398), and taking care of his brother Conrad, who has suffered from insanity because of his "cure." Jamie says, "There is hope, therefore I live" (401). Despite everything, Jamie has hope, something that Lovecraft's protagonists never do. King's characters, on the other hand, hang on to life until the bitter end, and when they go down, they do so with a fight. This is a direct reflection of King's own beliefs and doubts. "I choose to believe in God because it makes things better," he says (qtd. in Greene 75). Yet he also admits that "uncertainty is good for things" (75).

The obvious subtext in *Revival* is the binary opposition of religion and science, and this is personified by the Reverend Charles Jacobs, the minister who preaches from both the Bible and from books on electricity. From a metalinguistic standpoint, it is important to note that the reverend has studied "forbidden" volumes such as "*The Grimoire of Picatrix*" and "*De Vermis Mysteriis*, which was supposedly the basis for H.P. Lovecraft's fictional grimoire, called *The Necronomicon*" (336). King uses a Lovecraft quote as the epigraph: "That is not dead which can eternal lie/And with strange aeons, even dreams may die." This couplet appears in "The Nameless City" (*Dagon* 99) and is attributed to "Abdul Alhazred, the mad poet" and author of Lovecraft's fictional tome *The Necronomicon*. In *Revival* the quote "was stolen from a copy of *De Vermis* which Lovecraft had access to." (337) *De Vermis* was actually not Lovecraft's creation but first appeared in Robert Bloch's short story "The Shambler from the Stars" in 1935, a story where Bloch fictionally "kills" his mentor, Lovecraft (who subsequently kills Bloch in "The Haunter of the Dark"). The mythical book, supposedly written by Ludvig Prinn, is called "the most dangerous book ever written," according to an antiquarian book blog cited in *Revival* (337).

The power of words, as we have seen, is a dominant theme in Stephen King's fiction. In previous chapters we have seen how words and writing bring life. In *Revival*, words also have the power to reveal truth and restore sanity. The novel is written in the first-person point of view of Jamie, who is writing the narrative "after the fact." He freely admits that he is under psychiatric care and that his psychiatrist "doesn't believe much of it" (388), which might make us question his reliability as a narrator. Despite his mental condition, however, Jamie does appear as a reliable narrator. "I remember a thousand other things, mostly good ones, but I didn't sit down at my computer to put on rose-colored glasses and wax nostalgic. Selective memory is one of the chief sins of the old, and I don't have time for it" (26). Jamie is true to his word as he writes the story. "I've told Dr. Braithwaite everything you've read in these pages. I've held back nothing" (388). Jamie doesn't make excuses for his drug addiction, but takes responsibility. He also takes responsibility for the role he played in the sins of Pastor Jacobs and feels that he has "a lot to atone for" (398). He tells the story in a straightforward way, and when there were times when he couldn't remember, he doesn't make up a narrative to fill in the blanks. Furthermore, he doesn't embellish the tale to make himself look good or to make the story more appealing. If he were writing a romance, he would have said that Astrid was still beautiful, despite the fact she was dying from lung cancer. "I wish I could, but if I begin lying now, everything I have told you so far becomes worthless" (312–13).

Jamie has several reasons for telling the story. First, he is using writing as therapy. Second, he is writing a cautionary tale, warning people not to experiment with "secret electricity." Finally, like Paul Edgecombe in *The Green Mile*, he is trying to comprehend the awful truth that he has experienced and make some sense of the universe.

Even though his psychiatrist doesn't believe his story—"The world's most brilliant confabulators are in asylums"—Jamie tells the story anyway: "what a relief in the telling!" (388). Unburdening his experience is one of the things that holds his sanity together, along with antidepressants. "That some of my sanity is gone forever—amputated, like an arm or a leg, by what I saw in Mary Fay's deathroom—is a fact I have learned to live with. And for fifty minutes every Tuesday and Thursday, between two o'clock and two fifty, I talk. How I do talk" (388–89).

Jamie also uses words and talk as therapy for both himself and Conrad when he visits his brother. "After my talks with Ed, I sit in the living room of my brother's suite and talk some more" (401). He tells Jamie about real things that are happening, but some of it is made up. "Our visits are monologues rather than conversations, and that makes fiction necessary. My real life just won't do, because these days it's as sparsely furnished as a cheap hotel room" (402). His fictions are harmless, though, about women he's supposedly dating and family life. He doesn't share the story of the reverend Jacobs with his brother, who he hopes will speak back to him one day—speech, words, are not only life but represent sanity. When his brother went temporarily mute as a boy, it almost drove him crazy, and when Jamie found him crying in his bedroom, Conrad exploded with anger (37). At the end of the novel, his mental condition is reflected in his inability to talk.

The second reason Jamie must tell his story is to help him understand and explain what happened and to articulate it as a warning to others. "It is hard for me to think of what happened next, let alone write it down, but write I must, if only as a warning for anyone else who contemplates some similar experiment in damnation, and may read these words, and turn back because of them" (378). While he tells his experience to his psychiatrist orally, he must put the story in writing as well, because writing makes things permanent. In this way, Jamie is very much like H.P. Love-craft's narrators, who must leave behind a written record as a cautionary tale. In "The Shadow Out of Time," for example, the first person narrator tells his story to "urge, with all the force of my being, a final abandonment of all attempts at unearthing those fragments of unknown, primordial masonry which my expedition set out to investigate" (*Dunwich* 368). This concept occurs in a number of other Lovecraft tales, including *At the Mountains of Madness* and "The Colour Out of Space." It is not a coinci-dence that many of Lovecraft's narrators also go mad after discovering cosmic truth. The opening line of Lovecraft's "The Call of Cthulhu" explains the madness that both Conrad and Jamie suffer from: "The most merciful thing in the world, I think, is the inability of the human mind to correlate all its contents" (*Dunwich* 25). When faced with a cosmic truth such as the reverend's victims have experienced, where the mind sees all of these contents correlated at once, the brain can't seem to handle the concept and insanity or suicide are the only options.

Jamie is also writing his narrative down in an attempt to discover and articulate the truth. "Writing is a wonderful and terrible thing. It opens deep wells of memory that were previously capped" (25). In exploring this avenue, he realizes the truth of what he has discovered—that reality is multi-layered. "Electricity is one of God's doorways to the infinite" (31), the reverend claims, and his "secret electricity" opens that door. Jamie struggles with the idea of whether the universe is governed by fate or ran-domness:

> Who is governing our lives? Fate or coincidence? I want to believe in the latter.... I can't bear to believe his [Charles Jacobs] presence in my life had anything to do with fate. It would mean that all these terrible things—these *horrors*—were meant to hap-pen. If that is so, we live in darkness like animals in a burrow, or ants deep in their hill [2].

As much as he wants to believe that life is random, however, his discovery of the Great Ones makes him fear otherwise. "Once upon a time I would have said we choose our paths at random: this happened, then that, hence the other. Now I know better. There are forces" (91). In the very first page, he equates our lives to the movies. "In one way, at least, our lives are like movies" (1), then elaborates: "In the movies this sort of character is known as the fifth business, or the change agent" (2). In Jamie's model, we are all under the control of the author, in this case, the screenwriter and director of the film, similar to the great powers that "authored" the world in *It* and the Gunslinger epic. Jamie, like most of us, believes he knows what reality is. The main horror in this story is when he learns that he does not. Hugh relates his experience in the revival tent, when he saw prism-like colors as the reverend healed those who came to him using the secret electricity. "It was as if I could almost look through the world, and there was another world right behind it. A *realer* world" (215).

At the story's climax, when the door to another reality opens and the Mother peers out and kills the reverend, those who were cured by the secret electricity all get a view into this other terrible universe. Most of them cannot handle it and either kill themselves or go insane. Jamie's brother Conrad, an astronomer who had discovered a "Goldilocks Planet" (79) possibly able to sustain life, cannot handle this reality, even though physics and astronomy have speculated on the possibility of multiple dimensions, wormholes, and alternate universes. Conrad loses his mind, and his voice, and he is institutionalized. This universe was beyond even what science could imagine.

Of course, a multiverse is a normal part of the Stephen King reality. We have seen this idea in previous stories (*It* and "Ur" are just two examples that I have discussed). And, as we have also seen, according to Wiater et al. and King himself, all of King's worlds are connected like spokes to a central hub, to the Dark Tower books. The threads between all of his books are everywhere. In *Revival*, even the amusement park from *Joyland* is mentioned (167), along with other local Maine landmarks. And the Great Ones, as we have seen, appear in the *Wolves of the Calla*, book V of the Dark Tower series as demons inhabiting *todash* space: "travelling *todash* is similar to the state of lucid dreaming. However, unlike lucid dreaming, both body and mind travel *todash*" (Furth 511); "*Todash* space is the void place between worlds" (Furth 512). This space contains "things in the darkness" that can eat people (King, *Wolves* 89), "looming shapes behind weird phosphorescent eyes, the sort of things you saw in movies about exploring the deepest cracks of the ocean floor" (90). These *Todash* demons also appear in "The Mist" where they leaked through a tear in reality created by the government (Furth 512).

To Jamie, the Great Ones appear as giant ants who torture their human slaves, who enter their world when they die. But to readers familiar with the Dark Tower books, it is obvious that the reverend's secret electricity is a way of entering this *Todash* space. And the "Mother" with a giant claw made from the faces of the dead, resembles the spider-like monster described in *It*, which also came from another universe. Jamie, of course, isn't privy to the Stephen King canon, so his mind cannot quite comprehend what he has seen.

If words and writing have the power to give life and to maintain sanity, they also have the power to hurt and destroy. And, in the hands of a man like Charles Jacobs, words become a tool to manipulate others.

On one level the Reverend Charles Jacobs represents the failure and fraud of religion, particularly preachers who use God as a tool to acquire fame, fortune, and power. As King has said, "My view is that organized religion is a very dangerous tool that's been misused by a lot of people" (Greene 74). While Charles Jacobs seems like a sincere man of God at the beginning of the novel, it soon becomes apparent that he is deceitful. Even the children can see through his parlor trick magic, with the mechanical Jesus walking on water. "'It's a big old fakeroonie,' Billy Paquette said to me one Thursday afternoon ... he was right" (23). After he was fired as the reverend, Jacobs worked in the Joyland amusement park doing tricks with electricity that looked like magic. "You went from preaching to huckstering?" Jamie asks him. He replies, "No difference.... They're both just a matter of convincing the rubes" (168).

Although he is no longer a reverend, Jacobs still uses religion as a way to get supporters who will finance his "research." He calls himself the "Evangelist C. Danny Jacobs" and invites the public to "witness God's power to change your life!" (197) in an advertising flier. He even twists the words of the Bible in the flyer, "God heals like lightening" (Matthew 24:27), which isn't about healing at all, as the verse states: "For as lightening that comes from the east is visible even in the west, so will be the coming of the Son of Man." Jacobs tells Jamie that he tricked his brother when he restored his voice. "I *conned* him. It's a skill they try to teach in divinity school, although they call it kindling faith. I was always good at it" (*Revival* 84).

Jacobs also knows how to use words to manipulate Jamie. Jacobs needs him to be the second key to unlock the doorway to *Todash* space, and he manipulates him by sending him the letter written by Astrid, who only has weeks to live unless the reverend heals her. Jamie realizes he is being blackmailed, but can do nothing about it, even though he tells Jamie the choice is his. "Astrid was a pawn. I, on the other hand, was one of the pieces in the back row" (299). Jamie has been manipulated in another way, though—Jacobs has fascinated him with his secret electricity. Jamie admits: "*I was also curious.* God help me, I wanted to watch him lift the lid on Pandora's box and peer inside" (338).

The reverend's words have also had a profound effect on his congregation when he preached "the terrible sermon," where he outlined the failure of religion: "religion is the theological equivalent of a quick-buck insurance scam" (73). When he finishes, forced to stop by the congregation,

Jacobs says, "'Nothing I say will make any difference, anyway.' But it did. To one little boy, it did." That sermon turned Jamie away from religion and ultimately led him to the end of the novel. It was a turning point in the boy's life, "the fifth business, a change agent" (1–2).

If religion has failed to explain the universe, science hasn't done much better in Stephen King's world. While religion has run amok in *Revival*, many of his books show science gone out of control. In "The Mist" scientists rip a hole in the fabric of reality and allow monsters to enter the world; in *The Stand* science creates a superflu that escapes and kills 90 percent of the world's population; and in *Firestarter* government agencies experiment with people, create deadly mutants like Charlie McGee and then try to capture her to use as a weapon. In the Gunslinger books, machinery breaks down, causing fatal malfunctions in the multiverse. Both religion and science are dysfunctional in King's fiction. Neither can explain the universe. The reverend admits that he doesn't understand "secret electricity" either from a scientific or a religious standpoint. And Conrad Morton, the astronomer, is driven mad when he experiences it. Jacobs tries to play both roles, first as a preacher, then as a scientist, and finally plays both roles in one, calling himself "Reverend Charles D. Jacobs, currently chief prelate in the First Church of Electricity" (212). Even in this role, he never understands the powers he is experimenting with, and they destroy him in the end.

Finally, we must examine the meaning of the book's title, *Revival*. On the one hand, it is a word for a religious festival or celebration where people find God, are saved, are "healed" and commit themselves to leading holy lives. The Reverend Jacobs has, of course, destroyed this meaning with his hypocrisy, as he holds revivals to heal people in God's name while no longer believing in God. The purpose of the revivals are to raise funds for his electrical research where, like a mad scientist, he hopes to communicate with the dead.

The other meaning for revival is to bring back to life. Jacobs hopes to learn the mysteries of death and the afterlife using his secret electricity, probably in the hopes of seeing his dead wife again and perhaps even bringing her back to life. We have already seen how this can go terribly wrong in *Pet Sematary*. When Astrid is cured, she mumbles something about a mother, "but not the one *you* want" (323). This revival of Astrid, who is almost dead, is a prelude to a reanimation of Mary Fay, who is dead, at the book's climax. By then the Reverend Jacobs has gone from being a man of God to a Dr. Frankenstein, who is meddling in science that is dangerous and unethical. Hence the dual nature of the word "revival" refers back to the extremes of religion and science—faith healing and uncontrolled scientific experimentation on things that should be left alone. We can contrast this to John Coffey's revival of Melinda in *The Green Mile*, which is successful because he reaches her before she is actually dead, and his motives are totally unselfish. One might wonder, however, if Coffey's apparent simplemindedness might not also be the result of secret electricity and a visit to the multiverse.

In *Revival*, Stephen King returns to his roots, supernatural horror in the vein of H.P. Lovecraft, Arthur Machen, Mary Shelly, Clarke Ashton Smith, and other giants of the genre who he names on his dedication page. He makes no apologies for being a horror writer and embraces his role as one of its leaders, someone who has taken horror and brought it into the mainstream, both as a commercial success, and, at a growing pace, a critical success. He has recently said, "To a degree, I have elevated the horror genre" (Greene 74) and that is no idle boast. The book has received positive reviews from the *New York Times*, *The Washington Post*, and *The Guardian*, which says:

> There are few writers able so effortlessly, so naturally and so intimately to lay out the details of a life. Perhaps that's why, when the book begins to slide away from our own reality, we're happy to follow where Jamie leads; we've been tricked, just like our narrator, into forgetting just what kind of a book this promised to be.

Indeed, King's strength in this novel is not only in creating horror, but, perhaps more so, in recreating the struggles of ordinary individuals faced with mundane life problems: drug addiction; loss of loved ones; growing old; financial problems.... Facing these everyday obstacles makes Jamie, and other characters like him, heroic in the word's true sense. Then, when faced with something truly horrible, it is easy for the reader to accept the supernatural and believe in whatever story Stephen King tells us.

King has effectively taken Lovecraft's concept of cosmic horror away from the stuffy academic narrators and placed it squarely in the hands of the average American citizen so that those of us who live in the real world of work and bills and love affairs may understand it firsthand as well. Lovecraft's concept is based upon the lack of characterization; if we are all just specks in the universe, then our personal lives certainly don't matter and, therefore, character development would contradict his theme. To King, though, the question isn't about how much people matter in the overall scheme of the universe, but how much they matter to each other *despite* their insignificance on the cosmic level. One theme in this book, then, is how we can *make* ourselves matter, and the answer is simple—by doing the right thing. In another theme, King once again revisits the opposition of religion and science and finds that neither camp provides any real answers. Organized religion is shown as a scam, and science seems ignorant of its own ignorance. Still, as Lovecraft has demonstrated in his stories, human beings are driven by an almost pathological curiosity that leads them to uncover secrets that can destroy them. The book is a cautionary tale, warning the audience not to play around with "secret electricity"; however, if King is correct about the way people behave, the narrative will, in fact, encourage them to pursue this forbidden knowledge.

Finally, in virtually all of his novels, Stephen King cannot help talking about words and the act of writing or communicating. In this novel, as we have seen in others, the telling of a painful story acts as a sort of therapy. By telling the story to others, and especially by writing it down, King's narrators are able to make some sense of their lives. We see this theme in "The Body," *The Green Mile*, and again in *Revival*, where Jamie is forced to come to grips with the realization that he is, indeed, a speck in an infinite multiverse. This realization is enough to drive one mad, but Jamie is able to carve out a place for himself, a place where he matters, despite the immensity of the cosmos. He matters because he has hope and because he is taking care of his brother. Jamie has, in essence, survived the hero's trip to the underworld and returned—and that is his revival.

CHAPTER 22

End of Watch: To Be or Not to Be

End of Watch, the third book of the Hodges trilogy (following *Mr. Mercedes* and *Finders Keepers*), was published by Scribner's in 2016 and received favorable reviews. The *New York Times* called the book "a great big genre-busting romp, a gloriously fitting end to the Bill Hodges trilogy" (Mina), and *Newsday* claimed that the book "gives us King at the height of his powers" (Wilwol). While the first two novels in the sequences were more traditional detective fiction—*Mr. Mercedes* won an Edgar Award from the Mystery Writers of America—this concluding novel finds its way back into the supernatural genre that King knows best. Brady Hartsfield, the architect of the Mercedes Massacre, has managed to wake up from his coma and developed telekinetic powers, which he strengthens until he can actually enter other people's minds and take over their bodies with the help of an electronic device and a video game. This psychopathic killer then orchestrates a plot to lure people, mostly teenagers, into killing themselves by putting them into a hypnotic state, then getting inside their heads and feeding them suicidal thoughts.

While this novel resembles King's earlier psychic novels (*Carrie* and *Firestarter*), it can also be thought of as a form of zombie novel, taking the zombie away from the now-familiar "walking dead" motif (which King himself used in *Cell*) and returning it to its Haitian roots where the zombie is an unwilling slave of a powerful sorcerer who uses magic or drugs to control his victims. As we have seen in the chapter on *Cell*, William Seabrook traveled to Haiti and his travel book on voodoo, published in 1929, launched the public awareness of the living dead, and inspired the first zombie film, *White Zombie*, in 1932. This initial zombie myth holds little resemblance to the flesh-eating zombie swarms that George Romero later brought into American popular culture. The original Haitian zombies were victims, resurrected from the dead to become mindless slaves to work on the sugar cane plantations.

> While the *zombie* came from the grave, it was neither a ghost, nor yet a person who had been raised like Lazarus from the dead. The *zombie*, they say, is a soulless human corpse, still dead, but taken from the grave and endowed by sorcery with a mechanical semblance of life—it is a dead body which is made to walk and move as if it were alive. People who have the power to do this go to a fresh grave, dig up the body before it has had time to rot, galvanize it into movement, and then make it a slave, occasionally for the commission of a crime, more often simply as a drudge around the habitation or farm, setting it dull, heavy tasks, and beating it like a dull beast if it slackens [Seabrook 93].

While Seabrook is reluctant to believe these supernatural stories, he soon has occasion to see one of the zombies for himself, and after consulting with a local scientist, he reaches the more logical conclusion that these so-called zombies have been drugged into an induced coma-like state that mimics death, then taken from the grave for use while still drugged into hypnotic state and drafted as workers. *White Zombie* took this one step further, and closer to home, so to speak, when the victim was a beautiful American woman who is drugged and zombified to be used, essentially, as a sex slave.

This representation of the zombie forms the prototype for Brady's victims in *End of Watch*. The constant reference to the letter "Z" (Zappit, Z-Boy, and Dr. Z) make this reference clear from the very beginning. Brady begins by inducing his victims into a hypnotic state not with drugs but with a video game that puts them into a trance. Then he invades their minds with his own, taking over their bodies and using them for his own purposes. His first victim, Sadie MacDonald, a nurse, is his experimental model; he is able to enter her mind as she has a mild seizure while looking out the window of his hospital room. After playing with her for awhile, entering her mind and walking around the hospital—even using her as a sex slave when he forces her to touch her own breasts (193)—he eventually begins to put thoughts into her mind and over a period of time he drives her to kill herself. His next victim, Al Brooks, does become his slave as he forces Library Al, Z-Boy, to discharge errands and do his dirty work, even forcing Al to drain his own bank account to do Brady's bidding. "Each time he got inside, his grip was stronger, his control was better. Running Al was like running one of those drones the military used" (200). Brady then turns to Felix Babineau, his neurologist, and makes him his unwilling zombie as well, taking over his mind and body completely once he realizes he no longer needs his own ruined body. The breakdown of Babineau's mind is a slow but steady process. "Every time he comes back to Babineau after being Dr. Z, there's a little less Babineau to come back to" (145).

The real zombification, however, occurs when Brady manipulates his victims into committing mass suicide. He begins with Barbara Robinson, Jerome's sister, who he uses as a "test subject" (141) and learns that he can control her. He puts her into a trance and tries to make her kill herself by jumping in front of a truck—only a lucky intervention by Dereece Neville saves her life. Barbara exhibits classic zombie-like behavior while Brady is controlling her. "She walks like a girl in a dream" (136) and Dereece describes her behavior as being "in a daze" (165). She, like the zombies of Haiti "plodding like brutes, like automations" (Seabrook 101), has no mind of her own and is merely following the directive of her controller, in this case Brady. Once Brady has practiced his techniques and perfected his suicide machine, he becomes quite accomplished at creating zombies who are all too willing to end their own lives.

In the traditional zombie scenario of Haiti, drugs were supposedly used to create zombies, but in an interesting twist in this story, Babineau's experimental drug is what turns Brady from a mindless zombie in a vegetative state into a mindful creator of zombies. Although there may be a question of the exact role that the drug played in the Mercedes killer's revival—Brady believes he came back to life completely on his own—without the drug, the neurologist would have had little interest in Brady once he's written him off as comatose. Furthermore, a writer as skilled with plot devices as Stephen King would not have mentioned the experimental drug at all unless he had a good reason. The drug provides a scientific explanation for Brady's rapid recovery and his sudden telekinetic talents, making them more plausible (though Johnny Smith, the protagonist of *The Dead Zone*, develops psychic powers after emerging from a four and a half-year coma). The drug also brings up the issue of experimental drugs in American society, both legal and illegal. Flakka, also known as "bath salts," was reported to have created cannibalistic zombie-like symptoms in its users, though this myth has since been debunked (Thompson). King also asks his readers to consider the role of the FDA and the pharmaceutical companies in medical discoveries and the possibility of unauthorized experimentation and unpredictable side effects. Had the drug not played a contributing role in Brady's recovery or in the theme of the novel, it would not have been needed as a plot device.

The real culprit in creating zombies, of course, is the electronic device, the Zappit, and its accompanying video game, Fishin' Hole (which, in a case of life imitating fiction, has been loaded on Stephen King's Facebook page as a trivia game about the Hodges trilogy). The game seems to already induce a trance-like effect, which Brady is able to magnify. "The idiots who had created this particular game had also created, certainly by accident, a hypnotic effect" (192). One study conducted by computer scientists in Brazil concluded that video games do cause players, especially children, to enter a semi-conscious state similar to that which King depicts in this novel:

> Automatic and rapid motor movements, elimination of conscious thinking and self-consciousness, and feelings of challenge stimulated by exact objectives leads us to characterize the player as an automaton: a machine that transforms restricted visual impulses into extremely limited motor movements [Setzer and Duckett].

Researchers have also observed that video games continue to affect the brain even after the player is finished, a phenomenon that psychologists have called "The Tetris Effect" (Sinicki), where subjects continued to look for shapes from the game (tetrominos) in the real world and even in their dreams. While these effects may be positive by increasing a person's spacial recognition, the phenomenon does show the power that video games may have on users. By enhancing the Fishin' Hole game and making it even more hypnotic, Brady invents a frighteningly effective suicide machine that not even Ruth Scapelli, the harsh head nurse, can fight off: "she resists, but not for long," the story says as Brady leads her to the kitchen and to her death.

If the game is powerful in an adult, it is even more so in teens, particularly those suffering from self-esteem issues and depression. Even Barbara Robinson, a well-adjusted teen, succumbs to it as Brady and the machine make her feel guilty about her being a black person who had privileges that the black kids in the gangster neighborhoods don't have. How much easier is it, then, to affect those who are already depressed and feeling bad about themselves? Brady knows that "everyone worries, and teenagers worry the most" (292) and that "ordinary fears, the ones kids like this live with as a kind of unpleasant background noise can be turned into ravening monsters" (294). Brady makes Ellen jump out of a window because she's worried about the SATs; he makes Jamie Winters kill himself because he's gay; and Jane Ellsbury overdoses on painkillers because she's obese.

Video games and electronics have been a concern of many people, and some have linked violent video games to mass shootings, such as the one in Newtown, Connecticut. The use of the electronic devices in *End of Watch* is similar to King's warnings about cell phones in *Cell*. In both novels, the "zombies" are created by electronic technology, the Zappits, the Fishin' Hole game, and the Zeethland web site. While the cell phone pulse may have been caused by terrorists or an out-of-control government, there is no question that the suicide epidemic in this novel is caused by Brady, a psychopath. The possibility of a psychopath or a terrorist (or both) obtaining and using technology has become part of a real fear that has resulted from the 9/11 terrorist attacks. The next major event could be electronic—the fictional "pulse" in *Cell*, or perhaps a malicious attack from a virus on the electronic grid or a nuclear power plant. Perhaps even more insidious is the issue of social media, which has been responsible for incidents of bullying too numerous to count—some of which have resulted in violence or suicide.

Perhaps what is more disturbing about Brady's attack is how quickly it can spread through the internet and could continue to spread even after he is gone. Bishop has termed this type of zombie story "the contagion narrative" (*American* 210) as a bio-virus. As Riley notes, "It is reasonable to suggest that more people have been affected by global *digital* virus pandemics than have been harmed by biological ones" (197) and that "digital viruses spread so rapidly we're relatively powerless to stop them." Bishop but also references a computer type virus in *Cell* (*American* 211). Once Brady's suicide "virus" is put on the internet and spread by teens through social media, it becomes a contagion narrative of its own as teens influence each other to commit suicide. "The ones who find it ... will spread the word on Facebook and all the rest" (303), Jerome says, and while Hodges doesn't understand how this will make kids kill themselves, Holly assures him that "teenagers are vulnerable to stuff like this."

While King is fictionalizing the problem of suicide using Brady and his Zappit, the problem is actually a disturbingly real one, real enough that he includes the real suicide hotline phone number in the book. According to the American Society for Suicide Prevention, suicide is the tenth leading cause of death in the United States, with more than 42,000 victims each year. The Jason Foundation statistics show that there are 5,400 suicide attempts made each day by teens in grades 7–12 and that suicide is the second leading cause of death among teens and college students. King cites figures of his own in the novel, figures that Brady used in a paper he wrote as a school project (288), and quotes a Raymond Katz, a "famous psychiatrist" who claimed that human beings are genetically programed to kill themselves. According to an internet search, however, there is no such famous psychiatrist, so either Brady made up information for his school report or Stephen King is having some fun with his readers. Regardless, King is addressing the problem of teenage suicide and is using the Zappit and the zombies it creates as a metaphor for social media, where cyberbullying is common. National Crime Victimization Survey data estimates that about 2.2 million ninth to twelfth grade students experienced cyberbullying in 2011 ("Cyberbullying"). Brady, the Mercedes Killer, takes cyberbullying to new levels with his enhanced Zappit-Zero and Zeethland web site, which convinces teens that they are worthless and that they should end their own lives.

The theme of life and death dominates *End of Watch*. The very first time we see Hodges he is in the doctor's office to learn the test results about the severe abdominal pain he has been suffering from. He worries that it might be something bad: "he's always afraid that they're going to find not just something wrong but something *really* wrong" (16). In order to create suspense and delay the answer to Hodges' test result, King inserts a text message that diverts the detective's attention, calling him away from the doctor before he can be given the bad news. But the reader learns soon enough that it will, indeed, be bad when the doctor remarks, "I love my job, but I hate this part of it" (21). Although Hodges gets caught up in a new case immediately, he still can't help worrying about his test results, though, and he purposely lies to Holly about them not being ready yet. He hides his concern from the reader, but he can't hide it from himself as he thinks "that an ulcer might be the best-case scenario. There's medicine for ulcers. Other things, not so much" (56). When the doctor's office insists that he come back the next day, he has a pretty good suspicion that something is terribly wrong, but he doesn't want to believe it. Once he learns the truth, it doesn't immediately sink in and he has the urge to laugh about it (95), and has to have time to think about whether he will accept treatment, and he again lies to Holly.

According to the American Society for Suicide Prevention, people over 85 years old have the highest suicide rate in the United States, presumably due to pain caused by health problems. Although Hodges is suffering from terrible pain, he never considers suicide as an option. He considers refusing treatment, but only because he doesn't believe it will do any good, and he puts off even making the decision because he still has been given an important case and feels a strong need to see the case through to its conclusion. He goes on a dangerous mission to find and kill Brady towards the end of the novel, but he never gives up. When he becomes Brady's prisoner and it looks like he's going to be killed, he doesn't give up hope, even when he wants to, when death would be the easy way out. "The pain is very bad and he would give everything he owns to get away from it ... he would give anything to just sleep, and sleep, and sleep. But he ... forces himself to look at Brady, because you play the game to the very end. That's how it works; play to the end" (402). Even though it seems that Hodges has nothing to live for except pain, he fights on. He is dying, but his will to live is strong. Later, once Brady is dead and the case is over, he agrees to the treatment, though the odds are stacked strongly against him. That is when he comes to the central insight of the book, that life is precious, and he understands the importance of living every moment as if it were his last. "And the thought that comes to him is too complicated—too fraught with a terrible mixture of anger and sorrow—to be articulated. It's about how some people carelessly squander what others would sell their souls to have: a healthy, pain-free body" (424). Ironically, Hodges, who is dying, desperately wants to live, while those who are young and living want to die.

This theme is introduced early in the novel as well, as we learn about Martine Stover, the woman who was paralyzed by the Mercedes killer when he ran his vehicle into a crowd of innocent people. As a paraplegic, she also seems to have nothing to live for and the detectives who investigate the murder-suicide assume that she wanted to die and enlisted her aged mother's help in carrying out a suicide pact. Martine's housekeeper can't believe that they committed suicide, though, and, in fact, speaks of them in the present tense, as if they're still alive: "they're *happy*.... You wouldn't believe it, but there's a lot of laughter in that house" (49). The detectives later find that it was the mother who killed her daughter and then herself because of the Zappit video game and not because her daughter was suicidal.

If we examine *End of Game* from a purely structuralist perspective, it is obvious that King is experimenting with narrative time through his use of verb tenses. The novel begins in a the traditional way, with the story told in the omniscient past tense, looking back on the day of the Mercedes massacre from the point of view of the paramedics who were the first responders to the scene. The reader settles into this traditional, comfortable method of storytelling for 11 pages. Then, as we see Hodges for the first time, the verb tense abruptly changes to the present tense, an unusual and unexpected verb tense for a novel: "a pane of glass breaks in Bill Hodges pocket" (15). As the novel progresses, the tenses change in a very predictable pattern. When we are in the narrative present, then present tense is used. When we are experiencing a flashback or backstory, the prose is written in past tense. Since all of Stephen King's novels are written in the traditional past tense, with the notable exception of *Black House*, written with Peter Straub, one must wonder why *End of Watch* is written in this nontraditional style.

In any form of art, structure and meaning are intertwined, and this is the case with *End of Watch*. Since the major theme of the novel is about life and death—and, more specifically, the preciousness of life and how each moment is to be treasured—the verb tense reflects this idea. By placing the narrative time in the present tense, the reader is forced to live each moment of the story as it happens, which, of course, is what Stephen King is telling us to do in our own, real lives. In fact, as we read the novel, we have no choice but to do as King says and live in the present as we make our way through the text. The flashbacks and backstory are memories that exist in the past tense. But the main story is told moment by moment, as it happens, not as something that has already occurred.

The use of the present tense also keeps the characters alive. As we have seen, Martine Stover's housekeeper spoke of the women in the present tense, even though they were already dead. This present tense keeps them alive for her. And since Hodges' treatment ultimately fails, writing about the hero of three of Stephen King's books in the present tense keeps him alive as well, at least until the very end, when Holly and Jerome speak of him in the past. Yet even their narrative time is in the present tense (425), because even with Hodges gone, life goes on, and these two characters have learned the lesson of treasuring every moment—even Holly has "Holly hope."

One final theme that *End of Watch* touches on is the idea of "privilege," a term that has become a part of American culture where it seems we are constantly told to "check your privilege." The Free Dictionary defines privilege as "a special advantage, immunity, permission, right, or benefit granted to or enjoyed by an individual, class, or caste" and "such an advantage, immunity, or right held as a prerogative of status or rank, and exercised to the exclusion or detriment of others." In *End of Watch*, privilege appears when Barbara Robinson, hypnotized by Brady's Zappit, finds herself in a poor, black neighborhood. Although she is black herself—"café au lait" (135)—she comes from a privileged black family who lives in a white neighborhood and has money. She is obviously out of place, and someone taunts her with the label "blackish" (137), the title of a popular television show about black people trying to act white. This is the trigger that Brady needs to get inside of her head and make her feel guilty for her privilege, guilty enough to kill herself. The guilt immediately eats into her: "she is blackish, a word that means the same to her as useless, and she doesn't deserve to live" (138). King deliberately uses a black female to highlight this theme in order to show that privilege isn't about race or gender but about advantages that people may enjoy simply because of where and when they were born. As the product of a loving, affluent family, Barbara no doubt enjoys more privilege than many white boys her age—in many ways she is more fortunate than Stephen King himself was at that age, since he grew up in a poor family and with an absent father. The point of this scene isn't to compare privilege, however. Rather, we are told not to feel guilty for advantages we have that have been come by honestly. Instead of feeling defensive or bad about ourselves, we are encouraged to get to know and help those who haven't enjoyed the advantages we have been given. Once Barbara is away from the influence of the Zappit, she becomes friends with Dereece and comes to understand his life.

End of Watch answers Shakespeare's age old question "to be or not to be." Using an innovative new type of zombie narrative, it explores life and death and, sometimes, what lies between. From its earliest days, the zombie story has served as an effective mechanism of social criticism, beginning with a critique of the exploitation of workers in *The White Zombie*. As Laudo has said, "the modern zombie took shape as a critique of science, or at least, an expression of anxiety surrounding the powers of scientific knowledge bestowed on humanity" (54). The zombies in *End of Watch* metaphorically critique the control of others by those in power, as Z-boy and Dr. Z become helpless slaves, and the danger of technology, since the suicidal zombies are created with the help of an experimental drug, an electronic device, a video game, a website, and social media. Rather than use a biological virus, such as that used in *The Walking Dead*, King postulates an electronic virus, both in *Cell* and again in *End of Watch*, where the suicide virus spreads electronically.

As we have seen, the book explores the irony of life and death in the characters of Hodges and in American teenagers. Bill Hodges fights for every moment of life and, despite enduring the unimaginable pain of pancreatic cancer, he fights on and never gives up. By contrast, teenagers who are young and healthy succumb to the suicide machine and take their lives. According to this novel, every moment of life is precious and is to be treasured, and no matter how bad things may get, there is always hope. Even Holly, who had attempted suicide twice in her past, understands this concept as she continues to have "Holly hope." The novel ends with her agreeing to enjoy a movie with Jerome and it ends in the present verb tense.

Finally, the novel warns about the dangers of feeling bad for oneself—whether this feeling comes from depression, a negative self-image, or guilt. The narrative recognizes these issues in our society, particularly among teens, and through the metaphor of the Zappit, foregrounds the threats that these negative emotions pose to our society. King graphically shows the cost of suicide in our culture where, as he says in the afterword, "the high rates of suicides—both in the United States and in many other countries where my books are read—is all too real" (432). His last word of advice, "things can get better, and if you give them a chance, they usually do," is a concise summary of what *End of Watch* is all about—the verb "to be," in the present tense.

Conclusion

Stephen King's work has been harshly criticized, and much of this criticism has come about because of his status as a best-selling author. Indeed, he has referred to himself in a self-deprecating way, as the "literary equivalent of a Big Mac and a large Fry." S.T. Joshi, generally considered one of the horror genre's most respected critics, doesn't think highly of King's work:

> King's writing, considered abstractly, is a mixture of cheap sentiment, naïve moral polarizations between valiant heroes and wooden villains, hackneyed, implausible, and ill-explained supernatural phenomenon, a plain, bland, easy-to-read style with just the right number of scatological and sexual profanities to titillate his middle-class audience, and subscribing to the conventional morality of the common people [Joshi 63].

Harold Bloom blames King for the dumbing down of America and was not happy with his winning the National Book Award. "The decision to give the National Book Foundation's annual award for 'distinguished contribution' to Stephen King is extraordinary, another low in the shocking process of dumbing down our cultural life" ("Dumbing Down"). According to Greg Smith, part of King's unpopularity with critics is because of bad adaptations of many of his films (334) coupled with the fact that horror fiction "has been traditionally maligned by the guardians of high taste, culture, and the public interest," a phenomenon dating back to the Puritans, who "eyed fictional tales suspiciously" and found "fictional tales involving supernatural happenings ... even more offensive" (337).

What Bloom and others also don't recognize, however, are the cultural and economic forces that influence publishing, the forces that would probably prevent a Faulkner or a Melville or a James Joyce from being published at all in today's market. "The conventionalizing forces of modern literature—the way, for instance, that an editor's policy and the expectation of his readers combine to conventionalize what appears in a magazine—go unrecognized," says Northrup Frye (96). However, popularity in and of itself should have no bearing on objective literary criticism. As Frye has said, "The simple truth that there is no real correlation either way between the merits of art and its public perception" (4). According to Waugh, popular forms

> not only are "appropriate" as vehicles to express the serious concerns of the present day, but are forms to which a wide audience has access and with which it is already familiar. The use of popular forms in "serious fiction" is therefore crucial for undermining narrow and rigid critical definitions of what constitutes, or is appropriately to be termed "good literature" [86].

Kelly Chandler notes that "the membrane between the high culture and popular culture is, in many cases, a permeable one" (113). In the afterword to *Full Dark, No Stars*, King himself makes an important distinction between his work and what he sees as literary fiction: "I have no quarrel with literary fiction, which usually concerns itself with extraordinary people in ordinary situations, but both as a reader and a writer, I'm much more interested by ordinary people in extraordinary situations. I want to provoke an emotional, even visceral, reaction in my readers" (365).

King is criticized for not having "real" enough characters. However, John Barth, considered a serious novelist by Bloom and other critics, admits that "the tragic view of characterization is that we cannot, no matter how hard we try, make real people by language" (qtd. in Ziegler and Bigsby, 38). Other critics, however, praise the strengths of King's characters. "One of King's strengths ... is based on a consistent understanding of how people think" (Bosky 217). King says that "bad writing usually arises from a stubborn refusal to tell stories about what people actually do—to face the fact, let us say, that murderers sometimes help old ladies cross the street" (*Full Dark* 366). In stories such as "A Good Marriage," *The Green Mile*, *Lisey's Story* and "The Body" (to name just a few), he does, indeed, tell what people actually do, and he does so in a way that helps the "Constant Reader" better understand and adapt to the world. In some cases, such as *Pet Sematary*, he uses the supernatural to enhance this meaning (really, what would you do if you could bring your dead child back to life?), and in others, such as "A Good Marriage," cold, harsh reality provides meaning enough (what would you do if you found out your spouse were a serial killer?).

Literary criticism has its place and obviously plays an important role in what is written and what is read. As Frye has said, "A public that tries to do without criticism, and asserts that it knows what it wants or likes, brutalizes the arts and loses its cultural memory. Art of art's sake is a retreat from criticism which ends in an impoverishment of civilized life itself" (4). While compiling a survey about English teachers' reactions to Stephen King, Chandler cites a case of an English teachers excluding him from the curriculum without even having read his works: "refusing to read King seemed like a point of honor, a figurative finger in the dike between popular culture and the classroom" (112). That is why it is important to apply critical theory to an author's work, and not merely make blanket statements about King's lack of characterization, or complain that "reading *Harry Potter* is not reading, and neither is perusing Stephen King" (Bloom, "Afterword" 207) without using at least some critical methodology to back up these judgments. On the other hand, a critic cannot proclaim an author's literary merit simply because the work is enjoyable. The process works both ways, and the judgments of a writer's "fans" are as unreliable as that of critics who are stuck in a Victorian past.

I believe that looking at a work through the lens of a linguistic-based critical theory can offer the kinds of insights necessary to judge a literary work, or the works of an author, and shed new light on their meaning and construction. The theories of structuralism, semiotics, poststructuralist, deconstructionism, and postmodernism, all developed from the pioneering linguistic work of Ferdinand de Saussure, have been proven effective in analyzing literary texts in a more informed, impartial manner than merely the likes or dislikes of an individual critic. And, though I freely admit that I do enjoy Stephen King's work, my intent was to analyze his fiction using established theory and to see where it led.

After extensively reading King's work and putting it to the test of critical literary theory, I believe much of the harsh criticism of his work is unjustified. While I admire and appreciate S.T. Joshi's work, especially on Lovecraft, Dunsany, and the weird writers of the past century, I must respectfully disagree with him when he says that King is just a "popular" writer.

Yes, Stephen King does speak to a "middle-class audience," which makes him the target for critics who may not understand the lower to middle-class culture of American society. King speaks to the "Constant Reader" rather than the academic, and in doing so he "take[s] a bright light, and shine[s] it everywhere" (*Full Dark* 366). He asks us to look into ourselves and confront tough realities and ask hard questions. He deals with real everyday problems, such as alcoholism, domestic abuse, bullying, mental illness, disease, suffering, and financial worries, problems that may not infect the ivy walls of Harold Bloom's Yale (irony intended) but which are a part of everyday life in the real world of real people. As Collings has said, he and other horror writers "have grappled with the fundamental societal problems we face today ... have explored these issues through the metaphor of the horrific, because AIDS, molestation, homelessness, physical and mental abuse, racism, sexism, and other frightening -isms of various sorts are indeed monstrous and horrific" ("King in the Classroom" 121).

One of the reasons I enjoy and admire King's work, and relate to it, is because he speaks to me, the son of a factory worker, educated in the public schools and in the state college and university system, not the Ivy Leagues. During my lifetime, I held every shit job imaginable (scatological reference intended): I was, at various times in my life, a farm worker, picking vegetables for a dollar an hour; a custodian, cleaning toilets for the factory owners after hours, and mopping up constant oil spills of the factory floor during business hours; and an assembly line worker in a factory I still refer to as "the Hellhole" that did, in fact, have terrifying machinery much like King's "mangler" that seemed, to me, to be just waiting to chop off a finger or a hand, or to grab me by a loose piece of hair and pull me into its jaws of spinning blades. I worked in retail, dealing with obnoxious, snobbish customers who thought they were better than me. I worked the graveyard shift as a phlebotomist at a hospital, where I saw death and tragedy and horror and mutilated people on a nightly basis in the ER (including a boy hit by a train, reminiscent of King's "The Body"). I worked as a high school English teacher (mercifully, for only a few months before my current university hired me in 1984, and which has been the best job I could have ever hoped for in my life) where students who wouldn't read would read Stephen King. I was a product of the public school system, where anyone with half a brain had to keep his head down and fly under the radar and not act too smart to avoid being picked on and bullied. I worked my way through state college (at many of those shit jobs I've already mentioned), and through graduate school at the state university—the Ivy Leagues didn't want any part of me, because I didn't have the right name, connections, or bank account, and, frankly, I'm better off for it—I think the state schools taught me more than I ever would have learned in the ivy-lined halls of Brown, and I'd still be paying off the student loans.

So, no, Stephen King probably doesn't speak to S.T. Joshi, or Harold Bloom, or the undergraduates at Brown, Harvard, or Yale. But he does speak to those who have attended the University of Maine, which held a conference in his honor in 1996, which I was fortunate enough to participate in and present a paper. And he does speak to the National Council of Teachers of English (he also spoke to the New England Council in the '90s, and I was fortunate enough to be in attendance for that as well), an organization that struggles to get students to read *anything,* and whose members find that while students will not read Shakespeare or Faulkner or even Lovecraft, they will actually buy a Stephen King paperback and read it. As Chandler says, "In an era when so many educators complain about how little students read, it seems senseless, even wasteful, to ignore an author whose work affects adolescents so strongly" (113).

Fortunately, I am not alone in my praise of King's work. Other academics are beginning to see beyond what Bloom calls the "sub-literary" genre of "Poe and H.P. Lovecraft" ("Afterword" 207) and are realizing that Stephen King does have something important to say about life and the human condition.

> By offering his readers quality narratives in which they can vicariously, through familiar settings and realistic characters who are set upon by culturally symbolic evils (supernatural or otherwise), escape perceived widespread American social corruption or be utterly decimated by it, King seems to provide a cathartic fictional outlet for a nation of people whose intense desire to live out the ideal of the self-reliant individual conflicts so glaringly with their being inextricably bound up in social reality [Smith 344].

While King may not reflect the culture of the Victorians, he does comment on the way life in today's modern world of brand names and technology.

> In his writing, King is encyclopedic ... recording all of the details of contemporary American life from the sublime to the ridiculous, or like those 19th century novelists drawn to both social realism and *copia* such as Theodore Dreiser.... King may well be read in universities next century for the reasons that Dresier continues to be read now [Bosky 210].

Anthony Magistrale has praised "the multi-leveled relationship between society and the self examined in *The Stand,* the moral implications of the dialectic between free will and determinism in *The Shining,*" and "the numerous mythological archetypes that are employed in *It*..." (*Moral Voyages* iii). And Michael Collings says that King's "story is based on terror or horror; yet invariably, beneath the horror lies an extraordinary talent for the tale well told" (*Many Facets* 14). Schuman says that "King is a master of plot and setting; a skillful and self conscious manipulator of the English language; a rather stern moralist; and a first-class creator of literary characters" (158). Chandler has used King's works in High School English classes and she notes that her students "have had diverse, insightful and provocative things to say about it.... I consider [these books] to be literature of merit. The themes are complex, the language is imaginative, and the characters are sharply defined" (114). In her dissertation for the University of South Florida, Jenifer Michelle D'Elia's intention was

> to find out if *The Stand* had the depth expected of a serious literary work—themes, imagery, symbols, a certain "arresting strangeness" and resonation with readers; that is, the things that a literary critic looks for when considering a text. In short, the answer is a solid yes. From considerations of politics and government to the nature of the soul and spirituality, King's novel covers a great deal of thematic material. His writing is filled with imagery that further expands his points, whether he is calling on readers' knowledge of Tolkien with his "red Eye" descriptions or the casual way he mentions a dead cat and a rat in order to suggest a litany of subtext. As for symbols, *The Stand* resounds with them, from corn to cars and dead electrical sockets to the full moon; each concept reminds readers of something else that further enhances their understanding of the story [149].

Stephen King's fiction has evolved as he has matured over the years, and as one of the world's best-selling novelists, he no longer has to worry about sales and royalty checks. While all of his books have been bestsellers, not all of them have been of exceptional quality, as King himself admits— "*The Tommyknockers* is an awful book" (qtd. in Greene 77). Then again, Hemingway had his *Over the River and Into the Trees* and still won the Nobel Prize. But King's best work rises above the typical genre novel, and, in some cases ("The Body," "Rita Hayworth and the Shawshank Redemption" and *Cujo*, for example), are not genre novels at all. And in his newer works, including *Lisey's Story*, which he considers his best novel, he has turned his attention to the serious questions in life and seems to be writing the kind of book that he wants to write rather than the kind of book demanded by his fans and publisher.

Despite the objections of some critics, Stephen King has begun to receive accolades, including the National Book Award's Medal for Distinguished Contribution to American Letters and the O'Henry Prize in 1996. Serious critical studies by serious scholars are being published about his fiction and theses and dissertations are being written about his work. His texts are discussed at academic conferences such as the Popular Culture Association and the International Conference for the Fantastic in the Arts. While some scholars may scoff and wish that Stephen King would go away and take his multiverse with him, it seems more likely to me that his reputation will grow with time, and his work will continue to be examined with new critical insight. As Chandler says, "I think we teachers need to quit taking the literary high ground. Trying to keep out the pernicious effects of popular culture is a losing battle" (113). I fully agree with this assessment, and would add that universities and literary critics need to follow suit and not exclude writers like Stephen King on the basis of his popularity and success.

Works Cited

Adkins, Dalya. "Christopher Marlowe Credited as One of Shakespeare's Co-Writers." *The Guardian.* 23 Oct. 2016. Web. 28 Oct. 2016.

Adkins, E. Stanton. "Pediatric Tectomas and Other Germ Cell Tumors." *Medscape.* emedicine.medscape.com. 28 April 2015. Web. 11 June 2016.

Alberico, Jennifer. "'The Word Pool, Where We All Go Down to Drink': The Irresistable Pull of Language in *Lisey's Story.*" *Stephen King's Modern Macabre: Essays on the Later Works.* Ed. Patrick McAleer and Michael A. Perry. Jefferson, NC: McFarland, 2014. 185–193. Print.

Anderson, James Arthur. "Morality in the Horror Fiction of Stephen King." *Studies in Weird Fiction* 22 (Winter 1998): 29–33. Print.

_____. *Out of the Shadows: A Structuralist Approach to Understanding the Fiction of H.P. Lovecraft.* Rockville, MD: The Borgo Press, 2011. Print.

Auerbach, Nina. *Our Vampires, Ourselves.* Chicago: University of Chicago Press, 1995. Print.

Austin, J.L. *How to Do Things with Words.* 2nd ed. Ed. J.O. Urmson and Marina Sbisa. Cambridge: Harvard University Press, 1962. Print.

Badley, Linda. "The Sin Eater: Orality, Post-literacy, and the Early Stephen King."

Bloom's Modern Critical Views: Stephen King. Updated ed. Ed. Harold Bloom. New York: Chelsea House, 2007. 95–123. Print.

Bailey, Julius H. "African Creation Myths." Lecture 26. *Great Mythologies of the World.* The Great Courses. Audio.

Barker, Ronald L. "The Role of Folktales in Place-Name Research." *The Journal of American Folklore* 85, no. 338 (Oct.–Dec. 1972): 367–373. Web. 18 June 2016.

Barthes, Roland. "Authors and Writers." *A Barthes Reader.* Ed. Susan Sontag. New York: Hill and Wang, 1982.

_____. "Change the Object Itself." *Image-Music-Text.* Trans. Stephen Heath. New York: Hill and Wang, 1978. Print.

_____. "The Death of the Author." *Image, Music, Text.* Trans. Stephen Heath. New York: Hill and Wang, 1978. Print.

_____. *The Pleasure of the Text.* New York: Hill and Wang. 1975. Print.

_____. *S/Z.* Trans. Richard Miller. New York: Hill and Wang, 1974. Print.

_____. "Textual Analysis of Poe's 'Valdemar.'" *Untying the Text.* Ed. Robert Young. London: Routledge & Kegan Paul, 1981. 133–161. Print.

_____. "Work to Text." *The Norton Anthology of Theory and Criticism.* Ed. Vincent B. Leitch. New York: Norton, 2001. 1470–1475. Print.

Baudrillard, Jean. *The Consumer Society:*

Myths and Structures. London: Sage, 1998. Print.

_____. *Simulacra and Simulation.* Trans. Shelia Faria Glaser. Ann Arbor: University of Michigan Press, 1994. Print.

_____. *The System of Objects.* Trans. James Benedict. London: Verso, 2005. Print.

Beahm, George. *Stephen King from A–Z.* Kansas City: Andrews McMeel, 1998 Print.

_____. *The Stephen King Story.* 2nd ed. Kansas City: Andrews and McMeel, 1992. Print.

Bellipanni, Jason. *The Naked Story: Fiction about Fiction, a Concise Guide to Metafiction.* Mount Vernon, NH: Story Review Press, 2013.

Bishop, Kyle William. *American Zombie Gothic.* Jefferson, NC: McFarland, 2010. Print.

_____. *How Zombies Conquered Popular Culture.* Jefferson, NC: McFarland. 2015. Print.

Blackwood, Algernon. "The Wendigo." *Ancient Stories and Other Weird Stories.* Ed. S.T. Joshi. New York: Penguin, 2002. Print.

Bloom, Harold. "Afterword." *Bloom's Modern Critical Views: Stephen King.* Updated ed. Ed. Harold Bloom. New York: Chelsea House, 2007. 207–208. Print.

_____. "Dumbing Down American Readers." *The Boston Globe.* Boston.com. 24 Sept. 2003. Web. 3 Oct. 2014.

Bosky, Bernadette Lynn. "The Mind's Monkey: Character and Psychology in Stephen King's Recent Fiction." *Kingdom of Fear: The World of Stephen King.* Ed. Tim Underwood and Chuck Miller. San Francisco: Underwood-Miller, 1986. 209–238. Print.

Brown, Stephen P. "The Life and Death of Richard Bachman: Stephen King's Doppelganger." *Kingdom of Fear.* Ed. Tim Underwood and Chuck Miller. San Francisco: Underwood-Miller, 1986. 109–128. Print.

Buchanan, Ian. *Oxford Dictionary of Critical Theory.* Oxford: Oxford University Press, 2010. Print.

Burns, Robert. "Ode to a Mouse." *The Poetry Foundation.* 2016. Web. 29 June 2016.

Campbell, Joseph. *The Hero with a Thousand Faces.* 3rd ed. Novato, CA: New World Library, 2008. Print.

_____. *The Power of Myth.* New York: Anchor Books, 1991 Print.

Carter, Bill. "ABC Cancels a Planned Reality Show." *The New York Times.* 22 Oct. 2001. Web. 16 Oct. 2014.

Chandler, Kelly. "Canon Construction Ahead." *Reading Stephen King: Issues of Censorship, Student Choice, and Popular Literature.* Ed. Brenda Muller Power, et al. Urbana: NCTE, 1997. 105–111. Print.

Charles, Ron. "Art of Darkness." *The Washington Post.* 29 Oct. 2006. Web 02 Dec. 2014.

Charney, Noah. "Charles Baxter: How I Write." *The Daily Beast.* 7 Aug. 2013. Web. 4 Oct. 2014.

Chlipala, Adam. "The Ur Programming Language Family." UR/Web. Impredicative.com. Web. 20 Oct. 2014.

Chomsky, Noam. "From Aspects of the Theory of Syntax." *Critical Theory Since 1965.* Ed. Hazard Adams and Leory Searle. Tallahassee: Florida State University Press, 1990. 40–55. Print.

_____. "Language and the Problems of Knowledge." *The Philosophy of Language.* 5th ed. Ed. A.P. Martinich. New York: Oxford University Press, 2008. 678–92. Print.

Clarke, A.C. *The Nine Billion Names of God.* New York: Signet, 1974. Print.

Collings, Michael R. "*Bag of Bones*: A Review." *Stephen King From A to Z.* Ed. George Beahm. Kansas City: Andrews McMeel, 1998. 12–15. Print.

_____. "King in the Classroom." *Reading Stephen King: Issues of Censorship, Student Choice, and Popular Literature.* Ed. Brenda Muller Power, et al. Urbana: NCTE, 1997. 117–125. Print.

_____. *The Many Facets of Stephen King.* Rockville, MD: Wildside Press, 2006. Print.

"Cyberbullying and Social Media." Megan Meier Foundation. 2016. Web. 26 June 2016.

D'Elia, Jenifer Michelle. *Standing up with the King: A Critical Look at Stephen King's Epic.* Dissertation, University of South Florida, 2007. Scholarcommons. usf.edu. Web. 2 Jan. 2015.

De Lint, Charles. "Books to Look For." *The Magazine of Fantasy & Science Fiction.* Feb. 1999. Web. 27 Nov. 2014.

De Man, Paul. *Allegories of Reading.* New Haven: Yale University Press, 1982. Print.

Derrida, Jacques. *Of Grammatology.* Trans. Gayatri Chakravorty Spivak. Baltimore: Johns Hopkins, 1997. Print.

Dick, Philip K. *The Simulacra.* New York: Vintage, 2002. Print.

Dowling, David. "Dreams Deferred: Ambition and the Mass Market in Melville and King." *Journal of Popular Culture* 44, no. 5 (Oct. 2011). SPORTDiscus. Web.

Dymond, Erica Joan. "An Examination of the Use of Gendered Language in Stephen King's CARRIE." *The Explicator* 71, no. 2 (2013): 94–98. *Academic Search Complete.* Electronic.

Dyson, Cindy. "Biography of Stephen King." *Bloom's Bio-Critiques: Stephen King.* Philadelphia: Chelsea House, 2002. Print.

Eads, Sean. "The Vampire George Middler: Selling the Monstrous in *'Salem's Lot.*" *Journal of Popular Culture* 43, no. 1 (2010): 78–96. *Academic Search Complete.* Web. 25 May 2016.

Eco, Umberto. *Travels in Hyperreality.* Trans. William Weaver. New York: Harcourt Brace, 1986. Print.

Fielder, Leslie. *Freaks: Myths & Images of the Secret Self.* New York: Simon & Schuster, 1978. Print.

Findley, Mary. "The World at Large, America in Particular: Cultural Fears and Societal Mayhem in King's Fiction Since 1995." *Stephen King's Modern Macabre: Essays on the Later Works.* Ed. Patrick McAleer and Michael Perry. Jefferson, NC: McFarland, 2014. 56–63. Print.

Fishoff, Stuart, et al. "The Psychological Appeal of Movie Monsters." *Journal of Media Psychology* 10, no. 3 (2005). Web. 26 May 2016.

Flood, Alison. "Readers Prefer Authors of Their Own Sex, Survey Finds." *The Guardian.* 25 Nov. 2016. Web. 8 June 2016.

———. "Stephen King Tells US to 'Cool the Clown Hysteria' After Wave of Sightings." *The Guardian.* 6 Oct. 2016. Web. 20 Oct. 2016.

Foucault, Michael. "What Is an Author?" *The Norton Anthology of Theory and Criticism.* Ed. Vincent B. Leitch. New York: Norton, 2001. 1622–1636. Print.

Fowler, Roger. *Linguistic Critism* 2nd ed. Oxford. Oxford Press, 1996. Print.

Fromkin, Victoria A., et al. *Linguistics: An Introduction to Linguistic Theory.* Malden, MA: Blackwell, 2000. Print.

Frye, Northrup. *Anatomy of Criticism.* First paperback ed. Princeton: Princeton University Press, 1971. Print.

Furth, Robin. *Stephen King's The Dark Tower: The Complete Concordance, Revised and Updated.* New York: Scribner, 2012. Print.

Genette, Gerard. *Narrative Discourse.* Ithaca: Cornell University Press, 1983. Print.

Goldman, David. "Your Smartphone Will (Eventually) Be Hacked." *CNN.* 17 Sept. 2012. Web. 27 Dec. 2014.

Grace, Dominick. "Writers and Metafiction in Three Stephen King Texts." *Critical Insights: Stephen King.* Ed. Gary Hoppenstand. Pasadena: Salem Press, 2011. 61–77. Print.

Greene, Andy. "Reader's Poll: The 10 Best Stephen King Books." RollingStone.com. 5 Nov. 2014. Web. 5. Nov. 2014.

———. "Stephen King: The *Rolling Stone* Interview." *Rolling Stone.* 6 Nov. 2014. 72–79. Print.

Hacker, Robert "Publix Marketing Strategy Changes for the Worse." *Sophisticated Finance.* 6 Jan. 2014. Web. 21 Dec. 2014.

Halliday, Mak. "Anti-Languages." *American Anthropologist* 78, no. 3 (Oct. 2009): 570–584. Web. 31 Dec. 2014.

Halliday, Mak, Angus McIntosh, and Peter Strevens. *The Linguistic Sciences and Language Teaching.* London: Longman, 1965. Print.

Heidegger, Martin. *Being and Time.* New York: Harper, 1962. Print.

———. "Language." *The Norton Anthology of Theory and Criticism.* Ed. Vincent B. Leitch. New York: Norton, 2001. 1121–1134. Print.

———. *On the Way to Language.* Trans. Peter D. Hertz. New York: Harper & Row, 1982. Print.

Heldreth, Leonard G. "The Ultimate Horror: The Dead Child in Stephen King's

Stories and Novels." *Discovering Stephen King*. Ed. Darrell Schweitzer. Mercer Island, WA: Starmont House, 1985. 141–152. Print.

Hemingway, Ernest. *A Moveable Feast*. Restored ed. New York: Scribner, 2009. Print.

Herron, Don. "King: The Good, the Bad and the Academic." *Kingdom of Fear: The World of Stephen King*. Ed. Tim Underwood and Chuck Miller. San Francisco: Underwood-Miller, 1986. 129–157. Print.

Hesiod. *Theogony and Works and Days*. Trans. M.L. West. Oxford: Oxford University Press, 2008. Print.

Hilburn, Matthew. "Cyberattacks on Rights Group Likely Linked to Islamic State." *Voice of America*. 27 Dec. 2014. Web. 27 Dec. 2014.

Hohne, Karen A. "The Power of the Spoken Word in the Works of Stephen King." *Journal of Popular Culture* 28, no. 2 (Fall 1994): 93–103. *Academic Search Complete*. Electronic.

Indick, Ben. "What Makes Him So *Scary*?" *Discovering Stephen King*. Ed. Darrell Schweitzer. Mercer Island, WA: Starmont House, 1985. 9–14. Print.

Jameson, Fredric. *The Prison-House of Language*. Princeton: Princeton University Press, 1972. Print.

Janicker, Rebecca. "'It's my house, isn't it?' Memory, Haunting, and Liminality in Stephen King's *Bag of Bones*." *European Journal of American Culture* 29, no. 3 (2010): 183–195. *Academic Search Complete*. Electronic.

Johnstone, Barbara. *Discourse Analysis*. 2nd ed. Malden, MA: Blackwell, 1008. Print.

Jones, Louis Thomas. *The Quakers of Iowa*. Transcribed by Elaine Rathmann. Iowa History Project. Part V, Section IV "Quaker Manners and Customs." Iagenweb.org. 1914. Web. 22 Sept. 2014.

Joshi, S.T. *The Modern Weird Tale*. Jefferson, NC: McFarland, 2001. Print.

Jung, Carl Gustav. "On the Relation of Analytical Psychology to Poetry." *Critical Theory Since Plato*. New York: Harcourt Brace, 1971. 810–818. Print.

Keyser, Wayne N. "Carny Lingo." www.goodmagic.com. N.d. Web. 31 Dec. 2014.

Kid, James. Rev. of *Mr. Mercedes* by Stephen King. *The Independent*. 8 June 2014. Web. 22 Dec. 2014.

King, Stephen. "Acceptance Speech." *National Book Award Acceptance Speeches*. National Book Award Foundation, 2003. Web. 7 Sept. 2014.

_____. *Bag of Bones*. New York: Scribner, 1998. Print.

_____. *The Bazaar of Bad Dreams*. New York: Scribner, 2015. Print.

_____. "CBS This Morning." CBS.com. 7 June 2016. Web. 7 June 2016.

_____. *Cell*. New York: Scribner, 2006. Print.

_____. *Coffey on the Mile*. New York: Signet, 1996. Print.

_____. *The Dark Half*. New York: Viking, 1989. Print.

_____. *Different Seasons*. New York: Signet. 1998. Print.

_____. *11/22/63*. New York: Scribner, 2011. Print.

_____. *End of Watch*. New York: Scribner, 2016. Print.

_____. *Four Past Midnight*. New York: Viking, 1990. Print.

_____. *Full Dark, No Stars*. New York: Scribner, 2010. Print.

_____. *The Green Mile*. New York: Pocket Books, 1996. Print.

_____. "Introduction." *The Best American Short Stories 2007*. Ed. Stephen King and Heidi Pitlor. Boston: Houghton Mifflin, 2007. xiii–xvii. Print.

_____. *It*. New York: Signet, 1987. Print.

_____. *Joyland*. London: Titan Books, 2013. Print.

_____. *Lisey's Story*. New York: Scribner, 2006.

_____. *Misery*. New York: Signet, 1988. Print.

_____. *Needful Things*. New York: Viking, 1991. Print.

_____. *Nightshift*. New York: Signet, 1979. Print.

_____. "On Becoming a Brand Name." *Adelina*. Feb. 1980. Print.

_____. *On Writing*. New York: Scribner, 2000. Print.

_____. *Pet Sematary*. New York: Signet. 1984. Print.

_____. *Revival*. New York: Scribner, 2014. Print.

_____. *The Running Man*. In *The Bach-

man Books. New York: Plume, 1985. Print.

_____. *Skeleton Crew.* New York: Signet, 1983. Print.

_____. "Stephen King on the Kindle and the iPad." *Entertainment Weekly.* 26 March 2010. Web. 18 Oct. 2014.

_____. *Three Novels: Carrie; 'Salem's Lot; and The Shining.* New York: Random House, 2011. Print.

_____. *The Two Dead Girls.* New York: Signet, 1996. Print.

_____. *Ur.* New York: Ralph M. Vicinanza Ltd., 2009. Electronic.

_____. *Wolves of the Calla.* New York: Pocket Books, 2006. Print.

Klein, Amy. "Woman Sues Author Stephen King Again." *Sun Sentinel.* 20 June 2005. Web.

Kripke, Saul. *Naming and Necessity.* Rev. paperback ed. Malden, MA: Blackwell, 1981. Print.

Lant, Kathleen Margaret. "The Rape of the Constant Reader: Stephen King's Construction of the Female Reader and Violation of the Female Body in *Misery.*" *Bloom's Modern Critical Views: Stephen King.* Ed. Harold Bloom. New York: Chelsea House, 2007. 141–166. Print.

Leach, Maria, and Jerome Fried, eds. *Standard Dictionary of Folktale, Mythology, and Legend.* New York: HarperCollins, 1984. Print.

Lee, Benjamin. *Talking Heads: Language, Metalanguage, and the Semiotics of Subjectivity.* Durham: Duke University Press, 1997. Print.

Lehmann-Haupt, Christopher. "*Bag of Bones*: Death, Torture, and Writer's Block." *The New York Times.* 21 Sept. 1998. Web. 2 Dec. 2014.

Lehmann-Haupt, Christopher, and Nathaniel Rich. "The Art of Fiction No. 189." *The Paris Review.* Fall 2006. Web. 22 Dec. 2014.

Lewis, Jordan Gaines. "Brain Babble: Why Are Clowns Scary?" *Psychology Today.* 30 Oct. 2012. Web. 5 Nov. 2014.

Lovecraft, H.P. *The Dunwich Horror and Others.* Corrected Tenth Printing. Ed. S.T. Joshi. Sauk City, WI: Arkham House, 1963. Print.

_____. *Selected Letters Vol. I: 1911–1924.* Ed. August Derleth and Donald Wan-

dari. Sauk City, WI: Arkham House, 1965. Print.

_____. *Selected Letters Vol. III: 1929–1931.* Ed. August Derleth and Donald Wandari. Sauk City, WI: Arkham House, 1971. Print.

_____. "Supernatural Horror in Literature." *Dagon and Other Macabre Tales.* Corrected Sixth Printing. Ed. S.T. Joshi. Sauk City, WI: Arkham House, 1965. 365–436. Print.

Lyotard, Jean-François. *The Lyotard Reader.* Ed. Andrew Benjamin. Oxford: Basil Blackwell, 1991. Print.

_____. *The Postmodern Condition: A Report on Knowledge.* Trans. Geoff Bennington and Brian Massumi. Minneapolis: University of Minnesota, 1991, 2000. Print.

Macherey, Pierre. *A Theory of Literary Production.* Trans. Geoffrey Wall. Routledge: London, 1978. Print.

Magistrale, Anthony. *Hollywood's Stephen King.* New York: Palgrave, 2003. Print.

_____. *Landscape of Fear: Stephen King's American Gothic.* Bowling Green, OH: Bowing Green State University Popular Press, 1988. Print.

_____. *The Moral Voyages of Stephen King.* Rockville, MD: Wildside Press, 2006. Print.

_____. *Stephen King: The Second Decade, Danse Macabre to The Dark Half.* New York: Twayne, 1992. Print.

Maglio, Tony. "Ben Affleck, Matt Damon Revive Reality Show 'The Runner' for Verizon." *The Wrap.* 16 March 2016. Web. 6 Dec. 2016.

Matthews, P.H. *The Concise Oxford Dictionary of Linguistics.* 3rd ed. Oxford: Oxford University Press, 2014. Print.

McAleer, Patrick. "The Fallen King(dom): Surviving Ruin and Decay from *The Stand* to *Cell.*" *Stephen King's Modern Macabre Essays on the Later Works.* Ed. Patrick McAleer and Michael Perry. Jefferson, NC: McFarland, 2014. 168–184. Print.

McKay, Brett, and Kate. "Fiction for Men as Suggested by Art of Manliness Readers." *The Art of Manliness.* 21 May 2013. Web. 29 April 2016.

McRobbie, Linda Rodriguez. "The History and Psychology of Clowns Being Scary."

Smithsonian.com. 31 July 2013. Web. 5. Nov. 2014.

Mina, Denise. Rev. of *End of Watch*. by Stephen King. *The New York Times*. 10 June 2016. Web. 25 June 2016.

Minzesheimer, Bob. "Horror's Home Run King Bats Again." *USA Today*. 2 Dec. 1999. Web. 27 Nov. 2014.

Murphy, Shaunna. "Stephen King Explains Why He Chose to Write the Screenplay for 'A Good Marriage.'" *MTV News*. MTV.com. 3 Oct. 2014. Web.

Mustazza, Leonard. "Poe's 'The Masque of the Red Death' and King's *The Shining*: Echo, Influence, and Deviation." *Discovering Stephen King's "The Shining."* Ed. Tony Magistrale. Rockville, MD: Wildside Press, 2006. 62–73. Print.

Nash, Jessie W. "Postmodern Gothic: Stephen King's Pet Sematary." *Bloom's Modern Critical Views: Stephen King*. Ed. Harold Bloom. New York: Chelsea House, 2007. 167–176. Print.

Norman, Howard. Trans. *Where the Chill Came From: Cree Windigo Tales and Journeys*. San Francisco: North Point Press, 1982. Print.

Perry, Michael A. "King Me: Inviting New Perceptions and Purposes of the Popular and Horrific into the College Classroom." *Stephen King's Modern Macabre Essays on the Later Works*. Ed. Patrick McAleer and Michael Perry. Jefferson, NC: McFarland, 2014. 24–40. Print.

Phillips, Gyllian. "*White Zombie* and the Creole: William Seabrook's *The Magic Island* and American Imperialism in Haiti." *Generation Zombie: Essays on the Living Dead in Modern Culture*. Ed. Stephanie Boluk and Wylie Lenz. Jefferson, NC: McFarland, 2011. 27–40. Print.

Pinker, Steven. *The Language Instinct*. New York: Harper, 2007. Print.

Plimpton, George. "Ernest Hemingway: The Art of Fiction No 21." *The Paris Review* 18 (Spring 1958). Web. 4 Oct. 2014.

Poe, Edgar Allan. *The Portable Poe*. New York: Viking, 1973. Print.

Rainie, Lee. "Cell Phone Ownership hits 91% of Adults." *PEW Research Center*. 6 June 2013. Web. 26 Dec. 2014.

Redfern, Nick, and Brad Steiger. *The Zombie Book: The Encyclopedia of the Living Dead*. Detroit: Visible Ink Press, 2015. Print.

"Revival by Stephen King Review—Stephen King Returns to the Horror Genre." *The Guardian*. TheGuardian.com. 7 Nov. 2014. Web. 16 Nov. 2014.

Riley, Brendan. "The E-Dead: Zombies in the Digital Age." *Generation Zombie: Essays on the Living Dead in Modern Culture*. Ed. Stephanie Boluk and Wyle Lenz. Jefferson, NC: McFarland, 2011. 194–205. Print.

Ringel, Faye. *New England's Gothic Literature: History and Folklore of the Supernatural from the Seventeenth Through the Twentieth Centuries*. Lewiston, NY: Edwin Mellen Press. 1995. Print.

Rodale, Maya. "The Real Men Who Read Romance Novels." *Huffington Post*. 4 April 2016. Web. 8 June 2016.

Rogak, Lisa. *The Life and Times of Stephen King*. New York: St. Martin's, 2009. Print.

Rousseau, Jean-Jacques. *On the Origin of Language*. Trans. John H. Moran. Chicago: University of Chicago Press, 1986. Print.

Ruggiero, Paul, and Jon Foote. "Cyber Threats to Mobile Phones." *US-CERT*. n.d. Web. 27. Dec. 2014.

Russell, Sharon. "Needful Things (1991)." *Bloom's Modern Critical Views: Stephen King*. Updated ed. Ed. Harold Bloom. New York: Chelsea House, 2007. 125–139. Print.

_____. *Revisiting Stephen King: A Critical Companion*. Westport, CT: Greenwood Press, 2002. Print.

Sanders, Joe Sutliff. "Closure and Power in 'Salem's Lot." *Journal of the Fantastic in the Arts* 10, no. 2 (1999): 142–154. *K-State Research Exchange*. Web. 25 May 2016.

Saussure, Ferdinand de. *Course in General Linguistics*. Ed. Charles Bally and Albert Sechehaye. Trans. Roy Harris. Chicago: Open Court, 1972. Print.

Schuman, Samuel. "Taking King Seriously: Reflections on a Decade of Best-Sellers. *Critical Insights: Stephen King*. Ed. Gary Hoppenstand. Pasadena: Salem Press, 2011. 157–167. Print.

Seabrook, William. *The Magic Island*. Mineola, NY: Dover, 2016, Print.

Searle, John R. *Speech Acts: An Essay in*

the Philosophy of Language. 27th Printing. Cambridge: Cambridge University Press, 2005. Print.

Setzer, Valdema W., and George E. Duckett. "The Risks to Children Using Electronic Games." *Institudo de Matemata e Estatistica*, 1993, updated 18 Jan. 2006. Web. 25 June 2016.

Sinicki, Adam. "What Is the Tetris Effect." *Healthguidance.org.* 2016. Web. 26 June 2016.

Smith, Greg. "The Literary Equivalent of a Big Mac and Fries? Academics, Moralists, and the Stephen King Phenomenon." *Midwest Quarterly* 43, no. 4 (Summer 2002): 329–345. *Academic Search Complete.* Electronic.

Snow, Shane. "This Surprising Reading Level Analysis Will Change the Way You Write." Contently.com. 28 Jan. 2015. Web. 8 June 2016.

Spender, Stephen. "All Life Was Grist for the Artist." *The New York Times.* 25 Oct. 1959. Web. 4 Oct. 2014.

Spignesi, Stephen. *The Complete Stephen King Encyclopedia.* Chicago: Contemporary Books, 1991. Print.

Stern, Philip Van Doren. "Introduction." *Tales of Horror and the Supernatural* by Arthur Machen. New York: Pinnacle, 1983. Print.

Strengell, Heidi. *Dissecting Stephen King: From the Gothic to Literary Naturalism.* Madison: University of Wisconsin Press, 2005. Print.

Stroby, W.C. "Book to the Future." *Fangoria Masters of the Dark.* Ed. Anthony Timpone. New York: Harper Prism, 1997. 75–82. Print.

Taylor, Troy. "The Windigo." *Ghosts of the Prairie.* American Hauntings. 2002. Web. 6 June 2016.

Texter, Donald. "'A Funny Thing Happened on the Way to Dystopia': The Culture Industry's Neutralization of Stephen King's *The Running Man.*" *Utopian Studies* 18, no. 1 (2007): 43–72. *Academic Search Complete.* Electronic.

Thompson, Helen. "No, 'Bath Salts' Won't Turn You into a Cannibal." Smithsonian.com. 20 Nov. 2014. Web. 26 June 2016.

Thury, Eva M., and Margaret K. Devinney. *Introduction to Mythology: Contempo-rary Approaches to Classical and World Myths.* 4th ed. New York: Oxford University Press, 2017.

Todorov, Tzcetan. *The Fantastic: A Structural Approach to a Literary Genre.* Trans. Richard Howard. Ithaca: Cornell University Press, 1975. Print.

_____. *Litterature et Signification.* Paris: Larousse, 1967. Print.

_____. *The Poetics of Prose.* Trans. Richard Howard. Ithaca: Cornell University Press, 1977. Print.

Trachtenberg, Jeffrey A. "Why E-Books Aren't Scary." *The Wall Street Journal.* 29 Oct. 2010. Web. 18 Oct. 2014.

Tucker, Joshua. "Tweeting Ferguson: How Social Media Can (and Cannot) Facilitate Protest." *The Washington Post.* 25 Nov. 2014. Web. 26 Dec. 2014.

Underwood, Tim, and Chuck Miller, eds. *Bare Bones: A Conversation on Terror with Stephen King.* New York: McGraw-Hill, 1989. Print.

_____. *Fear Itself: The Horror Fiction of Stephen King.* New York: Plume, 1984. Print.

Updike, John. *A&P. Literature: Reading Fiction, Poetry, and Drama.* Sixth ed. Ed. Robert DiYanni. New York: McGraw-Hill, 2007. 32–36. Print.

Ward, Glenn. *Understand Postmodernism.* New York: McGraw-Hill, 2010. Print.

Waugh, Patricia. *Metafiction: The Theory and Practice of Self-Conscious Fiction.* London: Methuen, 1984. Print.

Whitehead, Colson. *Zone One.* New York: Anchor, 2012. Print.

Wiater, Stanley, Christopher Golden, and Hank Wagner. *The Complete Stephen King Universe.* New York: St. Martin's. 2006. Print.

Wilwol, John. "End of Watch Review: Stephen King Delivers Scary Finale to Latest Trilogy." *Newsday.* 1 June 2016. Wed. 25 June 2016.

Windolf, Jim. "Scare Tactician." Sunday Book Review. *The New York Times.* 12 Nov. 2006. Web. 19 Oct. 2014.

Winter, Douglas. *Stephen King: the Art of Darkness.* New York: NAL Books, 1984. Print.

Wittgenstein, Ludwig. *Philosophical Investigations.* 3rd ed. Trans. G.E.M. Anscombe. London: Blackwell, 1986. Print.

_____. *Tractatus Logico-Philosophicus.* Trans. O.K. Ogden. New York: Cosimo, 2007. Print.

Yarbro, Chelsea Quinn. "Cinderella's Revenge—Twists on Fairy Tales and Mythic Themes in the Work of Stephen King." *Fear Itself: The Early Works of Stephen King.* Ed. Tim Underwood and Chuck Miller. San Francisco: Underwood-Miller, 1993. 45–55. Print.

Zax, David. "How Did Computers Uncover J.K. Rowling's Pseudonym?" *Smithsonian Magazine.* March 2014. Web. 19 Oct. 2014.

Ziegler, Heide, and Christopher Bigsby. *The Radical Imagination and the Liberal Tradition: Interviews with Contemporary English and American Novelists.* London: Junction Books. 1982. Print.

Index